Evidence-Based Education Policy

Evidence-Based Education Policy

What Evidence? What Basis? Whose Policy?

Edited by

David Bridges, Paul Smeyers and Richard Smith

WILEY-BLACKWELL

A John Wiley & Sons, Ltd., Publication

This edition first published 2009
Originally published as Volume 42, Supplement 1 of *The Journal of Philosophy of Education*
Chapters © 2009 The Authors
Editorial organization © 2009 Philosophy of Education Society of Great Britain

Blackwell Publishing was acquired by John Wiley & Sons in February 2007. Blackwell's publishing program has been merged with Wiley's global Scientific, Technical, and Medical business to form Wiley-Blackwell.

Registered Office
John Wiley & Sons Ltd, The Atrium, Southern Gate, Chichester, West Sussex, PO19 8SQ, United Kingdom

Editorial Offices
350 Main Street, Malden, MA 02148-5020, USA
9600 Garsington Road, Oxford, OX4 2DQ, UK
The Atrium, Southern Gate, Chichester, West Sussex, PO19 8SQ, UK

For details of our global editorial offices, for customer services, and for information about how to apply for permission to reuse the copyright material in this book please see our website at www.wiley.com/wiley-blackwell.

The right of David Bridges, Paul Smeyers and Richard Smith to be identified as the authors of the editorial material in this work has been asserted in accordance with the Copyright, Designs and Patents Act 1988.

Wiley also publishes its books in a variety of electronic formats. Some content that appears in print may not be available in electronic books.

Designations used by companies to distinguish their products are often claimed as trademarks. All brand names and product names used in this book are trade names, service marks, trademarks or registered trademarks of their respective owners. The publisher is not associated with any product or vendor mentioned in this book. This publication is designed to provide accurate and authoritative information in regard to the subject matter covered. It is sold on the understanding that the publisher is not engaged in rendering professional services. If professional advice or other expert assistance is required, the services of a competent professional should be sought.

Library of Congress Cataloging-in-Publication Data

Evidence-based education policy : what evidence? what basis? whose policy? / edited by David Bridges, Paul Smeyers and Richard Smith.
　　　p. cm.
"Originally published as Volume 42, Supplement 1 of The Journal of philosophy of education."
　　Includes bibliographical references and index.
　　ISBN 978-1-4051-9411-2 (pbk. : alk. paper)
1. Education and state–Great Britain. 2. Education–Research–Great Britain. I. Bridges, David. II. Smeyers, Paul. III. Smith, Richard.
　　LC93.G7E83 2009
　　379.41–dc22

2009001810

A catalogue record for this book is available from the British Library.

Set in 9 on 11pt Times by Macmillan Publishing Solutions
Printed and bound in Malaysia by Vivar Printing Sdn Bhd

01　2009

Contents

Acknowledgement

The authors gratefully acknowledge the support they received in the preparation of this material from the UK Economic and Research Council's Teaching and Learning Research Programme (TLRP).

Notes on Contributors

David Bridges is Professor Emeritus at the University of East Anglia (where he was previously Pro-Vice-Chancellor) and Emeritus Fellow of St Edmund's College, Cambridge, where he continues to direct the Centre for Educational Research and Development in the Von Hügel Institute. He was until recently Director of the Association of Universities in the East of England, based in the East of England Development Agency. He is a Council member of both the British and European Educational Research Associations and is an Honorary Vice-President of the Philosophy of Education Society of Great Britain. His publications include *'Fiction Written under Oath?' Essays in Philosophy and Educational Research* and, edited with Richard Smith, *Philosophy, Methodology and Educational Research*.

James Conroy is currently Dean in the Faculty of Education, University of Glasgow. He has previously held the posts of Head of Graduate School and Head of Department of Religious Education at the University, and has taught in Higher Education, Schools and Adult Education. He has served on the boards of a number of national and international education and academic bodies. He is currently President of the 'Association of Moral Education' and is visiting Professor in the Department of Educational Leadership at Fordham University, New York. James has published widely on the politics of Catholic education, sectarianism and liberal democracy in education including, most recently, *Betwixt and Between: the Liminal Imagination, Education and Democracy*.

Robert Davis is Professor of Religious and Cultural Education in the University of Glasgow. He has taught, written and broadcast widely on literature, religion, music and the cultural history of childhood. His work includes studies of the place of imaginative literature in moral education, the future of education for religious literacy and the history of faith-based schooling. He is Co-investigator for the AHRC/ESRC Religion and Society project on the effectiveness of Religious Education in British secondary schools and is also completing a new intellectual biography of the radical educator Robert Owen for the Continuum Library of Educational Thought.

John Elliott is Emeritus Professor of Education within the Centre for Applied Research in Education, which he directed from 1996 to 1999, at the University of East Anglia. He is well known internationally for his role in developing the theory and practice of action research in the contexts of curriculum and teacher development, for example through the Ford Teaching Project (1972–4) and the TTA-funded Norwich Area Schools Consortium (NASC) on the 'curriculum and pedagogical dimensions of student disaffection' (1997–2001). He was a consultant to the Hong Kong

Government on the strategic development of its curriculum reforms from 2001 to 2006. His recent publications include *'Reflecting Where the Action Is': the Selected Works of John Elliott*, in the Routledge World Library of Educationalists (2007).

Penny Enslin is Professor of Education at the University of Glasgow, where she is Director of the Ed. D. programme. Until 2006 she was a Professor in the School of Education at the University of the Witwatersrand, Johannesburg, where she now holds the position of Professor Emeritus. Her research and teaching interests lie in the area of political theory and education, with particular interests in democracy and citizenship education. She has published internationally on deliberative democracy and education, liberalism, gender and feminist theory, nation building, African philosophy of education, and higher education.

Lorraine Foreman-Peck taught in inner-city secondary schools before moving into higher education. She worked in teacher education and staff development for over twenty years in the UK. She has recently moved from the University of Northampton, where she was Reader in Education, to the Oxford University Department of Educational Studies, where she is a Research Fellow. She is currently a Visiting Professor at the University of Northumbria. Her interests and publications span the philosophy of education and practitioner research. She is currently engaged in action research projects in higher education and the museum service.

Morwenna Griffiths is Professor of Classroom Learning in the Moray House School of Education at Edinburgh University. She has taught in primary schools in Bristol, and at the University of Isfahan, Iran, at Christ Church College HE in Canterbury, and at Oxford Brookes, Nottingham and Nottingham Trent Universities. Her recent research has included philosophical theorising and empirical investigation, related to epistemology of auto/biography, social justice, public spaces, the nature of practice, feminisation and creativity. Her books include *Action for Social Justice in Education: Fairly Different*; *Educational Research for Social Justice* and *Feminisms and the Self: the Web of Identity*.

Dominik Lukeš is a researcher and educator, whose primary research interests are in policy discourse analysis, conceptual framing and philosophy of social science. He is co-editor of the online journal *Critical Approaches to Discourse Analysis across Disciplines* and has been an associate editor of the Benjamins' *Bibliography of Metaphor & Metonymy*. He co-edited *Cognitive Linguistics in Critical Discourse Analysis: Application and Theory*. He has had a long career in education as a teacher trainer, working in over fifteen countries in Eastern Europe, Central Asia and the Middle East, and has also taught Czech language and culture at the School of Slavonic and East European Studies and the University of Glasgow. His life and work can be found online on DominikLukes.net.

Gale MacLeod is a lecturer in primary education and Director of Postgraduate Studies in the School of Education, Edinburgh University. After studying Philosophy and Theology at Oxford University, she worked for fifteen years with young people described as having social, emotional and behavioural difficulties. Her PhD, completed in 2005, mapped the separate provision available in Scotland for these young people, and explored the experience of being educated separately with a group of pupils. More recently, she has enjoyed revisiting philosophy and exploring how it can inform and enhance educational research and policy-making.

Jane Murray is Senior Lecturer in Early Years Education and Early Years' Programme Leader at The University of Northampton. She spent the first twenty years of her career as a teacher in primary and early years' settings and as a music education consultant, during which time she gained an MA in Education and the National Professional Qualification for Headship (NPQH). Since moving to work in the higher education sector in 2003, Jane has published in the fields of early childhood and the philosophy of education. She is currently studying towards a PhD, exploring the research warrant of young children in early years' settings. Jane's engagement with the TLRP Epistemology project has supported her development as a 'new researcher' in the field of educational research.

Alis Oancea is Research Fellow at the University of Oxford, working on philosophy of research (with particular interest in epistemology), research policy and governance, and post-compulsory education. She is author and co-author of over thirty journal articles, books and book chapters, and of over fifty other publications. She serves as expert reviewer of grant proposals to UK and European bodies, including the European Commission, the European Science Foundation and the Wellcome Trust. Recent projects include: 'Quality in applied and practice-based research' (ESRC); Nuffield Review of 14–19 Education and Training in England and Wales (Nuffield Foundation); 'Educational research expertise in the UK' (BERA); and 'Research quality and evaluation in education and gerontology' (Oxford Institute of Ageing and Department of Education).

Richard Pring is Lead Director, Nuffield Review 14–19 Education and Training, England and Wales, a £1 million review funded by the Nuffield Foundation. He was Professor of Educational Studies and Director of the Department, University of Oxford, from 1989 to 2003, and is President of the Socialist Education Society. He received the Aga Khan's Annual Award of Distinction in 2007. His recent books have included: *Philosophy of Education: Aims, Theory, Common Sense and Research*; *Philosophy of Educational Research*; *Evidence-Based Practice in Education* (edited with Gary Thomas); and *John Dewey: The Philosopher of Education for the 21ˢᵗ Century?* He is currently working on the Runners' Guide to Oxford.

Lesley Saunders was until recently Senior Policy Adviser for Research at the General Teaching Council (England). From its inception in 2000,

Lesley was influential in promoting teaching as a research-informed profession. She served as a user member on the Education sub-panel for the Research Assessment Exercise 2008. Before joining the GTC, Lesley was head of the School Improvement Research Centre at the National Foundation for Educational Research. She is a Research Fellow at the Department of Education, Oxford University, and Visiting Professor at the Institute of Education, London. She recently edited *Educational Research and Policy-Making: Exploring the Border Country between Research and Policy*, which features accounts by leading figures in both policy and research. She is also an award-winning poet.

Paul Smeyers is Research Professor for Philosophy of Education at Ghent University and part-time Professor at the Katholieke Universiteit Leuven. Together with Nigel Blake, Richard Smith and Paul Standish, he co-authored *Thinking Again: Education after Postmodernism*, *Education in an Age of Nihilism* and *The Therapy of Education*, and co-edited *The Blackwell Guide to the Philosophy of Education*. Together with Marc Depaepe, he co-edited *Beyond Empiricism: on Criteria for Educational Research*; *Educational Research: Why 'What Works' Doesn't Work*; *Educational Research: Networks and Technologies*; *Educational Research: the Educationalisation of Social Problems* and *Educational Research: Proofs, Arguments, and Other Reasonings*.

Richard Smith is Professor of Education at the University of Durham, UK, where he was for many years Director of the Combined Degrees in Arts and Social Sciences. He is Editor of the new journal *Ethics and Education* and Associate Editor of the *Journal of Philosophy of Education*. His most recent authored book is (with Paul Smeyers and Paul Standish) *The Therapy of Education* (Palgrave Macmillan, 2006). His principal research interests are in the philosophy of education and the philosophy of social science.

Michael Watts is a Senior Research Associate at the Von Hügel Institute, St Edmund's College, Cambridge, where his work focuses on higher education policies. He has researched a range of widening participation issues, including access opportunities for refugees and asylum seekers, the pedagogic implications of widening participation and the aspirations of young people who reject higher education, and published widely in these fields. He is lead editor of the journal *Power and Education*.

Preface

There are many reasons to welcome this collection of essays and to applaud the support given by the Directorate of the Economic and Social Research Council (ESRC) Teaching and Learning Research Programme (TLRP) for the work that has led to its production. The TLRP has been concerned with the question of how to demonstrate the 'warrant' of its wide range of research projects, not only to satisfy the complex but intrinsic obligations of educational research as a multidisciplinary field but also to fulfil the expectations of decision-makers in education—from classroom teachers to ministers of state—for assurance and practical guidance about what sorts of knowledge and evidence they can have legitimate confidence in.

These are wholly defensible, indeed desirable, expectations on the part of those charged with either teaching or policy-making, given the amount of so-called research that is accessible and downloadable from the Internet. As Conor Galvin's work has made plain (Galvin, 2003, 2004, 2005) the opportunities (temptations, even) for policy and practice to be based on info-nuggets and evidence-lite, even downright misinformation, are growing all the time. I have argued elsewhere (for example, Saunders, 2004, 2007) that, however hedged about with theoretical and practical reservations and qualifications it may be, the rationalist ideal in public decision-making is to be cherished. The alternative is that public life be dependent on revealed or idiosyncratic knowledge, in which case there would be no bulwark even in principle against opportunism, corruption, ignorance, solipsism and collective amnesia. So the question of 'warrant', the assurance that the grounds of our belief are solid under our feet, is crucial to the continued and strengthened influence of educational research on education in an increasingly competitive knowledge market-place.

To judge by the approaches that have been taken by different TLRP project teams to warranting their findings, this assurance may be thought to rest on, for example, the protocols of peer review, on methodological propriety, on analytical cogency or on the utility and plausibility of the research findings and messages for non-research audiences. The chapters in this volume attempt to place these different approaches in a more general and theoretical context and, in so doing, to fulfil two rather different needs. The first is to set out—for non-specialists—the underlying reasons why different kinds of research in education can and should be deployed as forms of trustworthy knowledge, together with the conditions under which they may be trusted. This has entailed saying some very interesting and useful things along the way about the contexts, criteria, underpinning values, constraints and limitations, and the making of meanings, in educational research. The second need is to explicate some specialist topics and issues about the enduring concerns of 'validity', 'generalisability', 'truth', 'evidence' and 'knowledge', in order to advance the collective professional understanding amongst what is a very diverse research community in education.

A sub-text for both these purposes was the felt need by several of the writers to take several steps back from the 'what works' discourse that, with the extended exchanges between its proponents and critics, has managed to colonise much educational research writing over the last ten years. In the course of the stimulating discussions that went into the writing of the present chapters, I suggested that this discourse—and perhaps particularly the 'strong' version of it—was not wholly nor deliberately created by policy-makers, who, in my experience, continue to commission and to take more or less notice of a whole variety of qualitative and quantitative research studies. In any case, I think it behoves us as scholars to treat the issue of policy 'texts' as highly problematic: what a minister says in a speech that is going to be widely reported and whose main audience is not the one in the room is not necessarily to be taken as the worked-out and believed-in policy position that is being elaborated, negotiated, tinkered with, woven into or interrupted by people's behaviours and practices in a variety of textual and oral 'spaces'. In such spaces research has plenty of room for manoeuvre and influence.

I think it is arguable that educational research production, dissemination and engagement has developed considerably over the ten years or so since the Hargreaves and Hillage challenges—which were thrown down as much to the 'users', funders and commissioners as to the producers of research, and to which the TLRP was itself a response, unprecedented in scope and scale. Moreover, large numbers of researchers working in government and other national policy organisations in education (as well as in the private sector), and an increasing proportion of teachers, are becoming research-active—educational research is no longer (if it ever was) the prerogative of universities. We can no longer (if we ever could) construct 'the Other' with confidence that we know wherein the defining differences between research and policy and practice lie.

Of course, many problems continue to wrong-foot the relationship between research and policy, among them:

- the misdiagnosis of what research can deliver for policy (probably both less and more than may be claimed by either side on any given occasion);
- the very different 'discourse communities' of policy and research, where even what counts as an askable question may not be held in common;
- the lack of opportunities for encounters and conversations between policy-makers and researchers in which meanings might be co-constructed;

- different timelines and timescales: for example, the rate of 'policy turnover' (in terms of substance and/or personnel) compared with the time it takes to set up, undertake, complete and report a research study; or the point in the policy cycle at which research is expected to make a particular kind of contribution;
- the proliferation of research outputs in journals, books, websites, with which other researchers (let alone policy-makers) cannot keep up to date: 'selectivity' must be a relative term;
- different or unclear criteria for what can count as evidence.

It is this last issue with which the chapters in this volume are most concerned, of course, but it has proved difficult to exclude entirely from consideration the way other factors impinge on the central epistemological issues, just as it has seemed impossible to talk about 'policy' without thinking 'politics'. But my impression is that decision-makers remain hungry for evidence and ideas: when conditions are right, research can deepen, open up or even disrupt current policy thinking, and be welcomed for doing so.

Two things in particular therefore strike me about this volume: one is the sense I get (and I hope readers will too) of educational research, in its fullest and deepest exemplification, being practised as an art and a craft as well as a science. Since I regard both teaching and policy-making in this light too, it suggests to me that there can be meetings of minds in imaginative as well as rational ways and spaces. The trope or turn towards 'storying' in research, which many of the writers discuss, therefore seems to me to be very important to emphasise: narrative feels like an innate human need and capacity which we (quasi-)intuitively bring to bear even on the most unadorned numerical datasets. If a story is trustworthy and recognisable, there is an immediate generalisability to be derived from the very act of recognition. Moreover, part of the 'storying' impulse is to complicate simple notions of 'cause-and-effect', to make patent the contingent and contextual, and to reveal the intentions, beliefs, values and attitudes, as well as the actions, of the different characters/agents. In the human and social sciences, it cannot be scientific to ignore them.

The second thing that struck me may be less immediately obvious to readers, although I was delightedly able to witness it in our meetings, and this is the power of the encounter: the dialogic way in which knowledge and understanding are created and developed, and become common property through principled debate. I think one result of this can fairly be described as the 'philosophical composure' which a member of the group commended as being one of the affordances—or shall we say gifts?—of philosophy, which all educationists should hope to receive. The moral for me is plain: much more attention and resource needs to be devoted to creating occasions for encounters between researchers and policy-makers within a discursive and ethically-attuned public space. I hope these essays prompt such thoughts in others too.

Lesley Saunders

Correspondence: Professor Lesley Saunders, General Teaching Council for England, Whittington House, 19-30 Alfred Place, London WC1E 7EA, UK.
E-mail: Lesley.Saunders@gtce.org.uk

REFERENCES

Galvin, C. (2003) The New Public Life: Wired Communities and the Creation of Education Policy in a Digital Age. Paper presented at British Educational Research Association Annual Conference, Edinburgh, 10–13 September.

Galvin, C. (2004) The Making of Public Policy in a Digital Age: Some Reflections on Changing Practice. Paper presented at Market Research Society Conference 'Social Policy Research in the Information Age', London, 17 February.

Galvin, C. (2005) But All the Wrong People are Here . . .: Wired Networks, Social Capital and the Making of Public Policy in a Digital Age. Paper presented at British Educational Research Association Executive Conference, Oxford, 10–11 February.

Saunders, L. (2004) *Grounding the Democratic Imagination: Developing the Relationship between Research and Policy in Education.* Professorial Lecture (London, Institute of Education).

Saunders, L. (ed.) (2007) *Educational Research and Policy-making: Exploring the Border Country Between Research and Policy* (London, Routledge).

1

Educational Research and the Practical Judgement of Policy-Makers

DAVID BRIDGES, PAUL SMEYERS AND RICHARD SMITH

THE CONTEXT: WHAT EVIDENCE?

This publication arises in a context in which policy-makers and educational researchers are increasingly vocal in their demands that educational policy and practice should be informed by high quality research. In some renderings in the USA and the UK this has been translated into the language of 'evidence-based' policy and practice and in both countries this in turn has led to 'systematic reviews' of educational research aimed at sifting what is regarded as research which can reliably inform us 'what works' from that which is less deserving of attention. In the United States following the re-authorisation in 2001 of the Elementary and Secondary Education Act ('No Child Left Behind') only such research as compares with the medical double blind randomised controlled trials has been seen in government circles to be deserving of attention in terms of policy formation. Not quite so restrictively, the 'systematic reviews' favoured by UK government and carried out under the auspices of the Evidence for Policy and Practice Information Coordinating Centre (EPPI Centre: www.eppi.ioe.ac.uk) at the London Institute of Education have nevertheless—'systematically', one might say—excluded whole swathes of educational research from their consideration. These exclusions were especially significant in terms of research which indicated what policy should be as distinct from how a particular determined policy might be implemented or delivered, but they also put beyond the frame of consideration, for example, much research based on individual case studies or narratives, let alone philosophical work or critical theory.

However, as Whitty pointed out in his Presidential address to the 2005 BERA conference:

> Even research that is centrally concerned with improving practice and supporting teachers ... needs to be more diverse in its nature than the rhetoric of 'what works' sometimes seems to imply. Research defined too narrowly would actually be very limited as an evidence base for a teaching profession that is facing the huge challenges of a rapidly changing world, where what works today may not work tomorrow. Some research, therefore, needs to ask different sorts of questions, including why something works and, equally important, why it works in some

contexts and not in others. And anyway, the professional literacy of teachers surely involves more than purely instrumental knowledge. It is therefore appropriate that a research-based profession should be informed by research that questions prevailing assumptions—and considers such questions as whether an activity is a worthwhile endeavour in the first place and what constitutes socially-just schooling (published in Whitty 2006, p. 162).

In a context of increasing diversification, segmentation and hybridisation of educational research, the major ESRC-sponsored Teaching and Learning Research Programme in the UK invited philosophical consideration of what might more widely be regarded as the epistemological bases of educational policy (though we were not entirely comfortable with the foundationalism implied by the language of 'bases': see Smith and also Elliott and Lukeš in this volume). The central question was: what sort of research can and should inform such policy? What confidence can we have in different kinds of research as a basis for such policy?

The editors of this volume can share with the 'evidence-based practice' movement a concern that policy should in some sense be informed by research rather than, for example, rumour, prejudice or unexamined assumptions and we can also share the hope that such research should be good quality research. The trouble is that 'quality' can be—and is—easily and even unintentionally defined in a way that excludes many of the varied intellectual sources which can and do contribute to educational understanding.

In fairness, as the sources and methodologies which educational researchers have drawn on have become more and more diverse (a pattern echoed across the social sciences more generally) they have presented something of a challenge to anyone faced with judgements of quality. When he was editor of the American Educational Research Association journal *Educational Researcher*, Donmoyer wrote an article—almost a plea for help—under the title 'Educational Research in an Era of Paradigm Proliferation: What's a Journal Editor to Do?' (Donmoyer, 1996) in which he described the field of educational research in these terms: 'Ours is a field characterised by paradigm proliferation and, consequently, the sort of field in which there is little consensus about what research and scholarship are and what research reporting and scholarship should look like' (Donmoyer, 1996, p. 19).

The authors of the chapters in this volume tend to view the richness of the intellectual traditions which can contribute to educational understanding as a source of fascination rather than frustration, as a cause for celebration rather than despondency. At least, with Elliott Eisner (and this was in his presidential address to the American Educational Research Association) we hold that 'If there are different ways to understand the world, and if there are different forms that make such understanding possible, then it would seem to follow that any comprehensive effort to understand the processes and outcomes of schooling would profit from a pluralistic rather than a monolithic approach to research' (Eisner, 1993,

p. 8). Thus we set off with the supposition that the intellectual resources which could and should inform policy might be rather more diverse in character than the evidence-based practice movement seemed to suppose—or at least we wanted to test this belief through closer analysis and argumentation. So we are asking: can we derive useful insight from small scale case studies and biography as well as large population studies, from practitioner action research as well as academic institutional research, from philosophical and literary work as well as from empirical evidence? If so, how, more specifically, do these forms of enquiry relate to and inform policy?

THE CONTRIBUTIONS

This volume begins with a chapter by Alis Oancea and Richard Pring on 'The Importance of Being Thorough: On Systematic Accumulation of "What Works" in Educational Research', which reviews the developments around 'evidence-based practice' and 'systematic reviews', rehearses some of the criticism to which they have been exposed, and discusses the nature of research more generally. It recognises, more particularly, the different kinds of evidence that are related to different kinds of research questions and the consequent limitations of general research-based solutions to generalised problems.

The second chapter, 'The Epistemological Bases of Educational Research and Policy' by David Bridges and Michael Watts, considers whether there are any *general* principles one can advance as to what sort of evidence can and should inform educational policy. This invites a closer inspection of the kind of information and understanding which are required for any formulation of educational policy. It draws attention in particular to the inescapably normative character of such formulation and discusses the role of research in the context of such normativity.

We then proceed to look at some specific forms of research with a view to examining what sort of contribution they might or might not make to educational policy. The first of these chapters focuses on one of the longest established forms of educational enquiry and perhaps one of the least controversial—large population studies. In 'On the Epistemological Basis of Large-Scale Population Studies and Their Use' Paul Smeyers considers the ways in which such studies might inform policy and provides particular insight into the interpretation of causality in such research. We wanted to include in the suite of discussions at least one example of quantitative research methods, because these are often assumed to be relatively unproblematic as evidence which can inform policy, but, as Smeyers demonstrates, the derivation of policy from such evidence and the inferences involved have their own complexities.

We then move to two discussions of qualitative research methods focusing on individual cases or a small number of cases. John Elliott and Dominic Lukeš discuss the ways in which case study can inform policy in 'Epistemology as Ethics in Research and Policy: Under What Terms

Might Case Studies Yield Useful Knowledge to Policy-Makers', while Morwenna Griffiths and Gale Macleod consider the particular issues relating to 'Stories and Personal Narratives'.

Some of the same issues are raised in connection with practitioner and action research, which is the focus of a chapter by Lorraine Foreman-Peck and Jane Murray 'Action Research and Policy: Epistemological Considerations'. This chapter analyses, in particular, the different relationships which different conceptions of action research have with policy.

It would be part of our contention that policy must inescapably be informed by philosophical considerations and James Conroy, Robert Davis and Penny Enslin explore this relationship in more detail in 'Philosophy as a Basis for Policy And Practice: What Confidence Can We Have in Philosophical Analysis and Argument?'—a chapter that also explores in some detail the notion of confidence itself as an epistemological principle. Finally, we wanted to open the debate to consideration of some even more difficult bedfellows to educational policy and this is what Richard Smith contributes in his chapter 'Proteus Rising: Re-Imagining Educational Research' which considers the place of 'non-modernist' enquiry and 'the romantic turn' in the educational policy arena.

These chapter do not of course cover all of the diverse forms that are taken by contemporary educational research. They do, however, make a case in favour of the contribution to educational policy which can be made by a wider rather than a narrower range of intellectual resources. They also make it clear that the relationship between some of these resources and policy formulation is not necessarily a straightforward one and is not necessarily the same in all cases.

WHAT BASIS? HOW RESEARCH MIGHT RELATE TO POLICY

There is a widespread assumption that research provides an 'evidential basis' for policy or, more acceptably perhaps, that research 'informs' policy. The notion of research providing a *basis* for policy is especially problematic in so far as it suggests that the process begins with research which then points to the required policy. This is an empirically and logically unsound view of the nature of policy and its construction. Policy is an ongoing process: it is not a vacuum waiting to be filled. It has a history and a contemporary social political context. It is there before the research comes along: it is not waiting for research to bring it into existence. Equally, policy-makers are not empty vessels: they come with prejudice, experience, values they wish to realise and ideas for the future. Sometimes they may be unsure what to do and be looking for advice, but even then research has to engage with socio/historical systems and with people, in which and in whom belief, understanding and experience are already deeply embedded. Research may arouse interest, provoke debate, confirm prejudice, give new insight, challenge pre-existing beliefs but it will never stand alone in its informing of policy and will rarely even be the predominant informing resource, simply because there is already so much 'information' of one sort or another embodied in policy systems and in policy-makers themselves.

This sort of picture of the relationship between research and policy raises, then, the question of the nature of the 'informing': how does research inform, enter or otherwise engage with policy or policy-makers?

The evidence-based policy movement seems almost to presuppose an algorithm which will generate policy decisions: *If* A is what you want to achieve *and if* research shows R1, R2 and R3 to be the case, and *if furthermore* research shows that doing P is positively correlated with A, *then* it follows that P is what you need to do. So provided you have your educational/political goals sorted out, all you need is to slot in the appropriate research findings—the right information—to extract your policy. Elliott and Lukeš draw on Nussbaum's (1990) 'Science of Measurement' to identify this kind of 'scientific' conception of practical reason characterised by a concern to maximise a single instrumental value varying only in quantity that is common to all alternatives. As Elliott and Lukeš argue in their chapter, however, 'Streamlined rational judgement is often, and almost always in the context of policymaking, a convenient fiction, a ritual of justification'. 'Human beings continually elude systems. If rational persons did agree, they would assent to the same rational systems. However, they do not' (Griffiths and Macleod, this volume).

A number of the contributors to this volume point to more subtle processes at work in the interaction of research and policy. First, there is the observation that not all research is orientated towards solutions to educational questions or problems (albeit that this may be a source of irritation to impatient and solution-focused policy-makers). Research may show that you have problems you had not even thought about; it may critique your policy rather than tell you how to succeed with it (even if it is 'action' research as Foreman-Peck and Murray point out); it may help you see what you are dealing with in its historical or social context, perhaps even *sub specie aeternitatis* (Elliott and Lukeš write in their contribution to this volume of the interface between research and practice as 'a continuing conversation between the general and the universal'); it may help you understand the complexity of the problem (Conroy *et al.*); it may reveal the stark reality of the choices facing you (see on all this, in particular, Griffiths and Macleod's contribution to this volume).

Secondly, and by extension, you get a different perspective on research if you move from looking to it for 'information', scores, numbers or facts to looking for different kinds of cognitive objectives. The simple shift, which Hammersley (2002) proposed, towards looking for *understanding* rather than seeking solutions, and towards making claims that are tentative rather than advancing them with evangelical certainty, has quite radical implications for the research/policy relationship (see chapters by Griffiths and Macleod and by Smith). Elliott and Lukeš write of 'retrospective generalisations' and summaries of judgement' which 'allow people to anticipate rather than straightforwardly predict possible events' (this volume); Griffiths and Macleod employ Aristotelian distinctions to suggest that it is *praxis* (crudely, the practical knowledge reflected in how one lives as a citizen and a human being, but also a knowledge informed by *phronesis* or practical wisdom) on which policy-makers need to rely rather than on the one hand *sophia* and *episteme* or on the other *techne*. It is this sort of knowledge which can be informed by auto/biography (Griffiths and Macleod), individual case studies (Elliott and Lukeš) and locally applied action research (Foreman-Peck and Murray). Smith takes the argument about the kind of knowledge that is needed in a different, therapeutic (in the Wittgensteinian sense) or, as he suggests, a Romantic direction: 'Instead of knowing the world we might be attuned to it, sensitive to it. We might resonate with it, share its rhythms—the way we might with the natural world if we opened ourselves to it instead of approaching it as scientists' (Smith, this volume).

Thirdly, several of the chapters in this volume emphasise the point that research has a role in informing the practical wisdom, judgement or *phronesis* of policy-makers (who, we suggested earlier, are not exactly without all sorts of pre-existent understanding of their own), but cannot substitute for it. Smeyers argues that large-scale population studies may correct particular explanations which are generally given and which may turn out not to be correct, but much more will need to be said when applying these insights in a policy context. Elliott and Lukeš explicitly argue that single case portrayals have a particular contribution to make 'in a policy context that leaves cultural space for *phronesis* as a mode of practical reasoning' though they add that 'Stenhouse's conception of case study fits a context in which space for *phronesis* cannot be presumed but needs to be opened up' (Elliott and Lukeš, this volume).

Fourthly, a number of the chapters share a suspicion of generalised solutions to educational problems and policy requirements which are supposed to be applied across what all the chapters regard as diverse, complex (Conroy *et al.*), unstable (Smith), unpredictable (Elliott and Lukeš), and messy particular contexts. (Griffiths and Macleod's discussion of Arendt on this is especially illuminating.) Action research in the UK was indeed posited on the need to test general curriculum prescriptions against the evidence of their effects on particular classrooms (Foreman-Peck and Murray). Elliott and Lukeš describe 'case-focussed reasoning' as 'a process which . . . unifies universal and situational understanding' and Griffiths and Macleod invoke sources which speak of 'the capacity to attend to context as well as idiosyncracy' (Fraser, 2004, p. 181) and which commend biographical methods on the grounds that they can help 'restore the relationship between policy and lived experience by moving between the micro- and macro-levels' (Frogget and Chamberlayne, 2004, p. 62).

All of these considerations contribute to a much more diverse and subtle picture of the ways in which research may inform policy than is suggested in the discourse of evidence-based policy. They are also a reminder of the mass of human experience and of research insight into that experience which will be lost if we do not pay attention to the wider range of resources that the educational research community can offer. 'So much passes unnoticed and unremarked, and is betrayed' observes Richard Smith in a concluding paragraph to this volume, and he invokes Pieter Brueghel's painting *The Fall of Icarus*, reproduced on the cover of this book, and Auden's reflection on it as a metaphor for what we miss when, like Brueghel's ploughman, we are too narrowly focused on the immediate job in hand or, like the ship that passes by unseeing, we have 'somewhere to get to'.

WHOSE POLICY?

Bridges and Watts (in this volume) emphasise that policy is not just what is constructed at national level by politicians and ministries (still less, in the UK context is it simply what happens in London, given the jurisdiction over educational affairs which is held—in different ways—in Scotland, Wales and Northern Ireland). It is legitimate to talk of policy at regional, local and school levels and even, by extension, at the level of the individual classroom, though it is more commonly applied to collective action. However, the discourse of 'evidence-based' policy is primarily a response to the demands of national ministries in a context (in England especially) in which power has been systematically sucked from local government and schools to centralised administrations.

Some of the problems about connecting research with policy are the direct result of this centralising tendency. This point bears emphasising. There is irony in the way that, in many parts of the world, governments have increasingly arrogated power to themselves or to central agencies operating under their direction in the educational field, and then expressed surprise that educationists are not providing them with the 'research findings' they seek in order to re-connect with the education communities they want to command and have in many cases alienated. This centralising tendency forces those at the centre to seek generalised policy imperatives which are increasingly removed form the variety of social situations to which they are addressed—and it creates a greater social distance between researchers and the policy-makers. In smaller political units—Scotland would be an example—researchers and policy-makers (and teachers) have much more natural interaction, and those responsible for the direction and administration of education are much closer to the social settings on which their policies are to bear. To take a second example, in the English region of the East of England all the researchers involved with research into widening participation in higher education meet annually with policy-makers and practitioners in the field to review the latest research work, to assess their implications for policy and practice and to identify what else needs investigating. The point of this last example is that the people thus assembled have both the capacity to determine their own priorities for action (at least within a broad national framework) and the capacity to commission and utilise locally applied research. Where policy is in the hands of central government neither opportunity is practically available.

Educational action research in a sense takes this logic one stage further. At least on one model (see Elliott, 2000 and Foreman-Peck and Murray in this volume) it brings the educational values and aspirations of the teacher ('policy' in a significant sense) and research together in the context in which those values and aspirations are to be realised. Where this is possible, as Bridges has argued elsewhere, it reaffirms the ownership by teachers of teaching and learning in their own classrooms, the integrity with which they can then carry out this teaching and their professionalism and responsibility in this task (Bridges, 2001). Again, the research/ policy gap and even the policy/practice gap are closed, by not being artificially brought into being in the first place, if you have the confidence or courage to locate them at the most local level.

Finally, several of the chapters link issues of the ownership of and participation in the processes of research and policy with the conditions under which a community may come to have confidence in the knowledge which is informing that policy. Pring and Oancea argue in their contribution to this volume that 'Reasonable policy and practice can arise only from a deliberation of these different sources of evidence [teachers, policy-makers, parents and pupils] and [their] logically different sorts of explanation—and, hence, in a context where this deliberation is democratised. By democratised we mean both that the different research and evidence voices are heard and that conclusions remain tentative and provisional, welcoming further dialogue and criticism'. Conroy, Davis and Enslin urge that 'philosophical analysis more widely conceived ought to be in permanent ongoing dialogue with the policy-making enterprise'. Smith reminds us in his contribution of Leavis' account of literary criticism as 'a collaborative and creative interplay. It creates a community and is inseparable from the process that creates and keeps alive a living culture' (Leavis, 1961, quoted in Matthews, 2004, p. 55). Elliott and Lukeš write of enquiry undertaken in 'the spirit of a conversation' which alerts participants to their prejudices. The reconstruction of such prejudices is, they suggest 'an alternative view of understanding itself', though it is one which seems at some distance from the kind of understanding required by systematic reviews.

It is a contemporary commonplace to imagine that if only researchers and policy-makers could simply talk to each other all would be well. Elliott and Lukeš warn, however, that the kind of conversation they describe,

> ... does not automatically lead to a 'neater picture' of the situation nor does it necessarily produce a 'social good'. There is the danger of viewing 'disciplined conversation' as an elevated version of the folk theory on ideal policy: 'if only everyone talked to one another, the world would be a nicer place'. Academic conversation (just like any democratic dialectic process) is often contentious and not quite the genteel affair it tries to present itself as (Elliott and Lukeš, this volume).

THE DEVELOPMENT OF THIS VOLUME

We hope that this volume gains particular strength and coherence from the way in which it has been developed. The authors worked collaboratively for twelve months, starting with a two-day seminar in the autumn of 2006 at which they presented outlines of possible essays and discussed them as a group. Authors then re-worked their plans in the light of this discussion and proceeded with the writing. A nucleus of the group presented their current thinking at the annual conference of the Philosophy of Education Society of Great Britain in April 2007. The group then circulated their first drafts for detailed critical scrutiny at a two-day seminar in Cambridge in June 2007. This was also attended by two colleagues from outside philosophy of education: Lesley Saunders, Research Policy Advisor for the General Teaching Council (who has contributed a Preface to this collection) and Alan Brown, Associate Director of the Teaching and Learning Research programme. The essays were then further re-worked for presentation at the annual conferences of the British and European Educational Research Associations in September 2007 where they benefited from joint sessions between the Philosophy of Education and the Policy and Politics special interest groups.

This work was supported by the UK Economic and Social Research Council (ESRC) through the Teaching and Learning Research Programme (TLRP) and we are very grateful for this support. We hope that it will prove to be the prelude to subsequent ESRC supported work in philosophy of education. TLRP has also supported the development of philosophical resources for research capacity building, and these are freely available along with short versions of this set of chapters at www.tlrp.org/capacity.

The chapters in this volume issue from debate among the contributors and the wider educational research and policy community and will, we hope, contribute to on-going conversations. To this end they do not necessarily assume a detailed knowledge of the philosophical literature (though they offer signposts towards it and have extensive references), but are written in a way that will, we believe, reach out to colleagues in the wider educational policy and research communities as well as those in philosophy of education.

The *Journal of Philosophy of Education* has now published the following special issues on the theme of philosophy and educational research, which have been issued in book form:

Volume 35, Issue 3	Michael McNamee and David Bridges (eds), *The Ethics of Educational Research* (2002)
Volume 40, Issues 2 and 4	David Bridges and Richard Smith (eds), *Philosophy and Methodology of Educational Research* (2007)
Volume 42, Supplement 1	David Bridges, Paul Smeyers and Richard Smith (eds), *Evidence-Based Education Policy* (2009)

We are grateful to the Editorial Board of the Journal and to Wiley-Blackwell for their support in bringing this material into the public arena.

REFERENCES

Bridges, D. (2001) Professionalism, Authenticity and Action Research, *Educational Action Research*, 9.3, pp. 451–464.

Donmoyer, R. (1996) Educational Research in an Era of Paradigm Proliferation: What's a Journal Editor to Do?, *Educational Researcher*, 25.2, pp. 19–25.

Eisner, E. (1993) Forms of Understanding and the Future of Educational Research, *Educational Researcher*, 22.7, pp. 5–11.

Elliott, J. (2000) Doing Action Research: Doing Philosophy, *Prospero*, 6, pp. 62–100.

Fraser, H. (2004) Doing Narrative Research: Analysing Personal Stories Line by Line, *Qualitative Social Work*, 3.2, pp. 179–201.

Frogget, L. and Chamberlayne, P. (2004) Narratives of Social Enterprise: From Biography to Policy and Practice Critique, *Qualitative Social Work*, 3.1, pp. 61–77.

Hammersley, M. (2002) *Educational Research, Policy Making and Practice* (London, Paul Chapman).

Matthews, S. (2004) The Responsibilities of Dissent: F. R. Leavis after *Scrutiny*, *Literature and History*, 13.2, 49–66.

Nussbaum, M. C. (1990) The Science of Measurement, in her: *Love's Knowledge: Essays on Philosophy and Literature* (Oxford, Oxford University Press).

Whitty, G. (2006) Education(al) Research and Education Policy Making: Is Conflict Inevitable? *British Educational Research Journal*, 32.2, pp. 159–76.

2

The Importance of Being Thorough: On Systematic Accumulations of 'What Works' in Education Research

ALIS OANCEA AND RICHARD PRING

This chapter outlines and appraises the considerable criticism of educational research, both in the United Kingdom and in North America, and shows how it has pointed to a narrowing of what counts as good or worthwhile research in the policy discourse. In particular, this involved prioritising research that purports to show clearly and unmistakably 'what works', and institutionalising this view of research in a range of centres that receive official approval. The chapter, though recognising the fruit of such centres, challenges the epistemological basis of such a narrowing of what counts as research, and, in doing so, analyses what is meant by evidence, the different kinds and strengths of evidence and the consequent need to democratise the search and appraisal of evidence in the constant refinement and criticism of the evidence.

INTRODUCTION

The task set before us by the Economic and Social Research Council's Teaching and Learning Research Programme was to scrutinise the epistemological basis of educational research findings, and explore the extent to which they can warrant policy trust and justify public investments and interventions. However, this scrutiny cannot be a one-sided assessment of the epistemic value of education research findings, but it needs to also engage with the moral and political context of policy-making, and the types of expectations that it places on research. Questions such as the following seem relevant to such an enquiry:

- What are the criticisms of research and how do they lead to the prioritising of a particular kind of research (namely, 'what works')?
- What types of assumptions and models of knowledge underpin the 'what works' context for education research policy?

- Is there a need to think more broadly about research and thus about what counts as evidence for policy? (More particularly, how can the concept of evidence-based policy be rescued from narrow interpretations of instrumental effectiveness?)
- What are the implications for the democratisation of research and thus for policy-making?

We begin this chapter by touching on the first two sets of questions, and we will then move to an exploration of the latter two, though only tentatively and with no claim to comprehensiveness.

1 CRITICISMS OF EDUCATIONAL RESEARCH AND THE ASCENSION OF THE 'WHAT WORKS' DISCOURSE

Throughout the 1990s and 2000s, on the background of what was presented as reasonable public expectations from research across a variety of fields (e.g. contribution to an evidence base for practice and policy, value for money, competitiveness), education research has been the object of harsh criticism. Education research was found lacking in all aspects that were high on the official agenda: relevance; cumulativeness and coherence; methodological rigour; and cost effectiveness (see also Oakley, 2003). In the United Kingdom, David Hargreaves 1996 lecture to the Teacher Training Agency (Hargreaves, 1996), the Tooley and Darby report (1998), commissioned by the then Chief Inspector of Schools, Chris Woodhead, and the Hillage et al. report (1998), together with remarks by Chris Woodhead and the Secretary of State for Education, David Blunkett (2000), were key elements in this discourse. And in the way of these things, despite the flaws, misunderstandings and intellectual vacuity of much of the substance of these elements, their effectivity cannot be denied. There have been a number of very significant consequences for the organization and conduct of educational research, and more to come (Ball, 2001). As argued elsewhere (Oancea, 2005), taken together, such documents epitomise an orthodoxy of education research common in policy circles in the 1990s and beyond and structured around expectations of cumulativeness, means-ends rationality, teleology, and convergence of knowledge creation and growth.

Over the same period of time, a particular strand of official discourse about education research gained power in the UK and the USA, and was articulated via a set of reports and interventions from within and outside the research 'community'.

In the UK, after an epoch of policy scepticism bordering on hostility about social research, New Labour came into power in 1997 with 'a renewed optimism about achieving more direct and instrumental use of research in policy-making processes' (Powell, 1999, p. 23). Its 1997 Manifesto endorsed the idea of a clear-cut separation between aims and ends in policy formation and implementation, as well as a focus on effectiveness and performativity: 'New Labour is a party of ideas and ideals but not of outdated ideology. *What counts is what works.* The objectives are radical. The means will be modern' (Labour Party, 1997, our emphasis). This was to become the mantra of at least the first New Labour mandate, and was repeated in various policy documents and speeches by key figures, from Tony Blair (see e.g. his 1996 Ruskin College speech expressing the belief that educational performance can be increased 'with the help of proper research and dissemination of what works'—Blair, 1996; or his January 1999 speech on Education Action Zones: 'We don't have a national blueprint—what matters is what works'—Blair, 1999) to the 2000 Education Secretary David Blunkett (in his now famous 'Influence or Irrelevance' speech to the ESRC, in which he exhorted the virtues of 'what works' as the way out from 'dogmatic', ideology-driven policy-making, and spoke of the government's 'clear commitment that we will be guided not by dogma but by an open-minded approach to understanding what works and why'[1]—Blunkett, 2000).

Many see this as part of New Labour's drive to 'modernise government' through a renewed emphasis on performance, effectiveness, transparency, and accountability (see e.g. National Audit Office, 2001, p. 26). For example, the 1999 White Paper *Modernizing Government* (Cabinet Office, 1999) (unlike its 1994 predecessor on the Civil Service—Cabinet Office and HM Treasury, 1994, *The Civil Service: Continuity and Change*) was enthusiastic about research evidence and evidence-based policy—though this was met with reservations by the research communities concerned, which worried about how exactly 'the underlying science' was to be turned into policy advice (Scott, 2003, p. 8). The enthusiasm was soon to become a mantra of education research, too. Soon, research 'evidence' ceased to be an open concept, and became increasingly regulated and weighed, as well as systematically reviewed.

The trend was inadvertently helped by the endorsement of evidence-based and evidence-informed practice by professional communities in, for example, medicine, nursing, and education (leading to the formation of the Cochrane Collaboration in medicine, and the Campbell Collaboration for social and economic fields). Government initiatives tried to build on this movement, and investments were made in setting up or developing centres such as the London Institute of Education Evidence for Policy and Practice Information and Co-ordinating Centre (EPPI-Centre), the Economic and Social Science Research Council (ESRC) UK Centre for Evidence-Based Policy and Practice and its Evidence Network, Queen Mary College, University of London (now at King's College London), or the Durham University Evidence-Based Education network (EBE). These centres and programmes took rather diverse directions—for example, the EPPI-Centre concentrated on mainstream systematic reviewing, building on pre-existing interest in evaluation and research synthesis at the London Institute, and maintaining a preoccupation with the codification and accumulation of knowledge (Oakley, 2003); while the Evidence Network engaged with reflection on realist synthesis and meta-analysis and on the role of evidence in the nexus policy-research (Boaz *et al.*, 2002; Pawson, 2002). The EBE centre built on the long-term interest at Durham in monitoring and evaluation research, but adopted a line that was closer to the official interest in 'what works': 'Evidence-Based Education' signifies the idea that educational policy and practice should be guided by the best evidence about what works' (Evidence-Based Education website, accessed 29 May 2007)—and to this aim the centre was prepared, not only to promote evidence-base initiatives and the use of experimental designs in research, but also, through its Evidence-Based Education Network, to actively campaign against 'non-evidence-based policy and practice'.

In the USA, the re-authorised 'No Child Left Behind' (NCLB) Act of 2001 included over 100 mentions of 'scientifically-based research' as the desirable basis for education, in general, and for schooling, in particular. Article 37 of the act defined such research as that which met the attributes of rigour, systematicity, objectivity, validity, and reliability, as warranted by the choice of method (empirical, experimental and quantitative designs, with 'a preference for random-assignment experiments'), and as accredited not only by peer review, but also by officially-designed agencies and clearinghouses.[2] The US National Research Council's (NRC) Committee on Scientific Principles for Education Research report (Shavelson and Towne, 2002) endorsed this definition, and, while acknowledging the complexity and qualitative depth of educational settings, argued that the answer to policy-originated criticisms of educational research was to build a *scientific* culture among research communities in the field. Such culture would stem from the premise that all scientific endeavour—education included—ought to be guided by six principles: pose significant questions that can be investigated empirically; link research to relevant theory; use methods that permit direct investigation of the question; provide a coherent and explicit chain of reasoning; replicate and generalise across studies; and disclose research to encourage professional scrutiny and critique (Shavelson and Towne, 2002, p. 52; see also Feuer, Towne and Shavelson, 2002, for further consideration of the NRC report and of its points of contact with, and of departure from, the 'what works' movement).[3] The report sparked extensive debate in the USA (see e.g. *Educational Researcher*, 31.8, 2002; *Educational Theory*, 55.3, 2005). In particular, the expectation that all research communities ultimately adhere to the same methodological and epistemological principles was thought dangerous and disempowering, and stifling of open critical debate about principles as well as techniques, particularly when endorsed by 'authoritative sources' such as the National Academy of Science (Moss, 2005, p. 280).

In such a context, the search for (research-based) evidence of 'what works', and the subsequent transfer of such knowledge (deemed inherently cumulative) into practice and policy, was gradually pushed into the centre of publicly funded research in education (as illustrated, in the US context, in the National Centre for Education Research's (NCER) call for proposals for education research projects and programs 2002–2006—see the NCER website). The preferred sources of evidence and tools of the 'what works' model are: experimental design interventions, with a predilection for Randomised Controlled Trials; systematic syntheses of research (systematic reviewing, meta-analysis), and in particular experimental research and quantitative findings; and realistic evaluation ('what works, for whom, in what circumstances, and why'—Pawson and Tilley, 1997). Each of these is a legitimate, worthwhile approach to research and to research synthesis, tackling important research questions and, in the process, supporting policy in its need to access and use research findings (see Slavin, 2002, 2004;[4] Taylor Fitz-Gibbon, 2003; Schwandt, 2005, on the importance of experimental research in answering the 'what works' questions of policy-makers and practitioners; Davies, 2000; Gough and Elbourne, 2002, p. 226; Oakley *et al.*, 2002; and Oakley, 2003, on systematic reviewing as a mode of codifying and managing, rather than generating, knowledge; and Pawson, 2002, on the promise of realist synthesis). The problems seem to stem not from one particular model or design as such, but from the policy-driven filtering of evidence on technical grounds, the hierarchies of knowledge on which this filtering draws, and the standard-setting exercises that narrow the contribution of research to policy and practice to a purely instrumental role.[5]

In the late 1990s and early 2000s, the so-called What Works Clearinghouse (WWC) was created with public funding in the USA, and is administered by the US Department of Education's Institute of Education Sciences through a joint venture contract with the American Institutes for Research and the Campbell Collaboration.[6] Both the WWC, in the USA, and the EPPI-Centre, in the UK (though the latter is university-affiliated and has a different history), are involved in weighing, judging and systematising research, though the ways in which they pursue their aims are distinct. What the two initiatives seem to have in common is the strong policy, and political, support that they enjoy (see for example No Child Left Behind, in the US case); an ideal of cumulative knowledge inspired by the medical model; as well as explicit references to the evidence-base movement epitomised by the Cochrane and Campbell collaborations. The EPPI centre's systematic reviews hold at heart values such as explicitness (of methods, strategies, criteria etc.); standardisation of procedures (keywords, searches, reporting); objectivity (unbiased searches, treatment, assessment); comprehensiveness (breadth, descriptions); cumulativeness (of data, leading to synthesis—as structured narrative, summary tables, meta-analysis; of quality assessment—leading to an overarching judgement of 'weight of evidence'); transparency (generally treated as a technical matter);[7] classification; and user involvement (see EPPI-Centre website; also, Oakley, 2003, pp. 23–24). The What Works Clearinghouse is more explicitly interested in effectiveness (of educational interventions), causality, validity, and scientific rigour (see the WWC website). The two initiatives also differ in the sense that, whilst the US initiative emphasises the value of 'scientific' education research about what works in practice and policy, as measured against certain methodological standards and hierarchies of evidence, the UK initiative favours research synthesis, quality assurance and evidence weighing (in a process that was originally called 'systematic reviewing').

At least in their original manifestos,[8] both initiatives seemed to privilege:

- *first*, a view of knowledge that favoured commensurable standards of scientificity across the natural and social sciences: 'ultimately, we failed to convince ourselves that at a fundamental level beyond the differences in specialised techniques and objects of inquiry across the individual sciences, a meaningful distinction could be made among social, physical, and life science research and scientific research in education ... Thus the committee concluded that the set of guiding principles that apply to scientific inquiry in education are the same set of principles that can be found across the full range of scientific inquiry' (Shavelson and Towne, 2002, pp. 51–52);
- *second*, a hierarchy of modes of knowledge and research designs that placed experimental work at its top—particularly in the form of RCTs (the medical research-inspired 'golden standard' for research);
- *third*, a combination of realism (of the studies included in a review), in the sense of knowledge of the world as given (with an in-built aspiration towards objectivity), and instrumentalism (of the review itself and its uses, as well as of the overall role attributed to research), in the sense of pre-defined practical ends and deliberation about the means to attaining them (see also Hodkinson and Smith, in Thomas and Pring, 2004);
- *fourth*, a view of the dynamics of knowledge as controllable systematic accumulation of findings, shaped by the pursuit of external aims, rather than fuelled by an internal logic of practice and of research; and
- *fifth*, an emphasis on thoroughness, rigour, and explicitness as core dimensions of research quality, coupled with a technical view of quality assessment that centred on explicit external criteria, accuracy of measurements, and public accreditation (see, for example, the Educational Underwriters' 'verified research' stamp of approval).[9]

Clearly, despite the fact that some of the current models of systematic review place themselves in explicit relationship with the 'what works' discourse (see e.g. the What Works Clearinghouse's reviews), systematic reviewing has a much longer history in education research, preceding the current policy-led drive towards instrumental effectiveness of research findings (see for example the early work of Glass, McGaw and Smith, 1981); as such, it arguably has the potential to be a politically cleaner, readily available, and practice-oriented tool. Oliver, Harden and Rees (2005) even seek to show how systematic reviewing may help us move 'beyond' the limitations of the 'what works' discourse; this would be enabled by, they argue, an opening of perspective from conventional systematic reviewing (focused on data extraction, quality assessment and narrative synthesis, exhaustiveness of searches, and quantitative reporting) towards cross-study design syntheses (immersion in the data; juxtaposition and constant comparison between several parallel synthesis of different types of evidence; theoretical sampling; combination of quantitative and qualitative synthesis of findings) (see also Nind, 2006; Andrews, 2005; Bennett *et al.*, 2005; Oakley, 2003; Boaz *et al.*, 2002; Evans and Benefield, 2001).

Gough and Elbourne (2002) attacked what they called the 'false dualism' between a 'positivistic' view of systematic synthesis of research and 'interpretative' qualitative synthesis and argued for reviews that strived to be 'dynamic', 'critical', and 'productive', rather than aspiring to become faithful mirrors of reality. The issue of accumulation, they claim, ceases to be an insurmountable problem if one realises that research synthesis does not necessarily have to mean accumulation of factual evidence and quantitative aggregation (meta-analysis), but could well amount to a 'meta-ethnography' and the development of interpretative explanations (pp. 232, 234).

However, the version of systematic reviewing that has been pulled into the mainstream of current research and education policy lent itself with ease to more instrumental filtering and digesting of evidence down to manageable, 'quality certified', chunks. 'What works' defines the values and sets the standards against which research evidence is to be judged. The aspiration towards (policy-driven) cumulative growth of a body of instrumentally effective research evidence is what we referred to as 'systematic accumulations of "what works"' in the title of this chapter.

2 ACCOUNTS OF KNOWLEDGE AND THE LIMITS OF 'WHAT WORKS'

In a sense, recent policy-originated criticisms of education research, such as those mentioned at the start of this chapter, were 'captive' within this discourse, which acted as the source of both prompts for, and pre-defined responses to, criticism (see also Smeyers and Depaepe, 2006, p. 11). Both the WWC and the EPPI models were particularly powerful responses to such criticisms precisely because they shared with them a set of assumptions and values. The push for their generalisation as the 'golden' standard for policy-relevant and policy-recognised research is however open to challenge, from the more obvious charges (such as the limitations of the underlying analogy with medical and natural science research, or the questionable hierarchies of evidence and of sources that privilege excessively experimental designs and quantitative evidence) to concerns about the definitions of knowledge, research and practice that the model takes as a starting point. The critical comments below will address mostly the restrictive 'what works' discourse, and will only touch on systematic reviewing to the extent to which some of its models share similar assumptions.

The view of knowledge adopted by the 'what works' movement (and partly by some models of systematic reviewing) does not accommodate well modes of research that embrace non-cumulative, divergent, or non-teleological views of knowledge. For example, it does not fully account for knowledge of the world as 'taken' by the person, rather than 'given', or for research that aims to destabilise taken-for-granted concepts and frameworks rather than replace them with equally closed alternative systems. As such, it is a restrictive model that, though potentially technically sound in its own terms, fails to respond to the needs of policy and practice and to capture the diversity and openness of the research enterprise and of the forms of evidence it produces. Sanderson (2003) links this to further concerns about the assumptions underpinning the effectiveness-centred model of the research- practice- policy relationship, particularly in relation to its predilection for research that provides evidence of strong, linear causal linkages between observed interventions and observed effects; its instrumentalist-rationalist conceptualisation of the role of research and research findings; and the aspiration for certainty that often obliterates the complexities of particular situations.

'What works' conceptualises practice and policy as interventions to which research is expected to make instrumental contributions. It thus fails to recognise the ethical and social nature of educational practice, and the creative encounters of practical wisdom and technical rationality within it (See Oancea and Furlong, 2007). Biesta (2007) argues that the movement misconstrues the nature of the practical epistemology underpinning educational practice as inquiry about means (to achieve pre-defined ends) that translates straightforwardly into rules for action (the 'cookbook' approach). In an attempt to build viable alternatives to the 'what works' discourse, Biesta draws on insights from Aristotle, Dewey and de Vries and supports a view of research as source of hypotheses and evidence about what may be possible, in order to inform intelligent problem-solving and open normative debate. In addition, rather than making merely instrumental contributions to practice, research fulfils a cultural, as well as a technical, role, and so it supports open and democratic debate about the definitions, aims and ends of education.

Further, the 'what works' movement places the emphasis on public accreditation, rather than on intrinsic excellence in research, and so it is not only research that is instrumentalised, but also the official concept of 'quality', as well as the assessment of evidence that is embedded in practice and policy (a point developed in Oancea, 2007). Rather than focusing excessively on technology and morally-neutral expertise, Sanderson (2003) suggests that our understanding of the role of research in practice and policy should focus on intrinsic excellence (MacIntyre, 1985) and the balance between epistemic, technical, and phronetic reasoning (Toulmin, 2001). Such a shift in perspective would bring to the foreground aspects of research that, though crucial for its relationship with policy and practice, have been so far neglected in the public discourse, such as the social, institutional and organisational context of decisions (Majone, 1989) and the communicative processes involved, based on dialogue and argumentation; the normative order of obligation and necessity (rather than the logic of hierarchy, calculation and causes-effects) in making judgements, including moral-political judgements, about what it appropriate in particular contexts (March and Olsen, 1989; Schwandt, 2000); the uncertainty and pluralism of praxis; and the need for free, open normative debate to replace the mechanistic appeal to pre-determined standards likely to privilege the more powerful. If all this is taken into account, Sanderson argues, 'the question for teachers is not simply 'what is effective', but rather, more broadly it is, 'what is appropriate for these children in these circumstances' (Sanderson, 2003, p. 341).

Last, though not least, the definitions of good education research which characterise the 'what works' drive, tend to exclude (or at least marginalise) the concern for what may be 'educationally worthwhile'. For Biesta (2007), 'what works'-focused definitions and assessments of practice ignore (or relegate to a marginal position) core considerations of educational value and ethics, and place undue emphasis on effectiveness, factual judgement, and instrumental knowledge. Elliott (2001) links the 'engineering model' of educational research (i.e. an instrumental model of evidence-based practice) to the notion of outcomes-based education stemming from the work of Benjamin Bloom (a point developed further in Elliot and Lukeš' contribution to this volume). As such, the central assumptions of the model are concerned with effectiveness and efficiency in the production of outputs; a contingent relationship between ends and means; and the pre-specification of ends as quality standards (p. 560). He opposes this to an ethical perspective on educational research, inspired by MacIntyre (1985) and Stenhouse (1975), and emphasises the educational value of practice and research and the aspiration towards internal excellence that underpins professional judgement.

The above comments converge to indicate that, while the systematic accumulation of validated evidence about 'what works' may have been an *effective* response to recent criticisms of education research (and one likely to gain policy endorsement), as well as an effective way of discarding certain instances of poor research practice, at the same time it furthers a discourse that is based on *narrow* assumptions about knowledge, which run against some core principles of education research. As will be shown in the remainder of this chapter, the discourse ultimately constructs and promotes an impoverished view of research evidence and of how it may be brought to 'work' in practice and policy.

3 RESEARCH AND EVIDENCE

In the light of this privileging of certain modes of research, it is important to reflect upon the nature of research more generally, and in particular to recognise, first, the different kinds of evidence related to different kinds of research questions, and, second, the consequent limitations of general research-based solutions to generalised problems.

There are no doubt many definitions of research, but for our purposes it might be described as the systematic gathering of evidence (in the sense outlined below), or indeed (as in philosophical research) the systematic analysis of the conceptual framework within which that evidence is gathered, with a view to answering certain questions. In that sense, research might be understood partly in terms of what it is *not*: the expression or indeed development of unsubstantiated opinions; the immediate response to a query; the haphazard or uncoordinated gathering of data; the lack of rationale in the selection of data, and so on. But this leaves open the many ways in which research might be conducted—the many different ways in which one's search might be considered 'systematic'. There is a *prima facie* case for not confining research to one particular model of systematic enquiry.

There are, however, four aspects of this that immediately give rise to controversy.

First, what counts as 'evidence' is by no means clear. Very often it is interpreted to mean 'observable data'—what you get from 'going out to have a look', those observations then being organised within some very general explanatory framework. And, indeed, that, as is argued above, would seem to dominate the research that informs policy. But there is no reason why evidence should not include 'previous judgements' (as in legal research), documents (as in historical research), arguments that have survived critical scrutiny (as in philosophical research), personal accounts (as in narrative research), identification of implicit social rules and norms (as in ethnographic research), and expert judgements. What counts as evidence (and thus as research) depends on the nature of the question— and those questions can be of logically different kinds. Hence, it is necessary to clarify what is meant by evidence for a particular intervention having the desired effect—and that raises central issues about the foundations and nature of knowledge.

Second, however, it is not always clear as to what counts as a researchable question. Prior to research, there is often a state of puzzlement—perhaps very vague at its onset. That puzzlement might be at the personal level (e.g. how might I best put across the concept of osmosis to this group of learners?) or at the policy level (e.g. why do standards appear to be so low?). Half the battle in doing research lies in making explicit the basis of one's puzzlement (for example, the feeling that prior attempts at teaching a concept are not effective or that standards are lower than they should be), and then turning that puzzlement into questions that are specific enough for one to know what would count as evidence in this particular case. The puzzlement about 'low standards' provides a good example. There is no doubt from political pronouncements and from media coverage of education that (a) standards are not as good as they should be, and (b) certain interventions (for example, the literacy strategy) will lead to their improvement. But there is a need for a lot of prior conceptual work upon the meaning of 'standards'—clarifying what exactly one has in mind, disaggregating the concept from the performance indicators that have been politically adopted for measuring standards, and deciding thereby what would count as evidence for or against the belief that standards were low. However, that itself leads on to traditional debates on 'verifiability'—about the meaning of a question in that its meaning is logically related to the kind of evidence that would enable one to answer it.

Third, both the puzzlement and the attempt to overcome that puzzlement are shot through with problems associated with the different ways in which people (researchers and policy-makers) conceptualise the issues and particularly the different ways in which particular features of the situation are highlighted by some, and not by others, depending on the values they espouse. Take, for example once again, questions about standards. 'Standards' refers to benchmarks of good performance that are logically related to the nature and purpose of the activity. Different values, often implicit and unacknowledged, affect the understanding of the purpose of the activity, and thereby what are to be seen as appropriate standards. For example, the Nuffield Review of 14–19 Education and Training for England and Wales[10] starts with the question, *What counts as an educated 19 year-old in this day and age?*; the answers to this question entail different conceptions of appropriate standards and of the kind of evidence upon which to decide whether they are going up or down (Hayward *et al.*, 2006). Are standards of literacy improving simply because an increased number of learners reach 'satisfactory' grades in literacy, irrespective of whether they read books? The rival ways in which reality is conceptualised and evaluated raise perennial questions about the 'social construction' of that reality, about the objectivity of our knowledge claims and about the sociological critiques of the prevailing organisation of knowledge and of 'knowledge production'. And it may be the case that the failure of policy to appreciate what research says lies in its unquestioned, albeit questionable, way of conceptualising the issues and the data. The philosophical spirit is lacking.

Fourth, tied intimately to all these problems is the nature of explaining how things come to be as they are, because the need to explain is the driving force behind research. If you want to change things (and thus to put in place some 'intervention' such as the literacy hour), then it is first necessary to explain why things happen as they do and how a desired change is likely to overcome the problems encountered. But, just as there are many logically different kinds of question, and different kinds of evidence relating to these different questions, so there are different kinds of explanation. It is the failure to see this that so often leads to one dominant model of explanation, thereby impoverishing so much educational research.

The following enlarges upon these four points, bringing out the distinctive issues in the nature and relevance of philosophical theorising about knowledge.

Evidence

The first thing to say about 'evidence' is that it must not be confused with 'proof'—a mistake too often made by politicians in their search for certainty and for solid foundations for their policies. In adopting a policy, politicians want to appeal to evidence that demonstrates that a particular intervention will work. But there is little outside pure logic and mathematics that can be proved in the strict sense of that term. There is always something unpredictable about the consequences of what one does for several reasons. First, the future may not always be like the past even in the physical world. Second, however, in the world of persons, prediction is even more precarious; different persons might well conceptualise the situation differently from each other, thereby interpreting the intervention and reacting to it differently. It is for that reason that some argue that one can never provide general explanations for human behaviour—a fallacious implication from our point of view, but it does make the evidence a little less compelling in particular cases. Conclusions have to be more tentative, open to exceptions and open to refinement in the light of further experience.

Evidence can be weak or strong, invoked with greater or lesser degrees of confidence. It may have force for a variety of reasons arising from different forms of discourse—statistical probability or analogous circumstances or historical precedents or social norms or understanding of human motivation. Conflicting evidence needs to be weighed and deliberated upon. Furthermore, we often in life need to act on a range of evidence that, though weak, is stronger than the evidence for any alternative course of action. Teachers, faced with new classes, act according to the evidence gleaned from previous classes, from what they have read, or from discussions with other teachers, but they can never be certain that their classes are the same as the others in all relevant respects. The consequence is that the conclusions reached from previous evidence have to be tentative and tested out in the new situation. Indeed, Stenhouse (1975) referred to the curriculum as a hypothesis to be tested out by the teacher in a class that, though like other classes in some respect, was quite unlike them in others. If research is to inform teaching, then evidence of many different kinds has to shape the views (or 'hypotheses') of the teacher.

Exactly the same applies to policy formation. The Nuffield Review is seeking to understand the relatively low participation rate at the ages of 17 and 18 with a view to making recommendations to the Government. Difficulties lie in this not being a homogeneous group as far as different relevant explanations go—hence, the need to seek different kinds of evidence (economic conditions, social class, local culture, low expectations, pressure of peer group, influence of the media, family aspirations), knowing that any generalisation will be falsified in particular cases and knowing that even tentative conclusions will need to be refined in the light, not only of further experience, but also of changing conceptions of 'participation' and 'learning'. Indeed, Government policy, for which evidence is sought, is constantly changing, if not in words, then in the meaning attached to those words, as is illustrated in the Review's research into 'apprenticeship'.

However, the difficulties faced by the Nuffield Review lie deeper. In reviewing 14–19 education and training, puzzles do arise that need to be shaped into questions—why so many young people reject the educational opportunities open to them, how a system of education comes to be competitive and fragmented, what qualities, attitudes, skills and understanding should be nurtured. But such puzzlement—the mark of a good researcher—is sometimes alien to policy-makers who, being certain about the ends to be attained (translated into targets), puzzle about the means of achieving them—for which purpose they see the need for the researchers. Hence, so often evidence is 'filtered out' through policy assumptions, formally stated in party manifestos. Agendas are set independently of contrary evidence—for example, in pursuing a policy in assessment or in educational selection.

Research, therefore, cannot be seen as something that gives a firm foundation from which to proceed with absolute confidence either in the formulation of policy or in the pursuit of particular practices. At the same time, this does not entail that there is no such thing as research knowledge—that all accounts are but social constructions, relative to one's own particular standpoint and freely open to quite different social constructions. As we shall argue, the lack of conclusive verification, and the continuing possibility of the further refinement of one's conclusions in the light of evidence, does not entail that there are no truth conditions for what one claims and thus no way of falsifying the conclusions reached. The refinement of one's views presupposes a reality, independent of one's knowing it, which forces one to do the refining.

Questions—Meaning and 'Verification'

A. J. Ayer (1946) argued that the meaning of a statement lay in its mode of verification, and indeed that is seen as the distinguishing mark of logical positivism. However, there were seen to be only two modes of verification and thus two kinds only of meaningful statements—purely logical and mathematical statements, which were true by reference to the principle of contradiction, and empirical statements, which ultimately could be verified by reference to the observations that they described. All other statements were meaningless, which would include (as O'Connor, 1956, argued) most statements in education, especially those of educational research. The shadow of Ayer, O'Connor and others still hangs over educational research where the model of general statements, logically reducible to statements of the observations that could unambiguously be carried out, would seem to prevail, as reflected in the criticisms already referred to.

Within the educational research community there is, therefore, a divide between, on the one hand, those who seem to aspire to making a science of educational research, hypothesising the causes of events and thus of 'what might work', seeking to generalise, for example, about the 'effective school' or the 'good teacher' on the basis of unassailable observations, and, on the other hand, those who reject such a narrow conception, pointing to the fact that human beings are not like purely physical matter and cannot be understood or explained within such a positivist framework. This results in a dichotomy between quantitative and qualitative research designs—the former receiving the approbation of Government looking for the evidence for particular policies, the other generally embraced by practitioners but disdained by those who want general answers to generally conceived problems.

This dichotomy is quite unhelpful (see Pring, 2000). The mistake lies in rejecting the main point in Ayer's definition at the same time as his narrow conception of 'verification'. In making any claim, in pronouncing on any subject, we are implicitly indicating that we or others could be mistaken. If nothing could conceivably contradict or weigh against such a claim, then there would be no point in making it. Implicit, therefore, in making a statement is the assumption of a logical link between that kind of statement and a particular sort of evidence. For example, 'smaller classes enhance the quality of learning' presupposes that certain observations or ways of assessing performance would be relevant evidence for saying that this statement is true. And that would be compatible with maintaining a certain degree of uncertainty, since further evidence might make one withdraw the statement or refine it or limit it to only certain sizes of class or certain kinds of learner or certain kinds of class teaching.

The systematic search for evidence, therefore, depends on the sort of question being asked and the sort of discourse within which that question is being raised, for within different sorts of discourse the relation of judgement to evidence will be different and will be made with different degrees of confidence. In all research, therefore, it is necessary to clarify the sort of question being asked, the sort of discourse within which it is being asked and thus the sort of evidence that will be relevant to answering the question—with different degrees of certainty.

Values and Rival Conceptions of Reality

One objection already referred to is that, since research takes place within a particular way of conceiving reality, then conclusions reached must necessarily be relative to that conception—and there are rival conceptions. A particular behaviour might be conceived by one person as 'deviant', but by another as 'creative' or 'enterprising'. The failure to participate or remain in some form of education and training might be interpreted as an act of defiance or as a response to a boring curriculum or as a rational act in the light of personal economic aspirations. The world can be described in many different ways, and it might well be argued that no one particular way should be privileged over another. Disagreement in judgement (for example, that Mary is intelligent or that John is cheeky) may not be settled by further observation because 'intelligence' and 'cheek' are understood differently—those differences reflecting, possibly, differences in social background or gender or ethnicity. Indeed, the dominant language of management—of inputs and outputs, of performance indicators and audits, of curriculum delivery and targets, of economy gains and value added—creates a different way of describing education and thus of conceptualising both ends and the means for achieving those ends. It is a language that may find no room for research that has not adopted that way of describing the complex world of learning and motivation.

Often those differences in conceiving a situation arise from the different values that people hold and that permeate the judgements they make. To educate someone is to enable them to learn those things that are regarded as valuable in some way; the person is to some degree transformed for the better. 'Education' is in that sense an evaluative term. But there is by no means universal agreement on what those values are. People have different ideas of what constitutes an educated person—'intellectual excellence' according to Newman (2001/1852), an intelligent and active contributor to the wider community according to Dewey (1916; 1936), someone displaying practical capability, according to the RSA 1980 Manifesto, and so on. Deliberations over the aims of education are essentially moral—concerning the qualities and virtues, the capabilities and understandings that, under the banner of 'education', are thought worth promoting. Such values permeate the meanings attached to standards, successful learning, personal achievement, educational purposes, and so on.

There is a danger, therefore, as a result of the different ways in which people might and do conceptualise both descriptively and evaluatively the world we inhabit, of denying the value that gives a different account of the educational scene from that which is officially endorsed. Certain ways of describing the world dominate because of the power that some people have to define what counts as knowledge, reinforced through examinations and such like machineries of control. To reconcile these different accounts of the world and the different evaluations of things within those worlds so described, is essentially a philosophical matter, raising questions about the adequacy and consistency of the concepts employed and the objectivity of judgements made.

As is frequently pointed out, however, there are particular difficulties in accounts given of people and of the societies in which they live, because persons, unlike purely material entities, interpret situations and, therefore, in a real sense, those situations become different ones as a result of those interpretations. The social relations, for example, are not objective in the sense of existing independently of the conceptions one has of those relations. The *fact* of marriage is not independent of the social rules that constitute 'being married', and these change from society to society and indeed evolve within any one society. It is not just that different people interpret physical reality differently, but also that social reality is created by those interpretations. This quite clearly has a profound effect upon the nature of much educational research that, obviously, is concerned with learners acting within social traditions that shape their conceptions of reality and that in an important way create the reality they are to inhabit.

This limits the extent to which generalisations can be made in addressing perceived educational problems. To understand why participation in education and training is comparatively low, one needs, not to generalise about all young people—look for the causal factors, as it were, which then will enable the government to make the right causal intervention—but to understand the many different social norms that enter, community by community, into the ways in which young people see what is possible, desirable, manageable and worthwhile. The research somehow needs to get on the inside of such social understandings.

This does not mean that we ought to abandon all chance of reaching the kind of general conclusions that would inform central policy, and despair about the nature and role of research in relation to policy. As Peter Winch (1958) argued in his influential book, *The Idea of a Social Science*, the differences between different societies and social groups can themselves be understood within a recognisable form of human life (for example, shared needs for satisfying basic needs, for bringing up the young, for ensuring safety and basic health, for formalising relationships), and within a recognisable form of human motivation and tendencies (need for affection and recognition, virtues of loyalty and honesty, vices of jealousy and revenge).[11] It is logically possible to enter into and to understand a society very different from one's own by reason of one's common humanity.

However, this difference between the physical and the human world is crucial to understanding the possibilities of, limitations of and approaches to educational research, and this is reflected in the different kinds of explanation in answer to different sorts of questions—and thus the different sorts of evidence to be invoked in providing those explanations.

Diversity of Explanations

As was explained in the first part of this chapter, one major criticism of educational research has been that it has not produced the kind of generalised statements about educational processes and outcomes, based on accumulating evidence as a result of systematic enquiry, which would enable policy-makers to initiate the interventions that would make education 'work'.

That would seem not to be wholly true of the past. The research into IQ testing in the 1950s by Phillip Vernon demonstrated that coaching for the 11+examinations could affect a person's IQ score by as much as 15 points, thereby undermining the basis of selection at the age of 11, which was premised on fixed and detectable intelligence; selection was subsequently abandoned in most local education authorities. The 'political arithmetic' of Halsey, Floud and Anderson in the 1960s demonstrated the close correlation between social class and educational achievement, thereby giving evidence for the creation of Education Priority Zones. The more recent injection of money into Sure Start arises from the systematic collection of data on the effectiveness of early interventions in a child's social and educational development. Some, but by no means all, large-scale research required both control and experimental groups so that comparisons could be made between those with a particular intervention and those without it. There is danger, in the emphasis upon differences between young people, of dismissing the kind of research that presupposes a certain commonality between young people that does enable generalisations to be made, whilst accepting that there may be many exceptions to the generalisation.

Such statistical generalisations can, however, be too often treated as explanations of a causal kind—for example, the high correlation between poverty or social class and educational achievement, or between certain styles of leadership and 'effective schools', as though poverty causes poor achievement or leadership causes effectiveness. But this would ignore the several different ways in which distinctively human activity needs to be explained. Hence, it would be useful to map out the different kinds of explanation that logically relate to different sorts of question and that shape what is meant by evidence.[12]

Causal Explanation

The dominance of a research model that seeks the accumulation of knowledge through thoroughly tested general hypotheses concerning 'what works', often conducted through large-scale comparative and control groups, calls upon a view of causality such that the successful intervention in the experimental group could be said to be the cause of what works. The nature of this underlying view and the critical response to it are developed in much greater detail by Paul Smeyers in his contribution to this volume. The various theories of and research into behaviour modification illustrate this well. Indeed, such research should not be rejected out of hand. There are aspects of our behaviour where talk of causality would seem quite appropriate, but it would also seem that there are aspects of what it is to be human that limit the explanatory power of causality in this sense.

On the other hand, the recognition of such limitations should not blind us to the value of large-scale quantitative accounts. The Nuffield Review, for example, has been very concerned to find the statistical data on such matters as entry and completion of apprenticeships, the take-up or otherwise of particular subjects at A Level, or the number of young people not in education, employment or training (NEET). But the data so gathered provides not so much 'causal explanation' as a set of puzzles that require very different sorts of explanation.

Explaining Human Behaviour

To ask why a person acts in the way he or she does is logically very different from asking why the lights failed or why such a person has 'flu'. A different sort of explanation is required—one in terms of intentions and motives. There is a world of difference between a blink and a wink. To understand why the people in the 'NEET group' are as they are, reference would need to be made to their intentions—the reasons they would give for dropping out. And these reasons may be very different from one

'NEET' to another—in order to escape the constant experience of failure, in order to pursue a particular interest, in order to support the family. Such intentional differences are too often ignored in general policy interventions that presuppose a specific cause, requiring a specific intervention.

But intentions do not arise in a vacuum. They may arise from certain dispositions to behave in a certain way—to be honest or dishonest, to be self-sufficient or dependent—and these might be seen to be created within a particular climate of social expectations, whether those of the family or the wider social group.

On the other hand, there is little point in acting intentionally unless others are able to interpret one's intentions. I raise my hand, intentionally, in order to draw attention to me or to wave goodbye or to signal a revolution. The meaning of the hand-raising logically relates not only to my intentions but also to the social rules through which that intention is to be recognised for what it is. There is no point in signalling a revolution if others do not know what I am doing. Hence, a crucial element in understanding persons is an understanding of the rules and norms through which particular actions have meaning and are to be interpreted. Of course, there are different overlapping levels of such social rules that define the different social groups to which one belongs—the wider society, the family, the set of youths with whom one mixes, etc. Explanations of young people's behaviour and decision-making require reference to the social rules through which they interpret others' actions and expect to be understood by them in turn. The general explanation for underachievement, say, or for dropping out of school, which gives rise to a particular intervention, might well fail because it fails to take into account the many different ways in which the young people interpret the situations differently, have intentions that the interventions take no account of, and ignore the diverse social rules through which the social reality of the young people is defined.

4 DEMOCRATISATION OF RESEARCH AND POLITICAL FRAMEWORK

Research is the systematic search for answers in the light of relevant evidence. Relevance' is partly determined by the nature of the question and the kind of discourse—historical, interpersonal, scientific, comparative—within which it falls. But one thing is clear from the above analysis, namely that no search for evidence, however systematic, can give grounds for certainty in the conclusions reached. There is a need to live with uncertainty—to be open to further evidence, further reconceptualisation of the evidence received and further criticism of the interpretation of that evidence. The state of knowledge is always provisional. The world, both physical and social, to which that knowledge applies is itself changing in an unpredictable way—the social world in particular because of the inevitable evolution of meanings attributed to experience as each interacts with each other.

Given the provisional nature of our knowledge and the need, in testing that knowledge, to be open to criticism, especially the critical appraisal of those who are, by reason of their role, the creators of that knowledge—the teachers and the learners—then that knowledge is more likely to be accurate if the participants themselves are able to contribute to its testing, criticism and reproduction. In other words, the very tentativeness of the knowledge base requires what, in the not far distant past, was referred to as the democratisation of knowledge. And this was central not just to the philosophy of educational researchers (see Simons, 1995) but to policy-makers themselves. Recall the words of Derek Morrell, in effect the architect of the Schools Council established in 1964, and captured in his lecture to the College of Preceptors, *Education and Change* (Morrell, 1966). The problem (the initial puzzle, as it were) concerned the preparation of young people for an unpredictable future especially when there is little consensus in society as to what constitutes a worthwhile form of life. Morrell, the civil servant, reflecting upon the establishment of the Schools Council, speaks of the need to democratise the processes of problem-solving as we try, as best we can, to develop an educational approach appropriate to a permanent condition of change. He continues:

> Jointly, we need to define the characteristics of change—relying, wherever possible, on objective data rather than on opinions unsupported by evidence. Jointly, we need to sponsor the research and development work necessary to respond to change. Jointly, we must evaluate the results of such work, using both judgement and measurement techniques. ... Jointly, we need to recognise that freedom and order can no longer be reconciled through implicit acceptance of a broadly ranging and essentially static consensus on educational aims and methods (Morrell, 1966, pp. 12–13).

For educational research to be relevant to policy and to professional practice, there is a need for all to recognise the provisional nature of knowledge to recognise that in the further refinement of that provisional knowledge, there are different sorts of evidence that need to be weighed and balanced, and that those different sources lie in the large-scale accounts of interventions, in the understanding of social norms that shape personal interpretation, in the experience of the teacher whose judgement embraces the peculiarities of the situation and in the voices of the learner whose own distinctive interpretation of the classroom interactions gives particular meanings to the events, quite different from those of teacher and policy-maker. Reasonable policy and practice can arise only from a deliberation of these different sources of evidence and the logically different sorts of explanation—and, hence, in a context where this deliberation is democratised. By democratised we mean both that the different research and evidence voices are heard and that conclusions remain tentative and provisional, welcoming further dialogue and criticism—a point developed in much greater detail by Elliott and Lukeš in their contribution to this volume.

CONCLUSION

The criticisms of educational research, as outlined in the first sections of this chapter, needed to be taken seriously. They pointed out that much educational research failed to meet a range of criteria—clear relation of conclusions to evidence presented, clarification of the basis of the samples selected, accessibility to those who might benefit from its findings, addressing the problems to which policy-makers and teachers need answers (even if these have to be provisional). But, in response to these criticisms, there has been an often officially sanctioned impoverishment of what counts as research—a narrow understanding of 'what works'. That 'impoverishment' lies, not so much in the inadequacy or inappropriateness of method, as in the deeper philosophical problems that have been raised in this chapter. These are essentially about the nature of knowledge: what it means to know and to understand in the complex social world of interpersonal relations, partial knowledge, autonomous decision making, cultural influences upon individual preferences, the screening of facts through values held and frameworks taken-for-granted within particular communities.

These epistemological considerations are reflected in the concept of 'evidence' and the many ways in which different people distinguish between conclusive, good, supportive and poor evidence. The chapter argues that little evidence can be conclusive in the development of policy and practice. We have to live with uncertainty, and act upon the best evidence available, always open to criticism, revision and further refinement in the light of further evidence—a democratisation, therefore, of the decision making processes at every level of policy-making.

Correspondence: Alis Oancea and Richard Pring, Department of Education, 15 Norham Gardens, Oxford OX2 6PY, UK.
E-mail: Alis.Oancea@education.ox.ac.uk; Richard.Pring@educational-studies.oxford.ac.uk

NOTES

1. Critics of current policy regimes sharply discriminate between the rhetoric of 'what works' and the actual process of policy formation and implementation. For example, Dainton (2006) goes as far as claiming that the 2005 DfES 'Higher Standards' White Paper 'cherry picked' research that 'works' for ideological, rather than educational, purposes. Elliott (2001) claims that the 'what works' discourse is only 'histrionically' effective, 'as a masquerade for arbitrary preferences' (p. 560). Others have interpreted the 'what works' discourse as a challenge to research communities, and sought ways in which its principles may be put in practice collaboratively by researchers and users forming communities of practice with 'semi-permeable walls' (Webb and Ibarz, 2006, p. 218; see also Davies *et al.*, 2000; Thomas and Pring, 2004). For Smeyers and Depaepe (2006), the challenge is to investigate 'what surpasses the rather simple cause and effect rhetoric and thus transgresses the picture of performativity that keeps much of the talk about education captive' (p. 11).

2. For a critical take on the NCBL view of scientific education research, see Sternberg's (2004) concern about what he interprets as 'the assumption that good science should be politically guided'.

3. Erikson and Gutierrez (2002) deplore this perspective as 'a substitution of scientism ... for science itself', which is 'truly alarming in its naïvete and zeal' (p. 22). By contrast, Berliner

(2002) defends the NRC report and claims that, unlike the NCLB act, the report puts the emphasis on support for 'building a community of scholars', rather than on any particular method deemed most rigorous and worth funding (p. 20).

4. The chapter is a response to Olson's (2004) criticism of earlier advocacy of experimental treatments by Slavin (2004).

5. Many critics of the 'what works' or 'engineering' model of the research–policy relationship have voiced strong concerns about its instrumental assumptions and linear rationality, as well as about the political implications of its application (e.g. in terms of setting research agendas and filtering research for publication or funding). See, for example: Hammersley, 1997, 2001; Edwards, 2000; Elliott, 2001; Simons, 2003; Hammersley, in Thomas and Pring, 2004; Schwandt, 2005. Another common charge against the model is that of extreme 'positivism' (Hammersley, 2001).

6. Schoenfeld (2006) levelled criticisms at the WWC in terms of both conduct of reviews and transparency of findings; his piece was followed by a reply from the WWC in the same issue of *Educational Researcher*.

7. This prompted criticisms from, for example, MacLure, 2005.

8. It must be noted that the EPPI model in particular is still evolving and efforts were made to take on board some of its early criticisms (e.g. those regarding the place allocated to qualitative research). Oakley (2001, 2003) emphasises the fact that the roots of EPPI-style syntheses are not only in the policy requirements of the early 2000, but also in a longer-standing interest in evidence-based policy and practice and in knowledge management, codification and accumulation. She highlights the 'real' technical and conceptual challenges of systematic reviewing, but dismisses a whole range of criticisms of the EPPI model (such as Atkinson, 2000, Hammersley, 1997) as manifestations of an 'anti-evidence movement' (Oakley, 2003, pp. 26, 31).

9. In a rather bewildering example of where the drive for effectiveness and quality control may lead, Education Underwriters Inc describes itself as a nonprofit US organisation created 'due to the NCLB mandate that educational products and services be "research-based"' with the purpose of 'certifying' that educational research is NCBL 'compliant' and therefore worth investing in by schools. The certification process is summarised on the organisation's website as follows: 'Vendors must submit their research, the researchers' credentials, and other basic information. This, along with some basic assurances, will earn most companies an immediate 'EdU Pending' status. EdU then works very closely with the vendor throughout the process to ensure that the product earns full 'EdU Listed' status'. As such, the organisation 'serves as a watchdog for all educators, ensuring that products are backed by valid research. Whenever necessary, we contract with researchers to perform the review of vendors' educational research' (http://www.educationalunderwriters.org/index.htm). Tempting as it may have been, we have not investigated this any further.

10. The Nuffield Review is a six-year independent review of every aspect of 14–19 education and training for England and Wales, its final report due in 2009. The wide range of evidence informing the Review, together with its three Annual Reports, are available on its website, http://www.nuffield14-19review.org.

11. For a somewhat different interpretation of Winch, see Smeyers, 2006.

12. This is further developed in Pring, 2004.

REFERENCES

Andrews, R. (2005) The Place for Systematic Reviews in Education Research, *British Journal of Educational Studies*, 53.4, pp. 399–416.

Atkinson, E. (2000) In Defence of Ideas, or Why 'What Works' is Not Enough, *British Journal of Sociology of Education*, 21.3, pp. 317–330.

Ayer, A. J. (1946) *Language, Truth and Logic* (London, Penguin).

Ball, S. (2001) 'You've Been NERFed!' Dumbing Down the Academy: National Educational Research Forum: 'A National Strategy – Consultation Paper': A Brief and Bilious Response, *Journal of Education Policy*, 16.3, pp. 265–268.

Bennett, J., Lubben, F., Hogarth, S. and Campbell, B. (2005) Systematic Reviews of Research in Science Education: Rigour or Rigidity?, *International Journal of Science Education* 27.4, pp. 387–406.

Berliner, D. C. (2002) Educational Research: The Hardest Science of All, *Educational Researcher*, 31.8, pp. 18–20.

Biesta, G. (2007) Why 'What Works' Won't Work: Evidence-Based Practice and the Democratic Deficit in Educational Research, *Educational Theory*, 57.1, pp. 1–22.

Blair, T. (1996) Speech given at Ruskin College, Oxford, December 16th 1996. Available at: http://www.leeds.ac.uk/educol/documents/000000084.htm [accessed 28 May 2007].

Blair, T. (1999) Speech by the Prime Minister Tony Blair about Education Action Zones, 15 January 1999. Available at: http://www.number-10.gov.uk/output/Page1172.asp [accessed 28 May 2007].

Blunkett, D. (2000) Influence or Irrelevance: Can Social Science Improve Government? *Research Intelligence*, 71, pp. 12–21.

Boaz, A., Ashby, D. and Young, K. (2002) *Systematic Reviews: What Have They Got to Offer Evidence-Based Policy and Practice?* (Working Paper 2, ESRC UK Centre for Evidence-Based Policy and Practice, Queen Mary College, University of London, February 2002).

Cabinet Office and HM Treasury (1994) *The Civil Service: Continuity and Change* (London, The Stationery Office).

Cabinet Office (1999) *Modernizing Government*. Cm 4130 (London, The Stationery Office).

Dainton, S. (2006) What Works: Real Research or a Cherry Picker's Paradise?, *Forum*, 48.1, pp. 23–31.

Davies, H. T. O., Nutley, S. M. and Smith, P. C. (eds) (2000) *What Works? Evidence-Based Policy and Practice in Public Services* (Cambridge, Polity Press).

Davies, P. (2000) The Relevance of Systematic Reviews to Educational Policy and Practice, *Oxford Review of Education*, 26.3–4, pp. 365–378.

Dewey, J. (1916) *Democracy and Education* (New York, The Free Press).

Dewey, J. (1936) *Experience and Education* (New York, Macmillan).

Edwards, T. (2000) All the Evidence Shows …: Reasonable Expectations of Educational Research, *Oxford Review of Education*, 26.3–4, pp. 299–312.

Elliott, J. (2001) Making Evidence-Based Practice Educational, *British Educational Research Journal*, 27.5, pp. 555–574.

Erikson, F. and Gutierrez, K. (2002) Culture, Rigor, and Science in Educational Research, *Educational Researcher*, 31.8, pp. 21–24.

Evans, J. and Benefield, P. (2001) Systematic Reviews of Educational Research: Does the Medical Model Fit? *British Journal of Educational Studies*, 27.5, pp. 527–542.

Feuer, M. J., Towne, L. and Shavelson, R. J. (2002) Scientific Culture and Education Research, *Educational Researcher*, 31.8, pp. 4–14.

Fitz-Gibbon, C. T. (2003) Milestones En Route to Evidence-Based Policies, *Research Papers in Education*, 18.4, pp. 313–329.

Glass, G. V., McGaw, B. and Smith, M. L. (1981) *Meta-analysis in Social Research* (Newbury Park, CA, Sage Publications).

Gough, D. and Elbourne, D. (2002) Systematic Research Synthesis to Inform Policy, Practice and Democratic Debate, *Social Policy & Society*, 1.3, pp. 225–236.

Halsey, A., Floud, C. A. and Anderson, J. (eds) (1961) *Education, Economy and Society* (London, Collier-Macmillan).

Hammersley, M. (1997) Educational Research and Teaching: A Response to David Hargreaves' TTA Lecture, *British Educational Research Journal*, 23.2, pp. 141–162.

Hammersley, M. (2001) On 'Systematic' Reviews of Research Literatures: A 'Narrative' Response to Evans and Benefield, *British Journal of Educational Studies*, 27.5, pp. 543–554.

Hargreaves, D. H. (1996) *Teaching as a Research Based Profession: Possibilities and Prospects* (London, Teacher Training Agency).

Hayward, G., Hodgson, A., Johnson, J., Oancea, A., Pring, R., Spours, K., Wilde, S. and Wright, S. (2006) *The Nuffield Review of 14–19 Education and Training, England and Wales Third Annual Report 2005–06* (Oxford, Oxford University Department of Educational Studies).

Hillage, J., Pearson, R., Anderson, A. and Tamkin, P. (1998) *Excellence in Research on Schools* (London, Department for Education and Employment).

Labour Party (1997) Labour Party Manifesto. Available at: http://www.bbc.co.uk/election97/background/parties/manlab/9labmanconst.html

MacIntyre, A. (1985) *After Virtue. A Study in Moral Theory*, 2nd edn. (London, Duckworth).

MacLure, M. (2005) Clarity Bordering on Stupidity: Wheres the Quality in Systematic Review? *Journal of Education Policy*, 20.4, pp. 393–416.

Majone, G. (1989) *Evidence, Argument and Persuasion in the Policy Process* (New Haven, CT, Yale University Press).

March, J. G. and Olsen, J. P. (1989) *Rediscovering Institutions. The Organisational Basis of Politics* (New York, The Free Press).

Morrell, D. (1966) *Education and Change*. The Annual Joseph Payne Memorial Lectures, 1965–6 (London, College of Preceptors).

Moss, P. A. (2005) Understanding the Other/Understanding Ourselves: Toward a Constructive Dialogue about 'Principles' in Educational Research, *Educational Theory*, 55.3, pp. 263–283.

National Audit Office (2001) *Modern Policy-Making: Ensuring Policies Deliver Value for Money* (London, NAO).

Newman, J. H. (2001) [1852] *The Idea of a University Defined and Illustrated* (London, Routledge/Thoemmes).

Nind, M. (2006) Conducting Systematic Review in Education: A Reflexive Narrative, *London Review of Education*, 4.2, pp. 183–195.

No Child Left Behind Act (Elementary and Secondary Education Act), US, 2001 (re-authorized Jan 8 2002). Available at: http://www.ed.gov/policy/elsec/leg/esea02/index.html

Oakley, A. (2001) Making Evidence-Based Practice Educational: A Rejoinder to John Elliott, *British Educational Research Journal.*, 27.5, pp. 575–576.

Oakley, A. (2003) Research Evidence, Knowledge Management and Educational Practice: Early Lessons from a Systematic Approach, *London Review of Education*, 1.1, pp. 21–33.

Oakley, A., Harlen, W. and Andrews, R. (2002) Systematic Reviews in Education: Myth, Rumour and Reality (BERA Conference, Exeter, September).

O'Connor, D. J. (1956) *An Introduction to the Philosophy of Education* (London, Routledge and Kegan Paul).

Oancea, A. (2005) Criticisms of Educational Research: Key Topics and Levels of Analysis, *British Educational Research Journal*, 31.2, pp. 157–183.

Oancea, A. (2007) From Procrustes to Proteus: Trends and Practices in the Assessment of Education Research, *International Journal of Research & Method in Education*, 30.3, pp. 243–269.

Oancea, A. and Furlong, J. (2007) Expressions of Excellence and the Assessment of Applied and Practice-Based Research, in: J. Furlong and A. Oancea (eds) *Assessing Quality in Applied and Practice-Based Research in Education* (London, Routledge).

Oliver, S., Harden, A. and Rees, R. (2005) An Emerging Framework for Including Different Types of Evidence in Systematic Reviews for Public Policy, *Evaluation*, 11.4, pp. 428–446.

Olson, D. R. (2004) The Triumph of Hope Over Experience in the Search for 'What Works': A Response to Slavin, *Educational Researcher*, 33.1, pp. 24–26.

Pawson, R. (2002) Evidence-based Policy: The Promise of Realist Synthesis, *Evaluation*, 8, pp. 340–358.

Pawson, R. and Tilley, N. (1997) *Realistic Evaluation* (London, Sage Publications).

Powell, M. (ed) (1999) *New Labour, New Welfare State? The 'Third Way' in British Social Policy* (Bristol, The Policy Press).

Pring, R. (2000) The 'False Dualism' of Educational Research, *Journal of Philosophy of Education*, 34.2, pp. 247–260.

Pring, R. (2004) *Philosophy of Educational Research*, 2nd edn. (London, Continuum).

Royal Society for the Encouragement of Arts, Manufactures and Commerce (RSA) (1980) Education for Capability Manifesto, *RSA Journal*, March.

Sanderson, I. (2003) Is it 'What Works' that Matters? Evaluation and Evidence-Based Policy-making, *Research Papers in Education*, 18.4, pp. 331–345.

Schoenfeld, A. H. (2006) What Doesn't Work: The Challenge and Failure of the What Works Clearinghouse to Conduct Meaningful Reviews of Studies of Mathematics Curricula, *Educational Researcher*, 35.2, pp. 13–21.

Schwandt, T. A. (2000) Further Diagnostic Thoughts on What Ails Evaluation Practice, *American Journal of Evaluation*, 21, pp. 225–229.

Schwandt, T. A. (2005) A Diagnostic Reading of Scientifically Based Research for Education, *Educational Theory*, 55.3, pp. 285–305.

Scott, A. (2003) *A Review of the Links Between Research and Policy* (Sussex, SPRU and The Knowledge Bridge). Available at: http://www.sussex.ac.uk/spru/documents/post_longer_e-report_on_science_in_policy.pdf [accessed 1 June 2006].

Shavelson, R. J. and Towne, L. (eds) (2002) *Scientific Research in Education* (Committee on Scientific Principles for Education Research report) (Washington, DC, National Academy Press).

Simons, H. (1995) The Politics and Ethics of Educational Research in England: Contemporary Issues, *British Educational Research Journal*, 21.4, pp. 435–449.

Simons, H. (2003) Evidence-Based Practice: Panacea or Over Promise? *Research Papers in Education*, 18.4, pp. 303–311.

Slavin, R. E. (2002) Evidence-Based Education Policies: Transforming Educational Practice and Research, *Educational Researcher*, 31.7, pp. 15–21.

Slavin, R. E. (2004) Education Research Can and Must Address 'What Works' Questions, *Educational Researcher*, 33.1, pp. 27–28.

Smeyers, P. (2006) What it Makes Sense To Say: Education, Philosophy and Peter Winch on Social Science, *Journal of Philosophy of Education*, 40.4, pp. 463–485.

Smeyers, P. and Depaepe, M. (eds) (2006) *Educational Research: Why 'What Works' Doesn't Work* (Dordrecht, Springer).

Stenhouse, L. (1975) *An Introduction to Curriculum Research and Development* (London, Heinmann).

Sternberg, R. J. (2004) Good Intentions, Bad Results: A Dozen Reasons Why the No Child Left Behind Act is Failing our Schools, *Education Week*, 27 October. Available at: http://www.edweek.org/ew/articles/2004/10/27/09sternberg.h24.html

Thomas, G. and Pring, R. (eds) (2004) *Evidence-Based Practice in Education* (Maidenhead and New York, Open University Press).

Tooley, J. and Darby, D. (1998) *Educational Research: A Critique* (London, Office for Standards in Education).

Toulmin, S. (2001) *Return to Reason* (Cambridge, MA, Harvard University Press).

Webb, S. and Ibarz, T. (2006) Reflecting on 'What Works' in Education Research—Policy/Practice Relationships, *Journal of Vocational Education and Training*, 58.2, pp. 205–222.

Winch, P. (1958) *The Idea of a Social Science* (London, Routledge and Kegan Paul).

WEBSITES

Campbell Collaboration http://www.campbellcollaboration.org/[accessed 5 November 2006].

Campbell Collaboration (2006) Approved reviews, Education. Online at http://www.campbell collaboration.org/frontend.asp#Education [accessed 5 Nov 2006] and Education Coordinating Group Systematic Review Checklist, at http://www.campbellcollaboration.org/ECG/ECGReview_checklist.asp [accessed 5 Nov 2006].

Campbell Collaboration (2006) Campbell Collaboration Guidelines for Systematic Reviews. Online at http://www.campbellcollaboration.org/guidelines.asp [accessed 5 November 2006].

Cochrane Collaboration www.cochrane.org [accessed 30 June 2007].

Educational Underwriters Inc http://www.educationalunderwriters.org/index.htm [accessed 30 June 2007].

EPPI-Centre http://eppi.ioe.ac.uk/[accessed 30 June 2007].

EPPI-Centre (2006) Systematic reviews: Methods. Online at http://eppi.ioe.ac.uk/cms/Default.aspx?tabid=89 [accessed 3 October 2006].

Evidence-Based Education website, University of Durham Curriculum, Evaluation and Management Centre http://www.cemcentre.org/RenderPage.asp?LinkID=30310000 [accessed 30 June 2007].

Evidence Network, King's College, London http://evidencenetwork.org/Mission.html [accessed 30 June 2007].

Institute for Education Sciences, USA http://www.ed.gov/about/offices/list/ies/index.html [accessed 30 June 2007].

National Centre for Education Research, USA http://ies.ed.gov/ncer [accessed 30 June 2007].

What Works Clearinghouse, USA http://www.w-w-c.org/[accessed 5 November 2006], now changed to http://ies.ed.gov/ncee/wwc/[accessed 6 January 2008].

What Works Clearinghouse (2003) What Works Clearinghouse Literature Search Strategy Handbook. May 29, 2003. Online at http://www.campbellcollaboration.org/ECG/documents/Policy%20Documents/What%20Works%20Clearinghouse%20Literature%20Search%20Handbook.pdf http://www.w-w-c.org/[accessed 5 November 2006].

What Works Clearinghouse (2006) The WWC Evidence Standards. Online at http://www.w-w-c.org/reviewprocess/standards.html [accessed 5 November 2006].

What Works Clearinghouse (2006) The WWC Intervention Rating Scheme. Online at http://www.w-w-c.org/reviewprocess/rating_scheme.pdf [accessed 5 November 2006].

What Works Clearinghouse (2006) The WWC Reports. Online at http://www.w-w-c.org/Products/BrowseByLatestReports.asp?ReportType=All [accessed 5 November 2006].

What Works Clearinghouse (2006) The WWC Review Process. Online at http://www.w-w-c.org/reviewprocess/review.html [accessed 5 November 2006].

What Works Clearinghouse website http://www.w-w-c.org/[accessed 5 November 2006].

3
Educational Research and Policy: Epistemological Considerations

DAVID BRIDGES AND MICHAEL WATTS

This chapter is centrally concerned with the sort of knowledge that can and should inform educational policy—and it treats this as an epistemological question. It distinguishes this question from the more extensively explored question of what sort of knowledge in what form policy-makers do in fact commonly take into account.

The chapter examines the logical and rhetorical character of policy and the components of policy decisions and argues that policy demands a much wider range of information than research typically provides. Either the research task or commission has to be substantially extended or the gap will be filled by information or thinking that is not derived from research.

One of the gaps between research of an empirical kind and policy is the normative gap. In the final section the chapter points to the inescapably normative character of educational policy. Of course the values that inform policy can be investigated empirically, but this kind of enquiry cannot tell us what we should do. There is a role for research/scholarship and more rather than less intelligent and critical argumentation in addressing these normative questions as well as the empirical questions that underpin policy.

1 IS THERE A PLACE FOR EPISTEMOLOGICAL CONSIDERATIONS IN EXAMINING THE RELATIONSHIP BETWEEN RESEARCH AND POLICY?

Most of the contributions to this volume consider how and whether particular forms of educational research—case studies, large population studies, local and particular stories etc.—might contribute to policy. However, as a preliminary to this more specific work, it seemed important to ask whether there were any more generic things one could say about this relationship.

More particularly we are concerned to see if there is anything one can say in the form of relevant *epistemological* considerations: about the kind(s) of knowledge that might or ought to inform educational policy and about the way(s) in which educational policy may or may not be derived from the very diverse sorts of knowledge generated by the educational research community. It may be helpful to identify this question by separating it from some others with which we are *not* concerned here, even if they are important questions in their own right.

First, we are, of course, aware of complaints from the policy arena about researchers' failure to provide the research that they think they need (Hargreaves, 1996, 1997; Hillage *et al.*, 1998; Tooley and Darby, 1998)[1] and complaints by educational researchers about the failure of policy-makers to take research findings properly into account. These concerns have not been limited to the UK. In France (Prost, 2001) and Australia (McGaw *et al.*, 1992) there have been reviews similar to those referred to above. In the United States there have been substantial and sustained attacks on both the quality and relevance of educational research (Coalition for Evidence-Based Practice, 2002). Levin (2004) refers to a website that he describes as closely linked to the US Department of Education (www.w-w-c.org/about.html) that observes in familiar terms: 'Our nation's failure to improve its schools is due in part to insufficient and flawed educational research. Even when rigorous research exists, solid evidence rarely makes it into the hands of practitioners, policy-makers and others who need it to guide their decisions' (cited in Levin, 2004, p. 3). The then Secretary of State for Education in the UK, David Blunkett, offered both critique and opportunity to educational researchers when, in 2000, he observed that: 'Too much social science research is inward-looking, too piecemeal rather than helping to build knowledge in a cumulative way' and that 'issues for research are too supplier-driven rather than focusing on the key issues of concern to policy-makers, practitioners and the public at large'. However he went on to urge that 'we need researchers who can challenge fundamental assumptions and orthodoxies . . . . If academics do not address it, then it is difficult to think of anyone else who will. We must recognise its importance' (Blunkett, 2000).

These complaints tend to focus on issues of the quality of research and its relevance. However, notions of quality are often confused with (narrow) expectations of what will count as research at all—as in the 'what works' movement discussed in Oancea and Pring's contribution to this volume—and the criterion of 'relevance' is riddled with questions rather than answers concerning what might *properly* be regarded as relevant to whom, where and when (see Bridges, 2003, pp. 120–122). In other words, the debate raises but has not satisfactorily answered questions about what sorts of research really are (or ought to be regarded as) relevant to policy and that have a contribution to make to its development.

Second, there is a good deal of interesting and important research that investigates what sources policy-makers do in fact draw on to inform their policy decisions and suggests that they rely primarily on commissions, trusted experts and think-tanks for ideas, and that academic research on social issues, including education, sits at the bottom of the list of resources drawn upon by policy-makers and below the media, constituents and consumers (see, for example, Edwards, Sebba and Rickinson, 2006). Whitty's account of New Labour's relationship with educational research supports these observations and concludes that 'in reality, policy is driven by all sorts of considerations, of which the findings of educational research are likely on some occasions to be pretty low down' (Whitty, 2006, p. 168). These are interesting findings in relation to the part that research does play in policy, but they open rather than answer the question: should research play such a minor role in the formulation of policy?

Third, it may be the case, as some empirical research suggests, that research better translates into policy if it is put to policy-makers without all the qualifications, if it is couched in non-technical language, if it can be summarised on one page of A4, if it happens to point in the direction that ministers have determined to be the right one, and if you know or get to know the right person in the minister's circle of close advisors (see on this Edwards, Sebba and Rickinson, 2006). These are interesting findings, and when we know what research deserves communicating we may want to take heed of this advice on how to do so; but knowing how to communicate it still does not tell us what to communicate.

Finally, and more fundamentally, we are of course aware of the intimate alignment of policy, politics and power and of the need to interpret policy decisions as, on the one hand, a function of particular distributions and structures of power and, on the other hand, a way of maintaining or shifting the balance in these structures. These are interesting and important questions within the field of political science and in the sociology of policy. We acknowledge that 'the contribution of research is always mediated through broader social and political processes with all their attendant limitations' (Levin, 2004, p. 1) and nothing in what follows is intended to set these considerations aside as unimportant.

These are not, however, the issues that concern us here. Hammersley has observed that some of the frustration in the debates about the relationship between research and policy are perhaps rooted in a failure to distinguish clearly between some different questions: 'factual questions about the roles that research has *actually* played, theoretical questions about the roles which it *can* play, and value questions about the roles that it *ought* to play' (Hammersley, 2002, p. 1). We are concerned less with the question 'what, as a matter of fact, *does* lead policy-makers to take notice of research in formulating policy?' and more with the questions 'what place can it *legitimately* occupy?' and 'what place *ought* research to occupy in the formulation of policy?'

The 'ought' here, which joins issues of moral responsibility with epistemology, is derived from a tradition of philosophical writing on 'the ethics of belief' illustrated by the following extract from William Clifford's essay with this title:

> Belief, that sacred faculty which prompts the decisions of our will, and knits into harmonious working all the compacted energies of our being, is

ours, not for ourselves, but for humanity. It is rightly used on truths which have been established by long experience and waiting toil, and which have stood in the fierce light of free and fearless questioning. Then it helps to bind men together, and to strengthen and direct their common action (Clifford, 1879, pp. 182–3 and see also James, 1937, and McCarthy, 1986).

The argument is that, in particular where the beliefs we hold have consequences for the welfare of other people, ensuring that these beliefs are well founded (which in Clifford's terms means that they have stood 'in the fierce light of free and fearless questioning', but we may have other requirements) is not just a functional requirement of a utilitarian character or an *epistemological* condition for claiming true belief: it is a *moral* duty. It is a matter of taking moral responsibility for our actions and, with this, for the quality of the judgements that underlie our actions. Such obligations have application in the private sphere, but have, surely, special significance in the context of national and other policy-making where the consequences of carelessly or inappropriately arrived-at opinion and misjudgement can be so far-reaching for good or ill.

In fairness, it should be acknowledged that the 'evidenced-based practice' movement has been motivated by much the same principles that we are indicating here. Most obviously, it is calling for practice (and policy) to be based on *evidence* as opposed perhaps to whim, prejudice or embedded custom. Second, the movement wants that evidence to be derived from rigorous or high quality research. We have no disagreement with these first two principles. Unfortunately, however, in some models (see the chapter in this volume by Oancea and Pring) it sees these principles as co-terminous with research that conforms to the manner of the double-blind controlled experiment. Other contributions to this volume demonstrate very clearly that we cannot follow this programme to its conclusion. Even the use of the term 'evidence' suggests in this context an empiricist and perhaps positivist set of assumptions that we cannot share. At least, we cannot accept that such 'evidence' is sufficient, even if it is necessary, for the determination of educational policy. It is part of the argument in this volume that those who have drawn such restrictive boundaries around the kind of research that ought to be taken into account in policy formation have themselves made a misjudgement that the ethics of belief requires us to challenge and them to correct.

What we do have in common with the evidence-based practice movement, however, is a belief that there are some considerations that ought to count for more than others in the shaping of policy and practice. How can one begin to draw this distinction? There may be some relatively easy cases of considerations that we could agree should not have a place in the forming of policy, though as we write this we can immediately imagine someone leaping to challenge even these. We suggest that we might feel that there was something wrong about education policy being based upon:

(a) the fact that a business, in which the policy-maker had a significant interest, would profit if this policy were introduced;

(b) the fact that the policy-maker had picked up a rumour about some flaw in the system;

(c) the fact that the policy-maker's child had come home from school upset at what appeared to be some manifestation of current policy;

(d) the fact that some other country had introduced this policy;
the fact that some friends in his/her pub or club had urged this policy direction;

(e) the fact that his/her boss had urged him/her to come up with something within 24 hours to grab the newspaper headlines.

If these bases of policy seem inappropriate, it is worth considering why. There seems to be a mixture of ethical and epistemological considerations. Some objections seem to be to do with the moral inappropriateness of acting on this basis (e.g. where there is a financial or other personal interest at stake). In some cases the concern might be with the insubstantial or unreliable character of the evidence that prompted the decision (a rumour, a single and unsubstantiated report, a pub conversation) though any of these might legitimately prompt some further enquiry. In the case of copying practice from some other country the concern might be to do with the insufficiency of the reasoning: one would want some reassurance that very different socio-cultural and historical circumstances had been taken into account. In the final example one might reasonably judge the decision to be ill-considered. We might have debates about the ethical or epistemological legitimacy or otherwise of particular examples, but we suggest that the intelligibility of such debates at least indicates the possibility and reasonableness of operating with both ethical and epistemological principles of the kind illustrated to discriminate between appropriate and inappropriate bases for policy formation.

One can acknowledge this and still recognise that there will be difficult cases where this distinction will be much less clear-cut. To take first the category of ethically unacceptable considerations, we might have a more difficult debate as to whether the following considerations provide an acceptable basis for policy formation or not:

(a) Support for the policy would virtually guarantee that the member (of Parliament or the County Council) would lose his/her seat at the next election.

(b) Evidence from focus groups and opinion polls suggests that this policy would win a lot of popular support.

(c) The policy would enhance the Minister's standing in contention for the party leadership.

Are we here looking at 'the real stuff of politics' stripped bare of ethical responsibility or at the legitimate working of a democratic political system and the ways in which a democratic citizenship properly exercises its influence in the system? To what extent, for example, is it right to take into account in policy formulation the popularity or unpopularity of a particular decision? Levin describes how:

Organizations which are in the public eye—governments, of course, but also many other large organizations—are inevitably sensitive not only to the views of their internal participants but also to larger political currents. One of the rules of the political world is that what is true is far less important than what people believe to be true. A government may be in a position where it is caught between what it believes to be the best course of action and what it believes to be publicly acceptable. In a world where public acceptance is the key to survival it is easy to predict which interest will dominate. It is only when public beliefs shift that government will feel required or able to move (Levin, 2004, p. 6).

At one end we may decry as pusillanimous the leader who is unwilling to take a stand on a matter where there is unequivocal evidence of public benefit: at the other end we might decry as authoritarian the leader who has no regard for public opinion. There is presumably a role for such 'leadership' in seeking honestly to persuade public opinion of what the evidence indicates or what morality demands to be the right course of action. We would distinguish between, on the one hand, a kind of single minded 'political expediency' linked to the desire for political survival whatever the policies that this might require and, on the other, a perfectly sensible concern for the extent to which the public (or a particular sub-set of the public e.g. teachers or parents) might be persuaded to accept a policy that research or other evidence indicated was the best. The latter seems to us to have a legitimate part in the determination of policy (politics being, after all, 'the art of the possible'): the former, while an understandable preoccupation for a political careerist, is a step too far in the direction of the corruption of the deliberative political process in the interests of personal ambition. In other words, political deliberation ought to leave at least some space for the consideration of reasons, evidence and arguments for doing this rather than that—and is *not just* a matter of finding out how many people want this or that, even if this is part of what has to be considered.

We have already indicated that we might reject some grounds for policy that, for example, lacked substance or were unreliable, that were insufficient for the purpose for which they were being employed, that were not properly thought through (what would be the consequences of doing this? what would be the cost? what are the alternative possibilities?) or perhaps were irrelevant—in short, we would reject them on the basis of considerations of an epistemological character

Again, we do not want to pretend that decisions as to what evidence is sufficient, what might properly be counted as relevant, what would be a legitimate inference from a particular set of information or what place ideological considerations might legitimately play in policy are always easily made. What we want to hold onto is the belief that we do, we can and we should make some such decisions in determining what ought to go into policy formation and that, at least in part, these rest on epistemological considerations. The alternative is a kind of reductivism that sees policy formulation only in terms of warring interest groups (among them, perhaps, the research communities) in an arena in which 'evidence', 'research' and 'argument' may have residual rhetorical functions, but where even these have lost the legitimacy they might once have had through their association with sound logical considerations.

So, we are assuming that, though the territory of policy formation is not unproblematic, there are conversations that we can have about what we might sensibly believe or do in the light of the evidence available and the argument that can be constructed around that evidence. Our concern is with understanding the logic of the determination of policy and its relation with these conversations, this evidence and this argument—and more particularly when such conversations take their most rigorous form as academic research.

2 WHAT IS 'POLICY'?

First, it is worth noting that policy can operate at all sorts of levels in an educational system as in any other public service: we can perfectly sensibly talk of national, regional or local government policy; about the policy of particular institutions or interest groups like the Confederation of British Industry, the Church of England, Universities UK or the National Union of Teachers; and about the policy of particular schools or their governing bodies. 'Policy research can be done within institutions or classrooms, as well as within local education authorities or government departments' (Ozga, 2000, p. 2). It perhaps sounds a little strange to speak of the policy of a particular teacher but only because the most common application of policy is in contexts of collective action.

This last observation is significant in terms of the relationship between research and policy formation. The complaints that we noted in our opening paragraphs are most typically associated with the failures or difficulties in applying research to the macro context of national policy-making in which research has to have maximal generalisability across diverse situations. The issue of applying research to much more local policy-making—e.g. at school level—is a rather different one. It is possible that small-scale local studies done at the level of the individual school more appropriately inform policy at this level than the larger scale studies that are more typically expected to inform national policy decisions, but the small-scale local study can also reveal something of the insecurity and untrustworthiness of larger scale prescriptions. Equally significantly, as Ozga suggests, engaging with policy at the local level in this way 'contributes to the democratic project in education' through the creation of an informed, active citizenry (Ozga, 2000, p. 2). These are issues that are explored more fully here in chapters by Elliott and Lukeš and by Griffiths and Macleod.

Second, it is worth asking: what is the status of 'policy' and how and where is it to be observed? If we take examples of policies such as those related to widening participation in higher education, developing nursery school provision for all or bringing children with special needs into mainstream education we can see that policy can be conceived of as a relatively systematic and sustained set of intentions or 'statements of prescriptive intent' as Kogan defined it (Kogan, 1975, p. 55). McLaughlin captures the same elements when he describes educational policy as 'a detailed prescription for action aimed at the preservation or alteration of educational institutions or practices' (McLaughlin, 2000, p. 442). In this sense policy is intimately associated with human agency, albeit that it may be the agency of human beings operating collectively, for example as a political party, a local authority, a charitable organisation or a school community. Like other forms of human intentionality it is typically revealed in what people say and in what they do; and, as in other forms of human agency, there is not uncommonly a gap between the intentions revealed by what people say and those revealed by what they do. For the sake of simplicity in this chapter we shall focus on examples of policy expressed in what people say, i.e. in explicit statements of various kinds.

3 THE LOGICAL AND RHETORICAL STANDING OF POLICY STATEMENTS

Different formulations of policy have different logical, rhetorical and functional standing.[2] For example, we might distinguish between the function of policy statements in:

(i) Expressing collective intentions and providing aims, aspirations

'My government will extend access to higher education to all those who have the ability to benefit from it independently of considerations of ethnicity, gender or social background.'
'This school is committed to involving parents as partners in the education of their children.'

(ii) Making rhetorical rallying calls:

'No child left behind.'
'We must educate our masters.'
'Education without boundaries.'

(iii) Providing rules that others have to follow or describing behaviours that others have to perform:

'Phonics methods of teaching reading will be employed in all schools at Keystage 1.'
'At least 60% of initial teacher training should take place in schools.'

(iv) Indicating outcomes that have to be achieved (while leaving it open as to how):

'Universal primary education by the year 2015.'
'50% participation in higher education by 2010.'
'90% with at least 5 GCSE passes.'

What is important in this context is that these different functions of policy make different demands on their evidence base. The first pair of statements are primarily normative in character and while research into e.g. the economic importance of a large graduate workforce may underlie the first statement and research indicating the value of engaging parents as partners might well lie behind the second neither actually requires research support (or at least, research of an empirical kind), since they are both essentially affirmations of certain things as being of value or importance. We shall argue, in fact, that such normative judgements are explicitly or implicitly central to all policy formation and that this feature of policy raises questions as to the extent to which policy can be informed by empirical research and questions of the kind of enquiry that can serve the intelligent formulation of policy thus conceived.

Similarly, it is difficult to see, for example, what empirical evidence might either confirm or upset the rhetoric of 'no child left behind' (though a bit of elementary conceptual examination might reveal its emptiness). These are essentially exhortations that have no real truth value and therefore are not open to scrutiny against an evidential base.

The third set of examples take the form of imperatives, which again have strictly no truth value, though it is easy to see how one might (and should) in each case ask 'why?' Indeed it is in particular this kind of policy statement that one might expect to be supported by an evidence base that indicated the benefits that would accrue from—in these examples—using phonics to teach reading, though agreement on a policy to improve the literacy scores of 11-year-olds by 10% may require little more than a level of political determination linked perhaps to evidence that this is not a totally unrealistic aspiration. Agreement to require that this should be achieved through the universal adoption of a particular practice would require a very different level and kind of evidence.

The fourth set of examples (expressed as goals or targets to be achieved) once again provides rather limited scope for research as to the rightness of the goals themselves (of course there may be a case for some empirical investigation of their realism) though they invite research into how they might best be achieved. Faced with targets for widening participation in higher education in the UK, for example, the HEFCE funded programme, AimHigher, launched a large programme of initiatives accompanied by packages of research and evaluation aimed at finding out what sort of interventions make an impact on the participation of non-traditional entrants in higher education.

In short, then, we have to observe that there are different forms of expression of 'policy' some of which are largely or entirely expressions of values and others that may invite (though they do not necessarily rest entirely upon) empirical investigation of one kind or another. In section 6 we shall look at elements of some of these policy decisions in more detail, but first let us turn briefly in the direction of the processes of policy-making.

4 THE PROCESS OF POLICY-MAKING

There is a substantial literature that focuses on the actual processes of policy decision-making and that combines a certain amount of empirical research into how people make policy with a level of prescription about the logical—perhaps rational—pathways that such policy-making *should* follow (see, for example, the contrasting approaches of Simon, 1960; Lindblom, 1959, 1968 and 1979; Finch, 1986; and Stewart Howe, 1986). These processes range from, for example, a model that supposes that policy is expressed through a statement of 'mission' translated into objectives and thence into actions and outcomes (a model that has become almost *de rigueur* in public service institutions including universities) to a more pragmatic approach that sees policy as emanating from perceived problems in particular situated and on-going sets of practice (see, for example, Pratt, 1999, 2000).[3] This contrast is sometimes expressed in terms of 'rationalist' and 'incrementalist' models of policy formation (Lindblom, 1968)—and these models clearly carry different implications for the way in that research-based knowledge might feed into the process, but this may not necessarily mean that they actually require different knowledge.

There is more to be said than we shall enter into here about the relationship between different conceptions of the nature of the judgement that is involved in policy-making and the nature of the knowledge that appropriately informs such judgement. We propose for the purposes of this discussion to by-pass the issue of the actual *process* of decision-making as a description or prescription of the recommended steps or sequence on the grounds that whichever process is employed there is still—at some stage[4]—a similar requirement both for normative orientation and empirical evidence. In all cases policy formulation is essentially a matter of deciding[5] what ought to be done. However one goes about such a decision, whatever the preferred sequence, the epistemological requirements are, we suggest, constant, even if there will inevitably be debate about what these requirements are. The methods of decision-making follow from the epistemological requirements of the decision, not the other way round. Thus, if situational understanding (or understanding of a particular situation) is a requirement of intelligent decision making, then we need to find an approach to decision making that can engage such understanding. If 'hard scientific evidence' is a requirement, then we need to find an approach that enables us to incorporate such evidence. This is the direction of the argument—and it is for this reason that we can focus on the epistemological requirements—on the components of policy decisions themselves—before engaging in consideration of decision making processes.

5 THE COMPONENTS OF POLICY DECISIONS

We need to look at the components of policy decisions themselves—not least because part of the disappointment of educational researchers with respect to the take-up of their research in policy circles is the result of researchers' under-estimation of the things that (quite legitimately) count in such decisions; and part of the disappointment of the commissioners of research with the information they get from researchers is that they underestimate the range of considerations that researchers need to investigate (and that need to be part of the commissioning process) if the research is to provide a solid basis for policy. One of the warnings to educational researchers emerging from a British Educational Research Association (BERA) colloquium on Educational Research and Policy Across the UK was that: 'researchers need to recognise that policy is shaped by many often conflicting interests and pressures so that even the "hardest" evidence can only be part of the shaping. It cannot be expected that policy will be necessarily read off from even the most rigorously conducted research because political considerations in today's world are always powerful' (BERA, 2002, p. 9). Of course, we acknowledge this warning, but the problem of the insufficiency of research is not just about its failure to take into account more narrowly political considerations (if it does indeed omit these). The problem lies often in a research brief that simply does not extend to all the information that someone who has to decide what to do will need.

Suppose, for example, a Government Minister received a research report that indicated persuasively that children learned a foreign language much more effectively through having intense programmes outside the normal school timetable than through the traditional extended time-tabled course. Suppose too that systematic research reviews lent support to this conclusion. Is this a sufficient basis for it to become government policy to shift the teaching of languages into this sort of delivery system?

Clearly not. Among the many (we would argue legitimate) considerations that would have to be taken into account before that conclusion could be reached are the following:[6]

- What would be the additional cost of such a change—and what analysis might be made of the cost/benefit relationship? Are there less complicated ways of achieving a similar or better cost-to-benefit ratio?
- How well equipped are teachers to re-orientate themselves to this kind of approach? What resistance might there be from teachers— and what might be the political cost of dealing with such resistance?
- What would be the teacher training requirements for such a change? What would these cost and how quickly could they be put in place?
- What are the plant utilisation implications of such a change? And the costs associated with these?
- What are the implications for parents—and especially for parents at work? How acceptable would such a change be to parents? What might be the political cost and benefit of carrying forward such a change?[7]

- Are languages the only subject that might benefit from this approach? If not, then what are the arguments for treating languages in this way and not other subjects?
- The research compares two alternatives—are there other options that ought to be considered?

The question that the original research addressed is, in this example, a relatively pragmatic one: do students learn a foreign language better under one organisational structure or another? The points above indicate that *either* the research needs to be much more wide ranging (more wide ranging than educational research conventionally is) in order to provide a sufficient basis for policy *or* it will be insufficient to provide a sound basis for policy determination. Unsurprisingly in these circumstances those responsible for policy may well take a view that is different from the direction in which the research points. A good deal of writing about educational research and policy bemoans this gap between research and policy. It follows from what we are saying here that the understanding that *should logically* inform policy depends appropriately on a considerably wider set of considerations than is conventionally covered by educational research, including matters to do with, for example, the level of political support for or the political cost of a particular policy. The fact that politicians draw upon such considerations is not necessarily a matter of political obduracy but of a proper understanding of the logical and epistemological considerations that need to inform political judgement.

There are three possible responses for educational researchers and research commissioners to this sort of analysis of the ingredients of educational policy-making decisions:

(i) They could take the line that this demonstrates that many of these ingredients fall outside the scope of educational research and that educational research can only ever make a limited contribution to such policy-making. Policy-makers will need to join the outcomes of educational research with other sources of intelligence provided, for example, by companies who conduct focus group sessions or public opinion surveys.

(ii) They could take the view that educational research and researchers need to be capable of engaging with all the elements of educational policy-making decisions and that, for example, the assessment of public opinion and the political costs and benefits of proceeding with a particular policy ought to be part of the competence required of educational policy researchers.

(iii) They could take the view that this sort of analysis of the elements of educational policy-making indicates the need for more narrowly educational researchers to work in multi-disciplinary teams with, e.g., political scientists and people who run public opinion surveys as well as experts on costing.

Each of these responses seems to us to be possible and coherent. Which is best depends in part on whom one considers best equipped to carry out the variety of tasks that, on our analysis, are involved in policy decisions. The problems in moving from research evidence to policy do not end there, however. Let us suppose that the research community has anticipated all the sorts of requirements indicated above and gathered all the necessary evidence. Can we or policy-makers now confidently derive from this evidence a view of what they should do?

Hammersley (2002) notes a number of limits to what, even in these circumstances, research can supply. These are especially pertinent here because they relate to *epistemological* features of research in relation to practice. His warnings deserve more detailed attention, but in this context let us just note some of the main points (and we have slightly re-ordered them too). First, researchers themselves will recognise that there is an inherent fallibility to their findings. Natural science and *a fortiori* social science-based knowledge can only be accepted provisionally and pending further enquiry. There are always elements of uncertainty and corrigibility and the possibility of human error, which put such knowledge on a continuum with everyday opinion, not on an entirely different plane. 'Common sense' has a place in policy deliberation alongside academic research, and there may be entirely legitimate reasons for deferring to the former rather than the latter in particular circumstances. This in turn reinforces a second point that is to do with the relationship between the level of evidence required and the risk attached to acting upon it—what Hammersley calls the 'acceptability threshhold'. Simply, if research indicates a course of action that we can readily undertake with relatively little risk and that perhaps, we can reverse quickly if things do not work out, then the level of evidence that we shall require will be less than we shall require if the recommendation is going to use up all our political and financial capital and if having taken the path suggested there is no going back. 'There will often be a mismatch between what the two groups [researchers and practitioners] treat as valid knowledge, *and with good reason*' (Hammersley, 2002, p. 43, his italics). Third—and this is illustrated by our example above—particular research studies tend to be focused on single issues, whereas practitioners (and *a fortiori* policy-makers) have to take a wider range of considerations into account in taking decisions. (One might hope, for example, that they are looking at the interaction and coherence of different policy decisions.) 'The perspectives of practitioners typically cover a broader range of considerations than the researcher focuses on, many of which will have to be taken into account in deciding how best to act on particular occasions ... Researchers are not able to supply practitioners with a replacement perspective, nor able to recommend a ready-made solution to their problems solely on the basis of research' (Hammersley, 2002, p. 44). Fourth, 'knowledge produced by research is usually general in character, and inference from it to conclusions about the particular situations in which practitioners operate is problematic' (ibid.). Of course, it is precisely this consideration (among others) that led to the development of classroom action research conceived of as the testing within the particular classroom of hypotheses drawn either from the wider theoretical and research literature or from practitioners' own professional beliefs. Fifth, the meaning and significance of any particular piece of research for policy or practice is not unequivocal:

> Even in factual terms every research report is open to multiple, more or less reasonable, interpretations and usually is interpreted in different ways by different people. It is not necessary to go to Derridean extremes about the 'dissemination' of meaning to recognise that there is a sense in which readers construct the meaning of any research report and may do so in diverse ways (Hammersley, 2002, p. 46).

There is a final point that Hammersley makes about the question of the insufficiency of research that we want to discuss more fully. He properly draws attention to what one might call the normative gap between what empirical research can provide and what is needed if one is required to decide what one ought to do, or, as he puts it, 'the relative autonomy of value conclusions from the factual knowledge that research provides' (Hammersley, 2002, p. 45). We readily acknowledge this point, but feel there is more to be said than Hammersely allows here about the contribution that research, more broadly conceived, can contribute to bridging this gap. We shall explore this issue more fully in the next section.

6 THE NORMATIVE BASIS OF RESEARCH AND POLICY

> Education ... has some particular characteristics that affect the role that research can play. It is a value-laden activity, inextricably connected to our broader aspirations for society (Levin, 2004, p. 2).

> Education is at least partly about the overall aims that society has for itself and how these aims are realised in practice. It cannot, therefore, be a neutral technical exercise, but is invariably a deeply ethical, political and cultural one bound up with ideas about the good society and how life can be worthwhile (Winch and Gingell, 2004, Preface).

Normative considerations are inseparable from educational choices, and educational policy: policy statements, even if they are no more than exhortations, are emphatically about either the sorts of ends that are desirable in themselves (in general or in a particular setting) or the sorts of actions that are likely to serve the ends that are desirable.

No one needs to apologise for this: this is what policy is. These values may play some different roles in policy statements. For example:

- They may be expressed as the categorical endorsement of certain moral or social principles: 'our educational policy will be founded on the principle that all children will have access to a high quality education till the age of 16 independently of considerations of race, gender, social class or accidents of geography'; 'we shall acknowledge parents' inalienable right to bring up their children in accordance with the moral and religious beliefs of their community'.

- They may be expressed as slightly more specifically educational principles: 'we shall seek to encourage in our pupils critical and independent thinking'.
- They may be expressed somewhat less explicitly, for example, in promoting practice that is explicitly or implicitly seen as advancing such principles: 'we shall use discussion rather than instruction as the primary form of teaching and learning in our classrooms'; 'we shall support the maintenance and development of faith schools'; 'we shall provide summer schools designed to enable children from ethnic minority communities to have some experience of higher education'.
- They may be almost totally concealed: 'all children will be subject to national tests on an annual basis' (where such a proposition is linked eg to a commitment to accountability to parents, to a belief that this is the way to raise the performance of the least able or to reduce gender differences in performance or whatever); 'we shall re-instate *Peter and Jane* as the standard text for the teaching of reading in all schools' (where this is linked, e.g., to a desire to restore traditional family values).

The first point to make here is that all educational propositions and policies have some normative—some might say ideological—framing or foundation. Kogan writes of policy as a matter of 'the authoritative allocation of values' (Kogan, 1975, p. 55), and Ball notes that 'policies are the operational statements of values' (Ball, 1990, p. 3). This normative framing may be discovered in the intentions of whoever promotes the policy; it may lie in an evaluation of the observable consequences of the policy; it may be discovered in the various readings of the policy that different stakeholders can provide. In other words, the 'normative framework' is open to interpretation, construction and reconstruction.

Part of the problem is that politicians and policy-makers tend to employ such norms rather crudely even if they do so explicitly at all. Some of the time they employ them in a rather sloganistic way in the hope of signalling their ideological credentials ('roll back the power of the state'; 'no child left behind'); at other times, however, they try to present educational policies as if they were purely pragmatic, simply a matter of 'common sense' concerned with 'what works'. As Saunders explains, 'One of the ostensible virtues of evidence-based education is that it is free of ideology, of pre-determined positions' (Saunders, 2004, p. 3)—but can any research live up to this claim? Saunders goes on to suggest that in the 'what works' discourse 'value positions disappear from sight as if by sleight of hand' (p. 8). Researchers, by contrast, have an irresistible urge to expose, critique, interpret, reinterpret, construct and deconstruct the normative assumptions of policy—to ask what might count as working and not (just) to ask what works. It is surely appropriate, as Whitty has argued, that a research-based profession 'should be informed by research that questions prevailing assumptions—and considers such questions as whether an activity is a worthwhile endeavour in the first place and what constitutes socially just schooling' (Whitty, 2006, p. 162).

The problem becomes more complex, however. Just as politicians and policy-makers quite legitimately approach their business within a normative framework of values, many researchers would acknowledge that they inevitably do the same. Minimally these may include ethical obligations to different kinds of participants in their research and to their colleagues in the research team; they will also extend to the kind of principles of truthfulness, honesty, reflexivity and criticality that are a *sine qua non* of research endeavour. More strongly, where researchers embrace an explicit ethical, social or political commitment, they may see themselves as having obligations to work for, for example, social justice or the empowerment of women through the very activity of their research—seeking to give voice to those who have not been heard in the conventional political processes; to democratise relationships in the organisational and political structures that they are entering; to challenge rather than to add legitimacy to the power structures over which the policy-makers preside; 'to speak truth to power' (Griffiths, 1998; Tierney, 1994; Gitlin and Russell, 1994). The ideological debates about educational policy become entangled with ideological debates about the character of educational research to the point that, as Levin observes, 'Many disagreements about educational research are actually differences over the substance of education policy' (Levin, 2004, p. 2).

The educational research community might divide fairly sharply in terms of how it thinks it should deal with the actual or potential normative and political dimension of research engagement. Some might claim that normative and political engagement is inappropriate for a researcher—a crossing of a line delimiting properly empirical enquiry. The BERA (2003) symposium on research and policy described such a 'fine line' that researchers crossed at some peril. Munn explained that 'where research spills over into advocacy an important boundary has been crossed' and she warned against researchers 'arguing for the desirable' (Munn, 2005, p. 24). Others, however, regard such engagement as both an appropriate and an inescapable feature of educational research (as significant when a researcher attempts to ignore it as when a researcher consciously seeks to adopt a political stance). Ozga is among those who argue for a very tight link between policy research and political intervention, defining educational policy research as 'an informed, independent contestation of policy by a research community of teachers and academics who have together developed capacities that allow them to speak with authority against a misguided, mistaken and unjust educational policy' (Ozga, 2000, p. 1; see also Griffiths, 1998, in her significantly entitled book *Educational Research for Social Justice*).

Whichever position one adopts educational research needs to be knitted together with the normative questions if it is to issue in policy. Even on a weaker analysis of the connection between research, normativity and politics, there seems to be an epistemological requirement for a dialogue between researchers and policy-makers around the normative issues rather than an attempt somehow to sanitise the research from such considerations. 'What works is a matter of discussion and debate, not simply of data; what works is a value statement not simply an empirical statement' (Morrison, 2001, p. 77).

Many researchers treat these normative considerations as matters that are open to portrayal or representation through research, but not as ones that research can help policy-makers to resolve in any sense. Even though Munn suggests that 'we need to engage with values issues and with . . . the why questions as well as the what questions in policy research' (Munn, 2005, p. 23) her approach to such engagement is still an essentially descriptive one focused on understanding the underlying value assumptions rather than one that can issue in anything to recommend (unless in conditional terms). The world of educational policy research is heavily dominated by people who bring a sociological perspective to their enquiry. The observation that an 'authoritative allocation of values' is at the centre of policy readily invites the questions: whose values? Whose interests are advanced and how? And these in turn draw attention to what Prunty has referred to as 'the centrality of power and control in the concept of policy' (Prunty, 1985, p. 136). Nothing we go on to say is intended to diminish the importance of this perspective. However, empirical and analytic sociological work does not tell us what we *ought* to do. Critical sociology might point in this direction, but only in so far as it has a declared or assumed normative position. Ball, for example, is at pains to declare his normative position in his 'policy sociology' (Ball, 1990) and this, along with his empirical data, provides a basis for something closer to policy prescription (at least by implication from the critique).

One can, of course, subject the normative elements of educational policy to all sorts of descriptive and analytic treatments, though again these all fall short of anything that might lead to prescription:

- historical analysis (how have these policies evolved over the years?)
- political analysis (what political interests do they serve? Through what power structures are they maintained?)
- discourse analysis (what is revealed about the underlying normative framework through an analysis of the language employed?)
- phenomenological enquiry (how are these or other values experienced by those whose lives they affect?)
- ethnographic enquiry (what can be revealed about these values by observation of the communities in which they are cultivated—by the rituals, symbols, behaviours and practices of these communities?)

All of this is possible. However, in so far as one might wonder whether a policy is the *right* policy, none of this research would actually address the central normative question. Hammersley emphasises rightly 'the relative autonomy of value conclusions' from the factual knowledge that he says research provides, and he infers from this that research is severely limited in what it can contribute towards the solution of practical problems concerning what ought to be done. We grant that this is the case so long as one regards research as providing only empirical evidence. However, as Davis points out, once one shifts the focus of one's enquiry from 'methods that work' to 'morally or educationally defensible principles' then 'these principles would not appeal to empirical evidence. They would rely instead on the reasoning peculiar to ethics, politics and educational philosophy' (Davis, 1999, p. 400). It follows that if one embraces these disciplines within the portfolio of educational research then additional possibilities are opened up to those that are offered by more restricted empirical enquiry.

Speaking about the way in which the Nuffield Review of 14–19 Education is tackling these expressly normative questions, Pring describes a process that is rooted in widespread opinion but that then exposes that opinion to a process of critique:

> In pursuing, therefore, an understanding of the overall aim of education in order to shape the review, the Review has solicited judgements, views or considered opinions very widely. The quality of those views does not matter. If they exist and are shaping practice then they deserve serious consideration. . . . The starting point (those judgements, views or opinions from many sources) is not what matters, but the process of criticism through which one progresses from those starting points. Such views have to be clearly articulated, opened to critical scrutiny, redrafted in the light of such criticism and challenged by evidence . . . (Pring, 2006, p. 10).

What form might such critique take? It might be worth indicating in conclusion at least the following possibilities for the treatment of values and norms in educational policy. First, one might ask: are the normative principles underlying any particular policy actually rendered in explicit or at least intelligible form? Part of White's critique of the UK national curriculum, for example, has been directed against its failure to explain the educational values or aims from which it is derived (White, 2007). Second, one might ask: are they in any sense justified? Is there a coherent rationale for them, which perhaps links them to a view of human nature, of societal good or of human flourishing? Again White's (2007) *Impact* pamphlet, one of a series aimed precisely at demonstrating the contribution that philosophy can make to educational policy, is an illustration of the way in which a rationale can be developed that makes a reasoned connection between certain fundamental values and educational policy even if it cannot in the end demonstrate conclusively why one should subscribe to those values. Third, one can ask whether the normative principles that are acknowledged are internally consistent and coherent, what is the nature of any conflicts between these principles and how conflicts between different *desiderata* are or can be resolved. Fourth, one can ask whether the acknowledged normative principles are consistent with the actions that are recommended or with those taken under the same policy framework. Arguably, these questions indicate what might be regarded as necessary conditions for the rationality of an educational policy even if they are not sufficient conditions for getting it entirely right.

In other words if policy cannot pass these critical tests it is arguably ill-prepared, but even a policy that can pass them is not guaranteed by that criterion alone to be the right policy. Such criteria do indicate, however, some work of a philosophical and ethical nature that the research community might contribute to policy debate alongside its more traditional empirical and critical contributions. Good judgement and sound belief are supported not just by appropriate evidence: they also require attention to reasons and what Phillips (2007) refers to as 'intelligent argumentation'—and there is scope for this around the normativity that is central to educational policy as well as the empirical evidence.[8]

7 SUMMARY AND CONCLUSION

The broader project of which this contribution is part was to examine what might be the epistemological bases of educational policy—what kind of research could and should inform educational policy-making? This chapter begins to address this question in general terms. We were at pains in some of the earlier discussion to emphasise that our question was not the one that a number of colleagues in the educational policy arena have addressed before about what sort of information presented by whom and in what form policy-makers do actually take notice of—but the question as to what sorts of knowledge could and perhaps should inform policy. It is, as philosophers are inclined to say, a further question how we persuade policy-makers to take notice of what they should take notice of. If this sounds a bit presumptuous, it is to say no more than is being said by anyone who thinks that excluding from attention anything but the double-blind controlled experiment is to be too restrictive in what you acknowledge as capable of informing policy.

We approached this question by looking at the nature of policy (as formulated in particular in policy statements) and the sorts of considerations that are appropriately and perhaps necessarily part of policy decisions (though acknowledging that the process of policy formation does not necessarily take the form of a clear-cut decision at one moment of time). This discussion pointed both to the breadth of considerations that might quite legitimately be involved in such an act or process and suggested that while all or most of these considerations might well be researchable in principle, few research briefs actually extended this widely. We drew from Hammersley's analysis, in particular, some further reservations of an epistemological nature about the limits of what research might contribute to policy.

Finally, we focused on the ingredient of normativity that we suggested was directly or indirectly part of any policy formulation. We noted some rather different responses to this observation within the educational research community itself, but tried to suggest researchers had a role to play not just in describing the operation of this normativity but in engaging with it through analysis, critique and 'intelligent argumentation'.

We hope that this discussion at least demonstrates in general terms the pertinence of epistemological considerations to debates about what can and should inform educational policy. Other contributions to this volume will explore this relationship with respect to more specific forms of educational enquiry.

Correspondence: David Bridges, Von Hugel Institute, St Edmund's College, Cambridge CB3 OBN, UK.
E-mail: db347@cam.ac.uk
Michael Watts, Von Hugel Institute, St Edmund's College, Cambridge CB3 OBN, UK.
E-mail: Michael.watts@uea.ac.uk

NOTES

1. Similar complaints have been made against a wider range of social science research—see, for example, the 2003 report of the UK's Commission on the Social Sciences, which speaks of 'significant problems with the exploitation of social science research in government, local government, commerce, the voluntary sector and the media' and observes that 'the caution of some academics towards close engagement with practitioners is a source of great disappointment to many users of social science research' (Commission on the Social Sciences, 2003, Executive Summary).

2. Terence H. McLaughlin drew a different set of distinctions from those that we employ here when he wrote of the different 'languages' of policy debate, which he labelled roughly as official, professional, research and popular (McLaughlin, 1999, pp. 37–38). Our distinctions cut across these and can be drawn in each of these contexts in one way or another.

3. 'By starting with the problems which policies are trying to solve, by testing policies as we would a hypothesis, by formulating alternative problems and alternative solutions, and by examining the outcomes, intended or not, a realist approach to policymaking and policy analysis can offer the hope of improvement' (Pratt, 2000, p. 146).

4. Furlong and White (2001), for example, describe a three stage model that includes (i) policy planning—putting issues on the agenda, helping policy-makers recognise their current and future information requirements and reviewing what is already known; (ii) policy development—piloting new initiatives; developing specialised policy instruments and developing specialised curriculum materials; and (iii) evaluation—finding out what worked and what did not and linking past experience to future planning.

5. Although we use the language of decision, we readily recognise that policy does not necessarily proceed on the basis of discrete and direction-making decisions. We are sympathetic to the incrementalist approach on this matter. As Finch explains: 'The incrementalist model emphasizes that there are seldom specific "decisions" taken by a clearly defined set of actors choosing between alternatives'. Rather 'change occurs cumulatively through a series of small scale decisions' (Finch, 1986, p. 150).

6. Saunders calls for more 'thick description' of what goes into the policy-making process (Saunders, 2004). While welcoming such empirical investigation we are attempting something different here in suggesting the kinds of considerations that in a sense have to go into or properly belong in a considered determination of policy.

7. 'One of the rules of the political world is that what is true is far less important than what most people believe to be true. A government may be in a position where it is caught between what it believes is the best course of action and what it believes is publicly acceptable. In a world where public acceptance is the key to survival it is easy to predict which interest will dominate. It is only when public beliefs shift that governments feel required or able to move' (Levin, 2004, p. 6).

8. Winch and Gingell's (2004) book *Philosophy and Educational Policy: A Critical Introduction*
    provides a good example of this sort of argumentation around a number of contemporary policy
    issues, though we are not assuming that such argumentation is the exclusive privilege of
    philosophers. See also, for example, Whitty (2002), *Making Sense of Education Policy*, which
    draws more heavily on sociological studies but is by no means limited to the reporting of
    empirical evidence. 'The modesty of philosophy,' suggested McLaughlin, 'must extend both to an
    acknowledgement that its contribution to educational policy is a partial one, and to its acceptance
    that its contribution must be offered in relation and dialogue with other reflective and critical
    resources and with the contingencies of circumstance and practice' (McLaughlin, 2000, p. 443).

REFERENCES

Ball, S. (1990) *Politics and Policy Making in Education* (London, Routledge).

Blunkett, D. (2000) Influence or Irrelevance? Can Social Science Improve Government?
Presentation at ESRC seminar, February (London, DfES).

Bridges, D. (2003) *Fiction Written Under Oath? Essays in Philosophy and Educational Research*
(Dordrecht and London, Kluwer).

British Educational Research Association (2002) Education Policy and Research Across the UK:
A report of a BERA Colloquium held at University of Birmingham, 7th and 8th November,
Nottingham, BERA.

Clifford, W. (1879) The Ethics of Belief, in: *Lectures and Essays*, Vol 2 (London, Macmillan).

Coalition for Evidence-Based Policy (2002) *Bringing Evidence Driven Progress to Education:
Report for the US Department of Education*, November 2002, www.excelgov.org

Commission on the Social Sciences (2003) Great Expectations: the Social Sciences in Britain.
Chaired by David Rhind. Available at http://www.acss.org.uk/docs/GtExpectations.pdf

Davis, A. (1999) Prescribing Teaching Methods, *Journal of Philosophy of Education*, 33.3, pp.
387–402.

Edwards, A., Sebba, J. and Rickinson, M. (2006) Working with Users: Some Implications for
Educational Research, *British Educational Research Journal*, 33.5, pp. 647–661.

Finch, R. (1986) *Research and Policy: The Uses of Qualitative Methods on Educational and
Social Research* (Lewes, Falmer Press).

Furlong, J. and White, P. (2001) *Educational Research Capacity in Wales: A Review* (Cardiff,
Cardiff University School of Social Sciences).

Gitlin, A. and Russell, R. (1994) Alternative Methodologies and the Research Context, in: A.
Gitlin (ed) *Power and Method: Political Activism and Educational Research* (New York,
Routledge).

Griffiths, M. (1998) *Educational Research for Social Justice: Getting Off the Fence* (Buckingham,
Open University Press).

Hammersley, M. (2002) *Educational Research, Policymaking and Practice* (London, Paul
Chapman).

Hargreaves, D. (1996) *Teaching as a Research Based Profession: Possibilities and Prospects*
(London, Teacher Training Agency).

Hargreaves, D. (1997) In Defence of Evidence-Based Teaching, *British Educational Research
Journal*, 23.4, pp. 405–419.

Hillage, J., Pearson, R., Anderson, A. and Tamkin, P. (1998) *Excellence in Research on Schools*
(London, DfEE).

James, W. (1937) *The Will to Believe and Other Essays* (London, Longman Green).

Kogan, M. (1975) *Educational Policy Making* (London, Allen and Unwin).

Levin, B. (2004) Making Research Matter More, *Education Policy Analysis Archives*, 12.56, pp.
1–20.

Lindblom, C. (1959) The Science of Muddling Through, *Public Administration Quarterly*, XIX,
pp. 79–88.

Lindblom, C. (1968) *The Policy Making Process* (Englewood Cliffs, NJ, Prentice Hall).

Lindblom, C. (1979) Still Muddling, Not Yet Through, *Public Administration Review*, 39, pp.
517–526.

McCarthy, G. D. (1986) *The Ethics of Belief Debate* (Atlanta, GA, Scholar Press).

McGaw, B., Boud, D., Poole, M., Warry, S. and McKechnie, P. (1992) *Educational Research in Australia: Report of the Review Panel of Research in Education* (Canberra, Australian Government Publishing Service).

McLaughlin, T. H. (1999) A Response to Professor Bridges, in: D. Carr (ed.) *Values in the Curriculum* (Aberdeen, Gordon Cook Foundation).

McLaughlin, T. H. (2000) Philosophy and Educational Policy: Possibilities, Tensions and Tasks, *Journal of Educational Policy*, 15.4, pp. 441–457.

Morrison, K. (2001) Randomised Controlled Trials for Evidence-Based Education: Some Problems in Judging 'What Works', *Evaluation and Research in Education*, 15.2, pp. 69–83.

Munn, P. (2005) Researching Policy and Policy Research, *Scottish Educational Review*, 37.1, pp. 17–28.

Ozga, J. (2000) *Policy Research in Educational Settings: Contested Terrain* (Buckingham, Open University Press).

Phillips, D. C. (2007) The Contested Nature of Empirical Research (and Why Philosophy of Education Offers Little Help), in: D. Bridges and R. D. Smith (eds) *Philosophy, Methodology and Educational Research* (Oxford, Blackwell), pp. 311–332.

Pratt, J. (1999) Testing Policy, in: J. Swann and J. Pratt (eds) *Improving Education: Realist Approaches To Method And Research* (London, Cassell).

Pratt, J. (2000) Research and Policy: A Realist Approach, *Prospero*, 6.3 & 4, pp. 139–149.

Pring, R. (2006) Reclaiming Philosophy for Educational Research: 'Educational Review' Annual Lecture. 11th October 2006, Birmingham (unpublished mimeo).

Prost, A. (2001) *Pour un programme stratégique de recherche en éducation* (Paris, Ministère de l'Education Nationale).

Prunty, J. (1985) Signposts for a Critical Educational Policy Analysis, *Australian Journal of Education*, 29.2, pp. 133–140.

Saunders, L. (2004) Grounding the Democratic Imagination: Developing the Relationship Between Research and Policy in Education. Professorial Lecture at the Institute of Education, University of London, 24 March 2004 (London, Institute of Education, University of London).

Simon, H. A. (1960) *The New Science of Management Decision* (Englewood Cliffs, NJ, Prentice Hall).

Stewart Howe, W. (1986) *Corporate Strategy* (Basingstoke, Macmillan).

Tierney, W. G. (1994) On Method and Hope, in: A. Gitlin (ed) *Power and Method: Political Activism and Educational Research* (New York, Routledge).

Tooley, J. and Darby, D. (1998) *Educational Research: A Critique—a Survey of Published Educational Research* (London, OFSTED).

White, J. P. (2007) *What Schools Are For and Why*, IMPACT Pamphlet No. 14 (London, Philosophy of Education Society of Great Britain).

Whitty, G. (2002) *Making Sense of Educational Policy* (London, Paul Chapman).

Whitty, G. (2006) Education(al) Research and Education Policy Making: Is Conflict Inevitable?, *British Educational Research Journal*, 32.2, pp. 159–76.

Winch, C. and Gingell, J. (2004) *Philosophy and Educational Policy: A Critical Introduction* (London, Routledge).

4

On the Epistemological Basis of Large-Scale Population Studies and their Educational Use

PAUL SMEYERS

This chapter attempts to take seriously the claim that we can look for causes in order to understand the reality we live (in), and focuses therefore primarily on 'the natural world'. It will be argued that even if we were to fully endorse the programme of looking for antecedents, a dominant driver for many educational researchers, this would still not solve the problems they commonly set out to address. It will illustrate the problem of contextualisation in using an example of educational research that uses the methodology of the randomised field trial. In these kind of studies the paradigm of causality and its experimental laboratory approach is modified to incorporate the exigencies of real life situations. The claim that these studies too do not put one in a position to derive straightforward conclusions for policy-makers or more generally for educational practitioners will be substantiated. Finally, some concluding remarks will be offered that indicate what may be expected from large-scale population studies and what their epistemological basis is.

INTRODUCTION

The need to apprehend the world one lives in is a fundamental part of the human condition. This apprehension includes understanding the meanings of various forms of expressions (concepts, symbol, art objects, rituals), of feelings and emotions, of actions in the world of human activity past and present (in terms of purposes, aims and more functional explanations), and last but not least the understanding of natural phenomena. In the context of the physical world for instance one may want to distinguish a unified style of explanation from explanations of a mechanical kind. The former explains in terms of basic comprehensive principles (for instance in biology: selection, mutation, heritability of traits), how in other words phenomena fit into an overall scheme; the latter answers questions of how things work (sometimes understood as what they are made of). Here what one is looking for is of a causal nature. In terms of understanding a society one may be interested in how it functions at large, what and why people do what they do, and 'who' they are. 'Understanding' here refers to knowing how things are for those who are involved, so that what one comes up with can be taken into account. In many cases, however, the concept of 'causality' seems to pervade our thinking about ourselves and others, about our environment, even concerning the entire universe we live in. Thus causal explanations appear fundamental to the intellectual under-standing of physical systems and living organisms, and also where our practical deliberations in these contexts are concerned. They are involved in the use of technology (where we attempt to achieve particular effects while avoiding undesirable ones) and in our everyday practical planning and dealings. Not only physicists and engineers, but social scientists too, have since the Enlightenment been occupied with finding causes in order to be able to manipulate particular outcomes. Evidently, psychologists and educational researchers are no exception to this general tendency. Here too, for many, to explain an event is to identify its antecedents, i.e. its causes.

It is often said that an educational research problem is an issue, topic or question that may be theoretical, practical, or a combination of both. However, in most cases, the starting-point for research derives from a particular educational reality that is unsatisfactory to the parties involved. In other words, the theoretical interest is secondary to dealing with the kind of educational reality one is confronted with. Examples are language learning, participation in higher education of particular social groups, implementation of educational policies, but also bullying in primary schools, the burn-out of teachers, the empowerment of parents etc. Generally educational research is grounded in the empirical traditions of the social sciences (commonly called quantitative and qualitative methods) and as such is distinguished from other forms of scholarship such as theoretical, conceptual or methodological essays, critiques of research traditions and practices and those studies grounded in the humanities (e.g., history, philosophy, literary analysis, arts-based inquiry). Since the early twentieth century, mainstream educational research has indeed been of an empirical nature and here—though qualitative research has gradually become more and more important—quantitative methods are still very much in use. In quantitative research, one typically looks for a distribution of variables (how many are there with this or that char-acteristic) and for explanations, which can be of a deductive-nomological kind, incorporating universal laws (A1), or of an inductive nature, employing statistics (A2). Due to being subsumed under its own set of laws, quantitative research can offer an explanation either in terms of an argument (a logical structure with premises and conclusions governed by some rule of acceptance), or as a presentation of the conditions relevant to the occurrence of the event and a statement of the degree of probability of the event given these conditions. Many writers have expressed doubts over whether it is possible to find universal laws within the context of the social sciences. But even if one accepts the more moderate approach, which argues that one can measure an event according to the degree of probability, most scholars will accept that contextualisation of theoretical insights is necessary, which comes down to a much more moderate version of what science is capable of compared to a stance where causality exclusively rules. Leaving aside the problem of determinism or indeterminism as the proper framework to deal with 'reality', it is clear that (A2) explanations are more of a descriptive nature, yet sometimes they are used in a quasi-causal framework awaiting (after much more research) the discovery of the 'real' causal structure of reality.

This is not different for large-scale population studies in the area of education. Pressed to make explicit what they are doing, many researchers will interpret what they are doing as descriptive: they are classifying in terms of a number of variables particular educational phenomena that are thought to be relevant for policy issues. How many cases of bullying are registered in primary schools? Do these occur typically more between particular kinds of children, within a particular group (boys or girls), between groups, etc.? Yet, at the back of the mind of many is usually not only an interest in generalisation from the observed phenomena but also a deeper 'causal' interest. It is presumed that one or more variables may be manipulated in order to avoid particular problems or to influence or act upon them. In other words, there looms a model of causality behind description. Now it goes without saying that to have an informed estimate of the frequency of the occurrence of a particular problem (as detailed as this can be) is quite essential in educational contexts. Policy needs to take this into account as it is sometimes for instance an element in determining how relevant the problem is. It is however a step further if these so-called descriptive studies are used in a general causal framework, where a means-end (sometimes even exclusively technological) rationale is used. This unfortunately is, however, often the case.

There is a strand of criticism against the use of 'cause' in the sphere of human explanations. This is not to deny that human beings are exempted from causal interactions generally; no one seriously denies that, for instance, bodily functions are subjected to physical and biochemical laws and processes. Nevertheless, once it is suggested that our behaviour itself can be understood either partly or exhaustively in terms of these kind of processes, human scientists and philosophers generally protest. Philosophers of human action in the continental and analytical traditions such as Dilthey, Gadamer, Ricoeur, in addition to Wittgenstein, Winch and Taylor have argued to the contrary that human beings *give* meaning to their lives. It behoves us to ask then, whether causal explanations still have significance or not, and in what sense, and for which contexts. And is it correct that if one accepts causal explanations of human behaviour there looms the threat of the disappearance of the ethical, thus inviting us to live 'beyond freedom and dignity'? Though these issues have typically been discussed within epistemological contexts, rather than in the Anglo-Saxon philosophy of education literature, nevertheless they are highly relevant to education and educational inquiries. Here I will not rely primarily on the criticisms of the philosophers of action I have mentioned above, who are critical of causal explanation. I will take a different line. For government and policy-makers educational research fails to provide the answers they are looking for. Worse, much research fails to enhance professional practice. Crucially, for the position developed here, educational research particularly that of a so-called qualitative kind is also criticised for being fragmented into myriad, incommensurable case studies that merely revel in their own uniqueness. On the one hand policy-makers are looking for a science of education, on the other hand it is widely argued that such an aspiration is based on false beliefs about what research can deliver.

In this chapter I will therefore attempt to take seriously the claim that we can look for causes in order to understand the reality we live (in), and I will focus primarily on the natural world. I will argue that even if we were to fully endorse the programme of looking for antecedents, a dominant driver for many educational researchers, this would still not solve the problems they set out commonly to address. I will then illustrate the problem of contextualisation in using an example of educational research that uses the methodology of the *randomised field trial*. In these kind of studies the paradigm of causality and its experimental laboratory approach is modified to incorporate the exigencies of real life situations. Yet it will be argued that these studies too do not put one in a position to derive straightforward conclusions for policy-makers or more generally for educational practitioners. Finally, some concluding remarks will be offered that indicate what may be expected from large-scale population studies and what their epistemological basis comes down to.

AN ANALYSIS OF THE PRESUPPOSITIONS OF QUANTITATIVE RESEARCH AND SOME OF ITS COUNTERARGUMENTS

Necessary and Sufficient Conditions, Determinism and Indeterminism

Paradigmatically one may want to start from Hume's insights on causation for which he uses the billiard ball example. As deductive logic cannot provide the answer (that explains why ball number 2 is set in motion after being hit by ball number 1), Hume turns to empirical investigations. On the basis of his observations he concludes that in situations where we believe that there is a causal relation, there is a temporal priority of the cause to the effect. There is furthermore a spatiotemporal contiguity of the cause to the effect and finally, on every occasion on which the cause occurs, the effect follows—there is constant conjunction. As there is, in his opinion, no physical connection between the cause and the effect (the connection does not exist outside of our own minds), the relation between cause and effect is to be found in custom and habit. As Hume could not find a necessary connection between cause and effect, neither in formal reasoning nor in the physical world, his lesson answers the question whether and how we can explicate the concept of causality in terms that do not surreptitiously introduce any occult concepts of power or necessary connection, which is exactly what he wanted to do.

The form philosophical discussions of causality take is usually as follows: there are two facts (or types of) C and E or two events (or types of) C and E between which there is a relation R. Questions are raised whether C and E should be taken to refer to facts or events, further, whether to individual facts or events or classes of them. Sometimes the logical structure of the relation is discussed in terms of necessary or sufficient conditions or a combination of both. Given the interaction of several conditions this leads to complex schemes to understand particular occurrences. Consider for instance the following example in which a cause is defined as a condition. If a barn burns down this might have been caused by a careless smoker, by embers from a nearby forest fire falling on it, by a stroke of lightning, or even from spontaneous combustion engendered by fermentation of fresh hay. None of these is a necessary condition, but any of them might be sufficient. Moreover, no fire will occur unless some additional factors are present (for instance, in the case of the incident of the cigarette, that it falls on some flammable material and that it goes unnoticed). These other conditions, however, would not suffice to start a fire. Each of them is a condition that is an Insufficient but Non-redundant (necessary) part of a condition that is Unnecessary but Sufficient (an INUS-condition). The dropping of the burning cigarette is an example thereof. Such a clear example is helpful in order to make the particular points concerning causality. As matters of 'meaning' are always involved where examples from social sciences are concerned, an analogous case from that context cannot easily be given. We will therefore continue a bit longer in the area of natural phenomena.

After this brief sketch of 'causality' and some of the (philosophical) problems that go with it, a move to the general level will take the argument forward to the relevance of causality in scientific explanations. The success of the development of more sophisticated experimental and mathematical techniques broadened the application of Newton's laws to new phenomena. The 19th century deterministic worldview has in some ways been confirmed and extended by 20th century science, for instance in the field of molecular biology, where the mechanisms of heredity are explained exclusively in chemical terms. Thus scientists find themselves just one step away from explaining learning in terms of specific chemical changes that occur in the brain cells and from chemical understanding of feelings and emotions in the field of psychology. To the determinist, the fact that we are unable to make perfect predictions in all cases is the result of human ignorance and other limitations, not because nature is lacking in precise determination—clearly, accuracy of prediction is irrelevant to whether determinism is true in principle. There is, however, another framework, that of indeterminism. The challenge of relativity theory is not simply that quantum mechanics is *prima facie* non-deterministic, but that under plausible constraints no deterministic completion of the quantum theory is possible. In view of this it seems inadvisable to accept determinism as an *a priori* principle—and of course the truth or falsity of quantum mechanics is a matter of physical fact. Concerning this it would not make much sense to step, as Wittgenstein would put it, outside of our form of life, i.e. to allow that our concepts amount to no more than whimsical social constructions. Doubts about the possibility of finding causes for everything, either on the basis of logical or empirical considerations or on the basis of relativity theory, have thus moved us to indeterminism as the more rational choice for the overarching framework. What are the implications of this for our understanding of scientific explanation?

Statistical and Functional Explanation, Causal and Pseudo-Processes

There are, of course, different sorts of explanation. A popular kind is the one where specific conditions obtaining prior to the event are cited (initial conditions) and general laws are invoked. Let me make this point clear. It is held that the occurrence of the event to be explained follows logically from those premises, ie those initial conditions and laws. One can distinguish between deductive explanations that incorporate universal laws (which hold without exceptions) and inductive explanations that employ statistical laws (which hold for most or many cases). According to Hempel (1965) scientific explanation consists in deductive or inductive subsumption of that which is to be explained under one or more laws of nature. This is referred to as the deductive-nomological model (D-N). For him, however, inductive-statistical explanations are essentially relativised to knowledge situations—he suggested the requirement of total evidence that took the form of the requirement of maximal specificity, where all possibly relevant knowledge is available. If there were an inductive-statistical explanation whose lawlike statistical premise involved a genuinely homogenous reference class then we would have an instance of an inductive-statistical explanation *simpliciter*, not merely an inductive-statistical explanation relative to a specific knowledge situation. However, as there are according to Hempel no inductive-statistical explanations *simpliciter*, ideally inductive-statistical explanation would have no place in his account. There is a striking similarity between this kind of explanation and Laplace's formulation of determinism. In view of this close relationship it is tempting to conclude that events that are causally determined can be explained, and those that can be explained are causally determined. And from this it is just one more step to say that when human actions and decisions can be explained, they are determined; this leads on to the conclusion that to explain human behaviour and choices is to show that they cannot be free (in which case moral responsibility disappears). However, it should be noted that in many cases *we do not have enough facts to be able to construct an explanation and we can never be sure that a new condition might not turn up* (one that in principle could not have been taken into account previously), that will jeopardise our D-N construction. Again, to put this in other words, one can never exclude whether a further relevant subdivision of a reference class might be necessary on the basis of additional knowledge. This problem is known as the framework problem. Another way to speak about this is that laws apply *all conditions being equal* (or *ceteris paribus*) but that it is impossible to spell out everything that has to be in place and everything that has to be absent. An important consequence is that this safeguards against a deterministic world view, as it is not possible to spell out the necessary *and* sufficient causes to explain a particular event. Indeed, it is not possible to predict precise outcomes with absolute certainty. This in turn implies that prediction cannot be a solid criterion to test a scientific theory nor to verify its truth—to say this is however different from saying that prediction is irrelevant in this context. I will return to this issue later, but there is also a further, even more worrying, problem.

The Inferential Conception Suffers from the Fact that it Seriously Misconstrues the Nature of Subsumption under Laws

If determinism were true then, according to Hempel, every future event would be amenable to D-N explanation. However, the explanation of past events confronts us with a problem: as explanations are essentially inferences they demand an asymmetry, which is simply not present in inferences. Explanation requires a sufficient condition that is based on empirical evidence that something actually happened. Inference on the other hand refers to something in the future. To infer something that lies in the future not only presupposes determinism, but also relies on the fact that everything relevant has been taken into account—a matter one can never be logically sure of. Indeed, inference (whether inductive or deductive) demands that all relevant evidence is mentioned in the premises. This requirement is automatically satisfied for deductive inferences. Explanation seems to demand further that only considerations relevant to the *explanandum* be contained in the *explanans*. As indicated, the *temporal asymmetry* reflected by inferences is precisely the opposite to that exhibited in explanation. Inference and explanation have opposing temporal direction. Another way to put this may point to the fact that *the future may be different*. Of course, if the future might always (or necessarily) be different, research to predict the future would not make sense. However, because the inferential conception demands that the future is in this sense not different, it relies on a claim that can never be met. Incidentally, when we relinquish the assumption of determinism the asymmetry becomes even more striking. Doubts about the fact that explanations are essentially arguments may follow from the impossibility of prediction as a consequence of the lack of all the facts and/or asymmetry of inferences—though this does not mean that we must give up the covering law conception, since subsumption under laws can take a different form.

It is interesting to notice that examples from the atomic and subatomic world show us that there is a limit to the joint precision with which two so-called complementary parameters can be known: there is an inescapable uncertainty if one attempts to ascertain the values of both the position and momentum of a particle, and similarly for energy and time. Ascertaining the position of an electron with great precision makes us unable to ascertain its momentum exactly, and vice-versa.[1] To offer an explanation here is something different: it comes down to the assembling of a total set of relevant conditions for the event to be explained, and to the citing of the probability of that event in the presence of these conditions. The explanation is in this case not an argument (a logical structure with premises and conclusions governed by some rule of acceptance), but rather *a presentation of the conditions relevant to the occurrence of the event, and a statement of the degree of probability of the event given these conditions*. Evidently, a persistent statistical correlation—a genuine statistical-relevance relation—is strongly indicative of a causal relation of some sort, but one should not confuse statistical correlation with genuine causation. This would be to conflate symptoms with causes.

When two types of events, A and B, are positively related to each other, we hunt for a common cause C that is statistically relevant. The statistical-relevance relations must be explained in terms of two causal processes in which C is causally relevant to A and C is causally relevant to B. This is the heart of the matter where it is claimed that a statistical explanation is based on causality. Now the question is, why should we prefer for explanatory purposes the relevance of C to A and C to B over the relevance of A to B that we had in the first place? The answer is that we can trace a spatio-temporally continuous causal connection from C to A and from C to B (while the relation between A and B cannot be accounted for by any such direct continuous causal relation). Recall that causal explanations present us, according to Hume, with a problem. Nevertheless, his criticism needs to be qualified. Indeed, it seems that Hume overlooked an important aspect of causality, i.e. that causal processes are capable of transmitting information.[2] A proper understanding of this will make it possible to distinguish between causal processes and pseudo-causal processes. This distinction emerged from Einstein's special theory of relativity that claims that no signal (no process capable of transmitting information) can travel faster than light. The so-called 'at-at' theory of causal transmission is an attempt to remedy Hume's criticism. The basic thesis about mark transmission can be stated as follows: 'A mark that has been introduced into a process by means of a single intervention at point A is transmitted to point B if and only if it occurs at B and at all stages of the process between A and B without additional interventions' (Salmon, 1998, p. 197).

Thus, Zeno's famous paradox of the arrow can be solved as follows: to move from A to B is simply to occupy the intervening points at the intervening moments. It consists in being at particular points at the corresponding instants. There is no question as to how the arrow gets from point A to point B. (There is no zipping through the intermediate points at high speed.) The arrow is at the points between them at the corresponding moment. And there can be no question about how the arrow gets from one point to the next, for in a continuum there is no next point. 'Mark transmission' is the proposed foundation for the concept of propagation of influence. The ability to transmit a mark is the criterion of a causal process; pseudo-causal processes may also exhibit persistent structure, but this structure is transmitted not by means of the process itself but by some other agency. The basis is thus *the ability of the causal process to transmit a modification in its structure resulting from an interaction (a mark)* without appealing to any of Hume's secret powers.[3] Whether the result of the interaction will be transmitted is a question that can in principle readily be settled by experiment (thus one will investigate whether the resulting modifications in the process are preserved at other stages of the process). The patterns in which we fit events and facts that structure our world, and that we wish to explain, are statistical and causal relations. Causal processes play an important role for they are mechanisms that propagate structure and transmit causal influence. This together with the 'at-at' theory answers Hume's question about the nature of the connections between causes and effects. One can therefore conclude that causal processes exist *besides* probabilistic or statistical causality. In indeterministic settings it appears that necessary causes have at least some degree of explanatory force, but sufficient causes do not. According to the causal conception, we explain facts (general or particular) by exhibiting the physical processes and interactions that bring them about, but such mechanisms need not be deterministic to have explanatory force — they may be irreducibly statistical. Thus a scientific explanation of a particular event is not rigidly determined by general laws and antecedent conditions.

To this different picture of causal processes and statistical explanation, finally another kind of explanation has to be added: *functional explanation*. An illustration of this is the following example from biology. Jackrabbits that inhabit the hot regions in the southwestern part of the U.S.A. have extraordinarily large ears. They constitute an effective cooling mechanism. There are of course many devices that can fulfil this function. It can be shown therefore deductively (or at least with a high inductive probability) that such animals will have some mechanism or other that enables them to adapt to the extreme temperatures, but it does not follow that the jackrabbit must have developed large radiating ears (nor that it is probable that it would do so). Explaining this particular cooling device (as opposed to explaining why it has some mechanism or other that fulfils this function) demands therefore a different kind of explanation. That explanation is labelled 'functional'.

In the study of social institutions by sociologists, anthropologists and other social scientists, many of these kind of explanations may be found. Again, it might be claimed that functional explanations are always illegitimate, or at best incomplete. But it is not clear why they should be ruled out on logical grounds. They offer a particular *kind* of explanation that the received view of scientific explanation (deductive certainty or high inductive probability) cannot account for, without necessarily invoking teleological and anthropomorphical elements—criticisms that are usually brought against this position. In this approach, difficulties with Hempel's model (where there is always a demand for a sufficient condition) are overcome (the functional explanation provides a necessary condition). The epistemic value of such an explanation is measured by the gain in information provided by the probability distribution over the partition. Similarly, in the statistical-relevance model it is the amount of relevant information that counts; it consists of a probability distribution over a (maximum) homogeneous partition of an initial reference class. Thus a unified style of explanation (using basic comprehensive principles) can be accommodated alongside explanations of a mechanical kind (how things work). Both of them may be compatible for a particular problem. Because of their focus on the question of what is intelligible these kinds of explanation resemble understanding and description as used in the human sciences.

So much for some of the seductive illusions and idle talk concerning scientific explanation of natural phenomena. What follows from all this for our ruminations on paradigmatic claims to *superior* scientific explanation—can the 'normativity' of the debate be brought to the foreground in this way? Clearly the paradigm of determinism in the material world has been shattered. For some, to explain an event is simply to identify its cause. Humean doubts about this possibility in terms of something more than contiguity, priority in time and constant conjunction were eased on the one hand by the so called 'at-at' theory, on the other by differentiating pseudo-causal processes from genuine causal processes in terms of the ability to transmit a mark. Contrary to Hume it was argued that there is *real causality* in the world of natural phenomena. But the *fundamental indeterminacy of nature* requires that different kinds of explanation are used for different domains. There are several examples in which there is a necessary but not sufficient cause that invariably produces the event to be explained. Elsewhere there is a sufficient cause but no necessary cause without which the event to be explained could not occur. This was made clear by referring to the fact that inference and explanation both have a *preferred temporal direction* on the one hand and that in many cases we do not have enough facts to be able to construct an explanation. There is room for statistical and functional explanation without thus rendering scientific explanation impossible or unintelligible. The general conclusion must be that if indeterminism is a feature of the atomic and subatomic world (i.e. causal indeterminacy—the truth or falsity of (in)determinism is a matter of physical fact), and if it cannot be ruled out on logical or metaphysical grounds, there is no reason to use determinism as the paradigm *par excellence* (or the only paradigm) for other domains of understanding— moreover, our everyday concept of human action also tells us differently: it refers to freedom and accepts responsibility for what we do in normal circumstances.[4] One way this problem has been handled is by using so-called randomised controlled field trials (RCTs). Although a number of the presuppositions of the causal model still pertain in this context, RCTs are supposed at least to come to terms with some of the contextual demands that are at stake when one is interested in a realistic picture of what works in educational practice. Here it is no longer about 'laboratory' conditions, and there is moreover the expectation that that one can come to grips to a large extent with the complex network of intervening variables (or conditions).

AN EXAMPLE OF A RANDOMISED CONTROLLED FIELD TRIAL: CLASS-SIZE RESEARCH

Class size and, more particularly, the reduction of the teacher-student ratio, has been discussed widely. There is indeed a widespread belief among parents, teachers and others that pupils learn most effectively in small classes. This is, according to Mortimore and Blatchford (1993), reflected by the fact that one of the main reasons cited for choosing independent schools is class size. That many people expect a lot from smaller classes is understandable as the size of a class is one of the most important means by which the school environment affects children's learning and behaviour. Yet some people are hesitant and argue that the cost of such an operation cannot be justified in terms of the benefits it generates for student learning (Slavin, 1990; Tomlinson, 1990). Though there is a lot of debate concerning this issue, some critics argue that there is not a wealth of evidence derived from well-designed studies to support size reduction. Most of the research is piecemeal and would not survive serious methodological scrutiny, at least not enough to corroborate a general conclusion concerning class size. As regards the U.K., Mortimore and Blatchford (1993) claim that typically only correlations or associations have been reported between class size and average pupil attainment, with little or no firm evidence on the impact of a particular class size on the achievements of its pupils. It is widely recognised, they say, that results from these studies are difficult to interpret because they do not account for intake (for instance lower attaining pupils can be concentrated in smaller classes). Furthermore, it should not go unnoticed that there have been instances of meta-analysis regarding this issue. But even if one takes these into account, it is not clear what conclusions should be drawn. The situation is somewhat different for North America where more research has been conducted on this topic, though again interpretations differ. Some argue that there is a clear and strong relationship between class size and achievement (Glass, Smith and Finley, 1982). Others criticise the idea that an optimum class size can be specified in isolation from factors such as the age of pupils or the subject matter being taught (Robinson and Wittebols, 1986). In conclusion, though a bibliographical search (ERIC) generates 456 references (to reports, journal articles, etc.) for the period 1966–2005 it is not, as many scholars have argued, transparently obvious that there is hard empirical evidence regarding the impact of class size on student learning.

Concerning class size, there seems to be one case many authors refer to due to its all-encompassing approach: the Tennessee Studies of Class Size, Project STAR (Student/Teacher Achievement Ratio). In this study moreover very clear conclusions are offered. It is described by Mosteller, Light and Sachs (1996) in an article published in the *Harvard Educational Review*, in which they use it to show that large, long-term, randomised controlled field trials can be carried out successfully in education.[5] Project STAR is seen as an experiment that starts from the idea that in smaller classes teachers have more time to give to individual children. This is to cope with a number of problems, as children face a great deal of confusion when they first come to school. For instance, they need to learn to cooperate with others, to get organised to become students, and of course they come from a variety of homes and backgrounds. In the experimental classes, the class size was reduced from around 23 to 15, by approximately one-third, in kindergarten, first, second and third grades (ages 5-8); the children moved into regular-size classes in the fourth grade. There were three kinds of groups: classes one-third smaller than regular-size classes, regular-size classes without a teacher aide and regular-size classes with a teacher aide. The experiment was carried out in 79 schools in the first year; both children and teachers were randomly assigned to the classes. In the second year it included 76 schools with 331 classes including 6572 children in inner-city urban, suburban and rural schools. It was continued for four years (1985–1989). After this period there was a second phase, the Lasting Benefits Study, which followed participating children into later grades and recorded their academic progress.

What are the major findings on class size? First, smaller classes did bring substantial improvement to early learning in cognitive subjects such as reading and arithmetic. Secondly, the effects persisted into grades 4, 5, 6, and 7, after pupils moved to regular-size classes. Students who had originally been enrolled in smaller classes continued to perform better than their peers who had started in larger classes. Incidentally, minority students gained twice as much as the rest during the first two years before settling down to about the same gain as the rest. Thirdly, the presence of teacher aides did not produce improvements nor did their presence seem to have as many lasting benefits. Some more detailed results will further corroborate this conclusion. Performance was assessed through the use of two kinds of tests: the standardised Stanford Achievement Test and the curriculum-based Tennessee's Basic Skills First Test:

> The effect sizes are around .25 for small versus regular-size class without an aide and around .10 for regular-size class with an aide compared to regular-size class without an aide. Thus the small class size advances the typical student an additional 10 percentile points, to the 60th percentile, while the aide advances the same student 4 percent, to the 54th percentile (Mosteller, Light and Sachs, 1996, p. 819).

The authors hasten to add that although '. . . not huge, these improvements are substantial; when applied to a large population, they represent a solid advance in student learning' (p. 819). Furthermore, it is encouraging to find that students' early experience of smaller size classes has lasting effects that can be observed when they move to regular-size classes—the measurable effect after the first year was .12 and in the fifth grade the effect was nearly .20.

Mosteller *et al.* finally indicate that there are many issues involved when a well-designed and well-implemented study comes out with a definite finding. Serious consideration has to be given to all the available alternatives, and to the costs and social consequences of implementing the new policy suggested by the findings. In this case, policymakers thought about the most effective place to introduce this intervention and decided to implement it in the seventeen districts with the lowest per-capita income. Thus the method was used in about 12 percent of the state's districts and reduced class size in only about 4 percent of all K-12 classes in the state. Mosteller *et al.* further point out that, at the time of the study (1996), no further information became available from the seventeen low-income districts after their students moved to regular-sized classes. Therefore, they stress that these findings do not automatically mean that reducing class size is the best way to improve schooling–this has to be compared with other measures (for instance, one-to-one tutoring by qualified teachers, peer tutoring or cooperative group learning).

As argued above, the matter of class size has been the focus of interest in various places. In the 1995 report 'Class size and the quality of education', the UK's Office for Standards in Education (Ofsted) used data from inspections to examine the possible relationship between class size and the quality of pupil's learning in U.K. primary and secondary schools. I will not go into details concerning this study, but it is interesting to examine the conclusions briefly. Some of the main findings are that:

- no simple link exists between the size of the class and the quality of teaching and learning within it;
- small class sizes are of benefit in the early years of primary education. Once pupils have achieved competency in basic learning, particularly in literacy, they are more able to learn effectively in larger classes;
- within the range of classes inspected, the selection and application of the teaching methods and forms of class organisation have a greater impact on learning than the size of the class (Ofsted, 1995).

There really is an abundant amount of research to select from. In some reports, attention is drawn to the fact that numerous aspects of the classroom are changed when the class size is reduced. Furthermore, teachers that have been assigned to smaller classes report that the classroom environment is better. There are fewer reports of distractions. The changes lead to the noise level being lower and the room arrangements are more flexible because there are fewer desks. Sometimes researchers observed that, in small classes, the majority of a pupil's time was spent in individual communication with the instructor, while most of a pupil's time in a large class was evenly split between individual and group instruction. Moreover, many forms of behaviour that are not tolerated in large classes because of the disruption they create, such as walking around the room, may be acceptable in small classes.

Though the results of the STAR Project have not generally been disputed, some critics have pointed out that the effects seem to decrease after a number of years. One may want to remark that this was probably to be expected in the sense that the experience of the initial class reduction was a one-off event that could not possibly produce the same effects the following years. Others have claimed that the reason for the limited benefits that derive from small classes may be found in the fact that teachers maintain their old methods of teaching and do not take advantage of the new opportunities small classes offer. Thus Mortimore and Blatchford (1993) argue:

> It is difficult to know whether it is the opportunity for more individual attention for pupils, more opportunities for pupils to become involved in practical learning tasks, or enhanced teacher motivation and satisfaction in small classes, which indirectly benefit pupils. It makes little sense, therefore, to consider class size in isolation from teaching practices, because the potential benefits of reducing class size will only occur if teachers alter their behaviour and classroom organisation (p. 4).

There may be other elements as well that have to be considered, such as the preparation time for teachers that is assumed to be higher for larger classes; whether larger classes are given to more experienced (or possibly better) teachers; and the views of pupils themselves (whether they feel happier, believe they are less likely to be bullied and are more confident about speaking up for themselves and participating in practical activities). Other more general issues have also to be taken into account: the relationship between class size, teaching methods and the age of the pupils. Therefore, it is suggested that the effects of class size may be different at various ages, a matter that will interact again with the kinds of teaching and instruction that are offered. For instance, it could be the case that class size reductions will be more effective in the first years of school when children are more dependent on adult help, whereas peer tutoring and computer-assisted learning are likely to be more effective once pupils have been in school for a few years. Therefore, it may also be the case that reduced class sizes can prevent problems but are not sufficient to remedy problems later on, and so forth. The complications are endless. Other issues that are suggested concern the relationships between pupil and teacher, attitudes and morale and the relationships pupils have with each other.

Given the success of the STAR Project some authors have drawn conclusions concerning the kind of research we need to conduct. Mortimore and Blatchford argue that a carefully controlled UK research study is long overdue (1993) and furthermore that what is needed is 'experimental research which compares the progress of pupils who have been randomly allocated to classes of different sizes' (Blatchford and Mortimore, 1994, p. 418) because it is the only research that can give us conclusive answers to the question of whether children in smaller classes do better. In the same vein, Mosteller *et al.* (1996) argue that having access to strong research and policy studies will enable educators to make wise choices. One should not forget that educators have to work with scarce resources and constrained budgets and must decide on how to organise students into classrooms. And they continue:

Hunches, anecdotes, and impressions may have been the only available options in the year 1900, but as we approach the year 2000, society has a broad set of analytic design techniques, widely accepted and effectively used in many fields, that can offer more reliable evidence than hunches and impressions ... Not all questions can be tackled using controlled experiments, but many can be. We need larger scale investigations because studies carried out in single schools always have the limitation of doubtful generalization (Mosteller *et al.*, 1996, p. 822–823).

They suggest a list of issues that may be tackled in a similar way (i.e. well-designed, randomised controlled field trials preparing for educational innovations) such as the appropriate amount of homework in different classes for children of different ages, the distribution of time to tasks among different school subjects and even the question of whether or not students are losing too much of what has been learned in the school year during summer months and vacations. I find these examples quite strange and it is not clear to me how they could be studied by randomised controlled field trials. Even more remarkable is the fact that Blatchford and Mortimore (1994) express some doubts about the results of (quasi-) experimental findings or randomised controlled trials, while on the other hand they do not give ample space for other alternatives. Though in my view they correctly point out that class size reductions and methods of teaching need to be considered together and that benefits are only likely to take place if we consider what kinds of teaching, classroom organisation and tasks are relevant to a particular size of teaching group, they insist that these issues should be approached in an experimental way – or how else, given their earlier statements, does one interpret their plea in the same article for *sound information* (p. 426)?

As I have noted, it is strange to find, on the one hand, pleas for well-designed (experimental) research while, on the other hand, these empirical researchers are aware of the multiple elements that have to be taken into account and the problems to be overcome. It is clear that they fully realise the limitations of the methods they want to follow. For instance, in a 1998 study, Goldstein and Blatchford discuss observational studies and randomised controlled trials, and argue for the assumption that the point of doing class size research is to make statements about causation: 'By causation we mean the inference that, from an observed 'effect' of class size on achievement estimated by research, we can assume that moving children from one class size to another will have a similar effect on achievement' (Goldstein and Blatchford, 1998, p. 256). Yet in the same study they argue: 'Even with the most carefully controlled study causal interpretations will be difficult, not least because we need to take account of the context in which the research has been carried out; and whether the 'effect' may vary across schools, educational systems and other contexts such as social background'(ibid.).[6] Goldstein and Blatchford draw attention to several problems that may arise because researchers have ignored the problematic aspects of measuring or defining certain concepts. The following list is long, though not exhaustive:

- the actual size of a class is not the same as the student-teacher ratio
- the number of students formally on the register may differ from the number of those being taught
- the experienced size is to be differentiated from the actual size
- the sample population may differ from the target population
- reduction of class sizes within a large school may not be the same as an equivalent change in a small school
- because of the unavoidably historical nature of all social research, by the time the results are available the context normally will have changed
- the institutions or populations that are most accessible for study are often atypical
- in the case of randomised controlled trials the expectations about the effects of class size may be partly responsible for observed effects
- teachers and children within a school in different class sizes may interact over time and possibly 'contaminate' the effects of the size differences
- a design where randomisation occurs only at the school level may not be representative of the real world where typically differential sizes do exist within schools
- teachers may alter their style of teaching (they might tend to use more whole-class teaching methods and concentrate more on a narrower range of basic topics), and consequently compensate in a number of ways with larger classes
- the role of 'mediating variables and processes' (such as quality of teaching, pupil attention, teacher control etc.).

Re-analyzing the data of the STAR Project, Goldstein and Blatchford (1998) identify other 'shortcomings'. For instance, they point out that 24% of the children were removed from the project after kindergarten and these had a markedly lower score than those who remained in the study. They also noted that problems regarding dropping out continued at grades 1, 2 and 3. In conclusion, one finds that, on the one hand, pleas are made for well-designed (mainly experimental) research, while on the other hand these empirical researchers are aware of the multiple elements that have to be taken into account and the problems to 'overcome'. Clearly they fully realise the limitations of the method they want to adhere, but, nevertheless, decide that it is still the best path to follow.

Of course, it is interesting to know that reductions in class size have no negative (and indeed have some positive) effects on student learning, but the question remains whether the level of those effects substantiates the claim for greater investment—resources are always scarce. This necessarily requires a different line of research and of argumentation. Many other issues are involved, which the STAR study does not go into, such as the workload of the teachers, the feelings of happiness of the students, and other issues that can hardly be measured in the same 'objective' experimental manner.

This is also a problem because the various elements that are involved relate to each other. It comes therefore as no surprise to find in many studies that it is not so much class size that is important, but the way the teacher deals with it, i.e. varies his teaching to accommodate optimal student learning. What lessons are to be learnt from this debate? Does it rule out experimental or even empirical research? I don't think so, but before going into that, I will first provide some more meta-level comments. Incidentally, what was observed in the above studies, in my view, holds for *all* empirical quantitative educational research in a paradigmatic way.

So what may be concluded on a meta-level as regards this kind of research? First of all, it seems that, in these studies, the benefits of reducing class size are determined in terms of factors (independent and dependent) that can be measured and manipulated in their constituent parts. What does not fit into this experimental pattern is simply left out. Although the wellbeing of pupils and teacher workloads are mentioned, there is no attempt to incorporate these factors into the design. Obviously it would be very difficult to analyse some of these relevant variables in random settings. Nevertheless, case studies are ruled out because the conclusions they offer cannot be generalised. It is true that most of the researchers working in this area accept that the higher cost of smaller classes is a relevant consideration. However, they are much more concerned with establishing whether or not there is an effect, rather than considering the strength of the effect that would justify higher spending on education.[7] The latter, much more political issue, is *irrelevant* for such researchers and is not dealt with. This generates a picture that suggests that once the facts have been determined, the conclusion (i.e. to decrease class size or not) follows on of its own accord. Second, it is difficult to see how long-term studies can accommodate situational and historical change. It is not only impossible to foresee which new elements have to be taken into account, but what is ignored are the different elements that, in their interaction with each other, create something new (which is not just the result of addition or subtraction of variables seen as separate and independent factors). Problems of discipline, for instance, may disrupt the interactions to such an extent that regularly observed relations between variables no longer hold. Conversely, we are told that one of the advantages of smaller classes is that many forms of behaviour, which are not tolerated in larger classes because of the disruption they create, may be acceptable in smaller classes. Third, and less technically but perhaps even more importantly, the favoured design seems to ignore the fact that teachers deal with class situations (or learning situations) in a creative manner. It comes as no surprise to find in many studies that it is not so much class size that is important, but the way the teacher deals with it, i.e. varies his or her teaching to accommodate optimal student learning. Teachers will look for opportunities for students to learn and thus act more in the spirit of 'making the most of it', rather than carefully following regularities or causal inferences. They realise that there are many roads to Rome, and also that it may not be the only place worth going to. All three of these conclusions could be seen as strengthening the case for a more holistic approach, where the relation of the elements that are involved is given a more prominent place. It seems that in educational contexts it is not so much factors or elements that have to be studied as such, but the complex relationships between them. Here the presence or absence of something may change the whole picture and, consequently, the conclusions that can be drawn from a particular setting. Yet from the position that is generally embraced, such studies are seen as irrelevant due to their lack of potential for generalisation.

What can be found in so-called quantitative empirical research is often of very limited use in a practical educational context. It belongs to a paradigm of causality, which cannot (or only at great pains and by changing the meaning of 'causality', i.e. incorporating 'reasons') give a place for the reasons human beings invoke for doing what they do. Or it is so piecemeal that it is hardly relevant given all other kinds of factors. Incidentally, so-called qualitative research does not do any better, as often the conclusions that are offered are so obvious that it is difficult to imagine disagreement. Yes, it is of course the case that people generally tend to find conclusions 'quite evident', and that sometimes, if asked beforehand, they are inclined to suggest something else that seems to them at that point intuitively obvious. So, for that matter, it is important to know the facts. But questions concerning how far these findings can go are quite another matter. How helpful is it to know that primary school teachers do not feel up to the task, or that new class sizes require adapting teaching skills and methods? Can it seriously be doubted that the number of students in a group will affect the teacher's workload or the wellbeing of the pupils *in some respects*?

LARGE-SCALE POPULATION STUDIES: ON THEIR EPISTEMOLOGICAL BASIS AND WHAT ONE MAY EXPECT FROM THEM

It may be clear from what has been argued that large-scale population studies flirt with the paradigm of causality. They generally tend to overstate their case that is in essence only descriptive. But even if one accepts that the problems of generalisation may be something that is in the nature of such kinds of studies, in other words, if one sets this aside, there is still an uneasiness behind the rhetoric that is used whether the insights tell us something about how things work. Correlations seem to invite the reader to see a mechanism that can in some way be used for particular purposes. It seems difficult to formulate a position from which one looks at the various elements involved, without at the same time putting everything within the context of a paradigm of causation. Often it is said that because so many 'factors' are at work, it might be difficult to formulate clear conclusions for practice. But this argument hides what is really at stake, which is a particular way in which understanding reality is conceived. Instead of a holistic approach, where different elements in their interaction with each other create something new, what is at the bottom here is a paradigm of addition or subtraction of variables seen as factors. What looms behind this may be captured by the following: not understanding everything is equated with not understanding anything. What is longed for is something similar to the law-like explanation and 'prediction' of the natural sciences. Here, for many to explain an event is to identify its antecedents, i.e. its causes.

What we do as researchers is constitutive of the reality that we shape together and that is unavoidably value-laden. If empirical research does not rise above the level of description, there is a danger it will degenerate into a kind of empty empiricism. It is therefore important to realise the centrality of theories and concepts for empirical research. Evidently, theories can be tested, but concepts cannot. Before observation can start, one needs a particular concept that does justice to the situation one is about to study. The discussion of these concepts is not itself something that belongs to empirical research. In *The Idea of a Social Science* (1958) Peter Winch emphasised this point several times. That is the reason why he says that it is all about 'what is real for us'. The matter is not only relevant for social studies, but even for physics and chemistry, but it is true that it carries a different weight in the context of understanding human interactions. The pitfalls of the positivist stance have for long become clear. We should therefore move in the opposite direction; that is, in accepting that concepts, theories, reasons etc. always presuppose a background in order to make sense. There is no need to rule out causes or observed regulations when explaining human action. They too presuppose a meaningful context. To give a causal explanation of human behaviour then only refers to the fact that it is described in certain terms, in the same sense as an explanation in terms of reasons presupposes a background of shared understanding. Some human actions may thus be characterised in terms of causes and effects, but it may also be possible to give descriptions in terms of regularities (how antecedent variables go together with subsequent conditions) or to refer to reasons. Some activities may almost exclusively be understood by using one type of explanation, while in other cases several will be possible. Thus whether something is *really explained*, or whether 'reality' here is merely a matter of not being fictitious, should not necessarily invoke a correspondence theory of truth where sense data are the exclusive building blocks. There is a kind of circularity involved that is not to be regretted, as it is characteristic of all explanation. Science, as for that matter any kind of explanation, will always take the data that are to be interpreted at a next higher step of abstraction, thus invoking a particular theoretical construction that makes sense. This is a circular process in which each level is taken to account for, to derive from, or to elaborate on the others. Thus instances are explained by patterns and patterns by instances. Moreover, in trying to be objective, and in identifying 'objective' with 'free of bias', the fact is concealed that we always and inevitably bring our pre-understandings with us into any situation.

Even if sense data and observations play an important role, this still does not jeopardise the claim that concepts are involved. Possible exceptions occur only at a very basic level, for example that light of a particular intensity is painful. In such cases one may argue that particular phenomena have 'meaning in themselves', that is, without presupposing a shared meaningful background. Obviously, what is 'shared' here is the human body and its particular physiology. These cases are rare, however, and once we start speaking about them, a language in which we can determine 'what makes sense for us' is implied. Again this has to be distinguished from a context in which reasons can be given. Physical objects may affect us in particular ways. It is therefore not correct to argue that phenomena with a 'meaning in themselves' play no role whatsoever in our understanding of human behaviour, but it would also not be correct to ignore that more is involved if they have a place in our lives. In that case they also presuppose some kind of shared meaning that will include elements above the physical, chemical, physiological or biochemical level. An adequate methodology of the social sciences should therefore combine causal and descriptive explanation with intentional understanding.

Large-scale population studies may direct our attention for instance to the fact that there are more delinquents in a particular region than anywhere else, more cases of leukaemia etc. They can give us detailed research questions and even clues to start dealing with these. They can also correct particular explanations that are generally given and that may turn out not to be correct (for instance, that these kind of children of this particular background or race are lazier, less intelligent). They may point us in a particular direction, but evidently much more, and that is complementary to what has been observed, will need to be said.

An interesting example is offered by the EPPE 3-11 study (2003–2008), which provides a five year extension to Europe's largest longitudinal investigation into the effects of pre-school education on children's developmental outcomes at the start of primary school: the Effective Provision of Pre-School Education (EPPE, 1997–2003) study.[8] In EPPE, more than 3000 children were assessed at the start of pre-school (around the age of 3), their developmental progress was monitored until they entered school, and then for a further three years until the end of Key Stage 1. The study applied an 'educational effectiveness' design to establish the factors related to children's progress, followed by intensive case studies to 'un-pack' effective practices. The EPPE 3-11 follows the same cohort of children to the end of Key Stage 2.

SAMPLE:

The research questions are answered from drawing different samples from three Tiers.

The Tiers are illustrated below in Figure 1.

Tier 1 enables the research to derive a series of 'value added residuals' for every primary school in England for three consecutive years (probably across 2001–2004). These scores (separating English, Maths and Science) would be linked with measures in other administrative databases including the Autumn Package classifications, Ofsted ratings (e.g. pedagogical

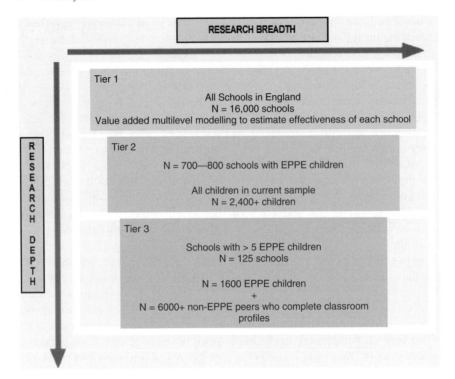

Figure 1

quality) and National Assessment Test Yr 6 data. Thus the effectiveness of every school in England is studied, using value-added measures over three years to identify trends in effectiveness in terms of academic outcomes. Following comparisons are made between the effectiveness and characteristics of schools in the EPPE sample with schools in England as a whole. Tier 2 enables the research to establish the long-term effects of pre-school on children's attainment, progress, attitudes, behaviour and SEN status. In Tier 2, EPPE 3-11 explores the continued cognitive and social behavioural development of different groups of pupils across KS1 and KS2. It establishes whether the influence of attending a more effective pre-school is lost or reduced for those who attend less effective primary schools. Likewise, do those who had no pre-school experience, or only limited or poor quality pre-school experience 'catch up' if they attend a more effective primary? This indicates to what extent later 'good' school experience can compensate for early lack of or poor pre-school experience. In addition, the Tier 2 study shows whether those children who attend both a more effective pre-school and a more effective primary obtain a greater benefit, and whether such experience has particular advantages for more vulnerable pupil groups. 'Out of school' learning at this stage is also investigated through pupil questionnaires, and thus its contribution to development at age 11 is established. Tier 3 builds on the essential analysis of Tier 2 and explores in more detail (through classroom observations and teacher questionnaires) the characteristics of primary school (including practice and ethos) that promote better developmental outcomes, including fostering pupil motivation and engagement as well as cognitive attainment, especially for more vulnerable groups. The study increases understanding of the way primary school practices interact with child, family and home learning environment to shape development. Such evidence informs practitioners and policy-makers about the extent to which pre-school and primary school can help pupil groups.

This is not the place to comment on the kind of methods (quantitative, qualitative) that the researchers used particularly in Tier 3 or to reiterate other issues of methodology that occupied me earlier in my discussion. The study exemplifies in my opinion in an interesting way how large-scale population studies can be complemented by more detailed approaches and shows thus indirectly the use that can be made of them.

Large-scale population studies may thus be an interesting starting point in attracting our attention to patterns that are not visible if one limits oneself to just a few cases. Thus they are part of the work that needs to be done to understand the phenomena on which we focus. It is not just a matter of taking into account the correct statistical rules or guidelines to be followed when generalisation is intended from a sample to a sampling frame (or from a sample to a population that is *not* a probability sample from that population) and articulating both the details of the investigation itself and the logic by which the findings of the investigations should apply to the domains intended. A large-scale population study is an interesting starting point that has to be complemented to make it educationally relevant, in other words, to do the job or make it work for educational purposes.

Correspondence: Prof Paul Smeyers, Faculty of Psychology and Educational Sciences, Ghent University, Dunantlaan 2, 9000 Gent, Belgium. *Email:* paulus.smeyers@ugent.be

NOTES

1. More precisely: when a photon strikes an electron, the direction in which the electron will go is not determined. There is a probability distribution over all possible directions. Furthermore, in this collision the amount by which the frequency of the photon will change is not determined. A probability distribution over all possible amounts exists. Because of the conservation of energy and of momentum, there is a perfect correlation between the direction of the electron and the change in frequency of the photon. The pair of values is however not determined. Incidentally, it is important in this context also to refer to problems with our instruments of measurement as well. The click that results from a genuine photon detection is utterly indistinguishable from the click that results from a spurious count. And finally, there is of course the presumption that conditions surrounding this particular occurrence can be specified in enough detail to establish the existence of a unique necessary and sufficient cause. (This example is discussed in Salmon, 1998.)
2. The development as before is mainly based on the position of Salmon (cf. Salmon, 1998).
3. The following example may illustrate this. Consider a rotating spotlight, mounted in the centre of a circular room, that casts a spot of light on the wall. A light ray travelling *from* the spotlight *to* the wall is a causal process: the spot of light moving around the walls constitutes a pseudo-process. The former process occurs at the speed of light; the latter 'process' can go on at arbitrarily high

velocities, depending on the size of the room and the rate of rotation of the light source. The speed of light places no restrictions on the velocity of the pseudo-process. The fact that the beam of light travelling from the light source to the wall is a causal process can be revealed by a simple experiment. If a red filter is interposed in the beam near its source, the colour of the spot of the wall will be red. This 'mark' is transmitted along the beam. It is obvious how the transmission of such marks could be employed to send a message:

Red if by land and blue if by sea.
And I on the opposite shore will be
Ready to ride and spread the alarm
To every Middlesex village and farm.

It is equally evident, I believe, that no information can be sent via the moving spot on the wall. If you are standing near the wall at one side of the room, and someone else is stationed at a diametrically opposite point, there is nothing you can do to the passing spot of light that will convey any information—e.g., 'The British are coming!'—to the other person. Interposing a red filter may make the spot red in your vicinity, but the 'mark' will not be retained as the spot moves on. (See Salmon, 1998, pp. 194–195.)

4. The concept of 'paradigm' is used here in a non-technical, general sense. One could also speak of the dominant belief in a certain world-view that sets the limits (or determines the frame-work) for paradigmatic approaches within a particular discipline.
5. In what follows I will draw mainly upon their characterisation of the project.
6. Causality here and elsewhere is conceptually identified as law-like generalisations paradigmatically used for instance in physics.
7. Recently Robert Coe (2002) has drawn attention to this problem. He writes:

'Effect size' is simply a way of quantifying the size of the difference between two groups. It is easy to calculate, readily understood and can be applied to any measured outcome in Education or Social Science. It is particularly valuable for quantifying the effectiveness of a particular intervention, relative to some comparison. It allows us to move beyond the simplistic, 'Does it work or not?' to the far more sophisticated, 'How well does it work in a range of contexts?' Moreover, by placing the emphasis on the most important aspect of an intervention—the size of the effect—rather than its statistical significance (which conflates effect size and sample size), it promotes a more scientific approach to the accumulation of knowledge. For these reasons, effect size is an important tool in reporting and interpreting effectiveness.

Yet he also observes that: 'The routine use of effect sizes, however, has generally been limited to meta-analysis—for combining and comparing estimates from different studies—and is all too rare in original reports of educational research'. I am grateful to Lesley Saunders who drew my attention to this.

8. The following is to a large extent quoted from the information that can be found at the website of the 'The Effective Provision of Pre-School Education (EPPE) Project' and the 'Effective Pre-School and Primary Education 3-11 (EPPE 3-11) Project' see http://www.ioe.ac.uk/schools/ecpe/eppe/eppe3-11/eppe3-11intro.htm and also http://www.tlrp.org/proj/phase111/AssocEPPE.htm I am grateful to Alan Brown who drew my attention to this study.

REFERENCES

Blatchford, P. and Mortimore, P. (1994) The issue of class size for young children in schools: what can we learn from research?, *Oxford Review of Education*, 20, pp. 411–428.

Coe, R. (2002) It's the effect size, stupid: what effect size is and why it is important. Paper presented at the Annual Conference of the British Educational Research Association, University of Exeter, England, 12–14 September 2002. Retrieved June 20, 2007 from: http://www.leeds.ac.uk/educol/documents/00002182.htm

Glass, G., Cahen, L., Smith, M. L. and Filby, N. (1982) *School Class Size* (Beverley Hills, CA, Sage).

Goldstein, H. and Blatchford, P. (1998) Class size and educational achievement: a review of methodology with particular reference to study design, *British Educational Research Journal*, 24, pp. 255–268.

Hempel, C. (1965) *Aspects of Scientific Explanation* (New York, Free Press).

Mortimore, P. and Blatchford, P. (1993, March) The issue of class size. *National Commission on Education* (NCE Briefing N° 12).

Mosteller, F., Light, R. J. and Sachs, J. A. (1996) Sustained inquiry in education: Lessons from skill grouping and class size, *Harvard Educational Review*, 66, pp. 797–842.

Ofsted (Office For Standards in Education) (1995) *Class Size and the Quality of Education* (London, Ofsted).

Robinson, G. E. and Wittebols, J. H. (1986) *Class Size Research: A Related Cluster Analysis for Decision Making* (Arlington, VA, Educational Research Service).

Salmon, W. C. (1998) *Causality and Explanation* (New York, Oxford University Press).

Slavin, R. (1990) Class size and student achievement: is smaller better? *Contemporary Education*, 62.(1), pp. 6–12.

Tomlinson, T. (1990) Class size and public policy: the plot thickens, *Contemporary Education*, 62.(1), pp. 17–23.

Winch, P. (1958) *The Idea of a Social Science and Its Relation to Philosophy* (London, Routledge).

5

Epistemology as Ethics in Research and Policy: The Use of Case Studies

JOHN ELLIOTT AND DOMINIK LUKEŠ

This chapter examines the ethnographic case study in education in the context of policy-making with particular emphasis on the practice of research and policy-making. The central claim of the chapter is that it is impossible to establish a transcendental epistemology of the case study on instrumental rationality. Instead it argues for the notion of situated judgement that needs to be made by practitioners in context, practitioners being both researchers and policy-makers. In other words, questions about the level of confidence or warrant that can be placed in different sorts of research evidence and findings cannot be answered independently of forming a view about the appropriateness of the policy culture that shapes political decision-making. The chapter draws a distinction between the general, which is internal to the data as construed by a particular discipline, and the universal, which is the result of embedded human deliberation. This applies to all research findings and not only to case study, although since case study has long had to defend itself against accusations of the lack of generality, it can be a useful starting point for the discussion. This chapter is not meant to be yet another defence of the case study research genre, although a summary of other defences is offered. Rather it focuses on how use of the case study points to the limits of epistemology as rationality and offers a view of epistemology as ethics.

INTRODUCTION

In considering the issues surrounding the question of case study epistemology we were mindful of the following points made by David Bridges in his proposal to the Economic and Social Research Council (ESRC) for the Teaching and Learning Research Programme (TLRP) for the project on *The Epistemological Basis of Educational Research*

Findings, defining the central questions to be addressed as: 'to do with the warrant or level of confidence which educational research (of different kinds) can provide for decisions about what should be done in terms of general educational policy across a whole system or practice at classroom level'. It will, therefore, Bridges argues,

> ... address specifically the claims made by contemporary discourses of 'evidence-based practice' and 'what works', but it will locate these within a wider framework of literature which examines the relationship between research, policy and practice (including considerations to do with the derivation of practice from policy as well as policy and practice from research).

The task assigned to us was specifically to address issues about the level of confidence one might have in case study research as a basis for both policy and practice in the field of education:

> What kind of confidence can we have in the ethnographic study and construction of a single case (or cross-site analysis of a limited number of cases) as a basis for policy and practice? What is the nature of the inference between evidence and recommendations for policy and practice in such studies?

In referring to 'case study', it is all too easy to engender terminological confusion. We will not attempt to provide a generative definition of 'case study', an exercise that has been well rehearsed (see Adelman, Jenkins and Kemmis, 1976; Stake, 1994, 1995, for more in-depth discussion). However, we believe that definitional questions are appropriately about how one characterises 'a case' as an object of inquiry and not about which method(s) are appropriate. Attempts to define 'case study' in methodological terms are all too often symptomatic of unproductive paradigm wars. Pole and Morrison (2003, p. 9) point out that in the educational context 'case study' is frequently a 'synonym for ethnography'. Indeed Bridges treats it as such in his proposal to the ESRC (see above). The term 'case study' appears to have been captured by ethnographers working in the education research field and cast as the bearer of an alternative qualitative methodology to quantitative methods. We see educational case study as a form of inquiry into a particular instance of a general class of things that can be given sufficiently detailed attention to illuminate its educationally significant features (see e.g. Parlett and Dearden, 1977; Simons, 1980). Such a view of case study is methodologically open. Methods need to be justified pragmatically in terms of their 'fitness for purpose' rather than in terms of *a priori* principles derived from a theory of knowledge. For some purposes ethnographic methods may illuminate the case, while for others narrative or even quantitative methods may be more appropriate (see the contribution by Griffiths and MacLeod in this volume).

Just as case study cannot be cast as a 'method of inquiry' neither can it be cast in terms of the scope, length or expense of the inquiry. The latter are dependent on the 'needs of the case'. The idea that case studies are always small-scale inquiries compared with sample studies and can therefore be carried out in a shorter time-period at less expense is biased by assumptions that shape the latter. Case study research in education was initially developed in the UK and USA to inform decision-makers about the way an educational change proposal shapes up in particular context of action. It strove for an increasing particularization of description in order to illuminate the complexity of the interactions involved in shaping actions to effect change and their consequences. Such case studies were extremely detailed and time consuming to produce. For example, the six case studies carried out in the context of the Cambridge Accountability Project (see Elliott, Bridges, Ebbutt, Gibson and Nias, 1982) took five researchers 18 months to complete. Moreover, as this example illustrates, much case-study based research in education was designed to address the information needs of decision-makers beyond the confines of the school, such as members of the wider policy community. From the 1970s, until quite recently, multi-site case study research—deploying a range of qualitative methods—emerged as a complementary and increasingly alternative paradigm of educational programme evaluation. This development was given considerable impetus by a group of evaluation specialists from the UK and USA who from 1972 onwards convened occasional meetings in Cambridge UK (see MacDonald and Parlett, 1973; Hamilton et al., 1977; Elliott and Kushner, 2007). A digital archive of case studies drawn from the work of members and associates of the Cambridge Conference, together with contextualising interviews, can now be accessed (http://www.caret.cam.ac.uk/tel). It was developed as part of an 18 month RDI project funded under the ESRC Qualitative Archiving and Data Sharing Scheme (QUADS). The impact of particular case study based evaluation and research projects and the issue of the generalisability of case studies are amongst the themes explored in the contextualising interviews. It should also be noted that uses of the term 'case study' to refer to subject presentation in business and professional training, and to problem-based learning or to purely quantitative pilot studies using smaller data-sets, are quite different from the use of the term to depict a form of research, as in this chapter.

Questions of warrant, confidence[1] and verifiability in the field of educational research generally are not new, or peculiar to case study. They are posed by the inevitable struggles for legitimacy of research paradigms in and across particular disciplinary contexts: the constant tug of war between qualitative and quantitative outlooks on the gathering and interpretation of data. A frequent source of confusion in these discourses is the use of the statistical metaphor to understand 'generalisability'. In large-scale population studies, the determination of whether a particular description is general, i.e. valid for the entire population, is a matter of well-understood mathematical procedures that have to do with properties of large random cohorts. Although the limitations of this approach are known (see below, and in more detail Smeyers, this volume), qualitative researchers are called upon time and again to demonstrate how the results of their inquiry can be verified with respect to a larger set. However, this is not the focus of our chapter. A virtually definitive treatment of how the validity of individual case study can be viewed with respect to the 'statistical metaphor' was provided by Kennedy (1979) who outlined how criteria for sample attributes in quantitative studies can be applied to individual cases and linking them to questions of verifiability and validity. A similar, albeit less formalized, view was expressed as early as 1961 by Becker *et al.* (1977 [1961]). From this perspective a case study is valid if it illuminates certain general features of the class of objects to which the case belongs (see Simons, 1996, for a critique of this perspective). In fact, it is astonishing how little has changed in both the rhetoric and the institutional context of case study and qualitative research in general. Justificatory tropes, dignified as 'methodology' and aimed at linking the particular to the general, can be found as a matter of course in research publications of qualitative research.

One area we believe has not been as thoroughly investigated is the situated ethics of the researcher and the research-user (see Pole and Morrison, 2003). One exception is in the field of educational programme evaluation (see Simons, 1971, 1980, 1987, Parlett and Hamilton, 1972; MacDonald and Walker, 1975; MacDonald, 1976; Kemmis, 1980; Adelman, 1984; Elliott, 1984, 1990; Kushner, 1993). While this is deeply intertwined with questions of verification and replication, we claim that any attempt to treat questions of warrant as transcending the individual and his or her embeddedness in their context are doomed to failure, and are in effect epistemologically naïve (see Elliott, 1984).

STENHOUSE ON VERIFICATION: FROM THE CASE TO THE CASE RECORD

One of the more explicit treatments of questions about the verification and warrant of case study findings can be found in the work of Lawrence Stenhouse in the late 1970s and early 1980s, before his untimely death in 1982 (see Stenhouse, 1978, 1979a, 1979b, 1979c, 1985). Stenhouse was keenly aware that in the UK case study had emerged in the fields of educational research and evaluation as an alternative to the then dominant psycho-statistical paradigm. In a lecture given at the Scottish Educational Research Association in 1979 he argued that: 'The illuminative tradition ... now seems to have got off the ground both in research and in evaluation. It no longer needs to fight to establish itself as an alternative to the "psycho-statistical paradigm" as worthy of consideration' (Stenhouse, 1979a, p. 1). Stenhouse pointed out that illuminative research and programme evaluation[2] was associated with the study of cases rather than the study of samples, as was the case with the psycho-statistical paradigm (p. 3). Although sympathetic to illuminative research Stenhouse expressed concern about the extent to which such studies conformed to his understanding of research as 'systematic inquiry made public' (p. 4). At the heart of this concern lay two major problems, those of the *verification of interpretations* and their *utilization* by others operating beyond the boundaries of the case. For Stenhouse, *utilization* depended on *cumulative* case studies such that a researcher undertaking a study of a comprehensive school could draw on other studies of comprehensive schools. From his point of view the study of individual cases only constituted research if it yielded insights that could be generally utilized in understanding to other cases that belonged to the same class of objects. Here Stenhouse was anticipating a problem about case study that is frequently posed from within and without the educational research community, and indeed by members of the policy community, who argue that one cannot use case studies as a basis for generalization beyond the boundaries of the case. What they appear to be claiming is that one cannot use case studies to cumulatively generate knowledge about education through research, implying that one cannot apply knowledge of particulars with confidence to general problems of practice and policy. On this view, case studies do not fit the knowledge requirements for effecting solutions to such problems.

Stenhouse's emphasis on the accumulation of knowledge through successive case studies is an issue that should not be left unexamined, mostly because of the great potential for misunderstanding. The cumulative nature of knowledge as such is both epistemologically and sociologically questionable.[3] While on the one hand knowledge does seem to accumulate over time in a society and an individual, significant portions of it also seem to disappear.[4] When case study (or any other research data) is being used to make policy and other practice decisions each individual teacher or policy-maker as a practical philosopher (see below) needs to disaccumulate knowledge as presented to them in research and apply it to their particular problem. The knowledge that is available to them at any moment is highly integrated and compressed rather than unproblematically accumulated. Indeed, it could be argued that it is the ability of the individual to reconstruct their 'cumulative' knowledge into workable parts that makes for an effective practitioner. Kennedy (1979) makes a similar argument when she postulates 'disaggregation' as a prerequisite to functional analysis. However, there is a very unproblematic sense in which Stenhouse's aspirations for 'cumulation' can be construed, and that is simply in the sense of assembling archival material for access and verification in the future. In that case, an easily accessible store (inventory) of past case study research can hardly be argued against. But the assumption that such an archive would serve as an unproblematic source of knowing about the world of education that is different from that available through the reading of a single case study is something that should receive more careful examination. It bears mentioning that one of the stronger arguments for maintaining such a store of case study material is the education of qualitative researchers.[5] Also a closer look at the US *Education Resources Information Center* (ERIC) and its real use by researchers, practitioners and policy-makers, could prove revealing, particularly as it pertains to the utilization of case-study data.

Underpinning the issue of case study and generalization is a strong epistemological boundary between knowledge of particulars and knowledge of general laws. It is reflected in the historian Wilhelm Windelband's distinction between ideographic and nomothetic methods. In this respect he was attempting to draw a boundary between the natural sciences that are concerned with formulating general laws and the human sciences, such as history, that he contended had their own methods and discipline. Hence, one can argue that case study methods are ideographic and concerned with generating knowledge that takes the form of *particularizations of descriptions* of things and events, while policy-makers need nomothetic knowledge in the form of general principles governing the relationship between causes and their effects. Only on the basis of the latter, some will argue, can the policy community formulate rational policies that are instrumentally effective in achieving desired educational outcomes. If one is justified in drawing a tight methodological boundary between ideographic and nomothetic methods then one can conclude that, while case studies may support judgment and action within the particular circumstances depicted, they cannot be accommodated as evidence in which to ground policy-making. Such an argument is underpinned by certain beliefs and assumptions about the *policy context*: namely, that *instrumental effectiveness* is the primary criterion for evaluating policy decisions and that this implies a clear and measurable specification of desired outcomes in the form of 'targets'. We will return later to the question of how the policy culture shapes the level of confidence and warrant that can be placed on different kinds of research evidence and findings.

Let us now return to Stenhouse's reservations (1979a) about the illuminative case study paradigm of educational research that had emerged in the wake of the critique of the psycho-statistical paradigm. Stenhouse was concerned that doctoral students and some post-doctoral researchers might declare themselves to be doing illuminative research in order 'to escape the pressure of standards' (p. 5). He was not convinced by arguments from within his own centre (CARE) at the University of East Anglia that case studies are analogous to works of fiction and therefore a kind of story that sheds any appeal to authenticity other than its power to emotionally engage the reader. For Stenhouse fiction aimed at a fuller truth about human experience than illuminative research that could only be realized 'by shedding the burdens of authentification' (p. 4). Good fiction for him was the creation of exceptional individuals, but he wanted good illuminative research to be the product of 'honest hard work because it has the support of a discipline' (ibid.). The idea that illuminative case studies should aspire to 'best seller status' was not one Stenhouse endorsed. Nor did he support a tendency to cast the role of the illuminative researcher in heroic mould, as 'speaking truth to power'. Some of his colleagues began to view illuminative research as analogous to investigatory journalism. He argued that such an analogy is only rarely appropriate. It presupposes a context in which hidden truth has to be exposed in the face of a powerful adversary who is attempting to suppress the evidence. Much illuminative research, Stenhouse argued, does not presuppose this kind of adversarial context, typically depicted as a situation in which the policy community abuses its power by suppressing evidence about the facts (ibid.).

Stenhouse was anxious to build an illuminative research tradition that was founded on clear procedures for verifying case studies and utilising their insights beyond the boundaries of the case they applied to. He proceeded to specify verification procedures in the form of constructing case records of evidence gathered from a range of sources in a variety of media (See Stenhouse 1978, 1979a). The function of the case record was to enable the interpretations in the researcher's case study to be replicated through an appeal to a systematically organised body of evidence—interview excerpts, observational notes, documentary evidence—that the researcher had drawn on in constructing the study. In this respect Stenhouse looked to history for a method of disciplining illuminative case study research (see Stenhouse, 1978, pp. 21–39, 1979a, pp. 5–9). However, he avoided implying that the use of historical case study methods excluded a concern for generalisation. Generalisations can be cumulatively constructed from cases retrospectively rather than taking the form of general principles that enable people to predict in advance how events will unfold in the cases they cover (Stenhouse, 1979a, p. 7). Stenhouse's retrospective generalisations are rather like the kind of 'universal principles' depicted by Nussbaum (1990). They link cases together by discerning their similarities without, in Nussbaum's words, 'dispensing with their particularity.' Retrospective generalisations constitute cumulative insights based on cross-case comparisons. They are couched in the form of *summaries of judgment*, which enable people to anticipate rather than straightforwardly predict possible events. Both Stenhouse (1978) and Nussbaum (1990) view their *retrospective generalisations* (Stenhouse) and *universal principles* (Nussbaum, 1990, pp. 67–69) as supporting rather than displacing professional judgment.

Stenhouse refuses to accept that case studies cannot be used to construct general insights in the field of education. If he is right then there are no good epistemological reasons for claiming that case studies cannot be used to inform the judgments of policy-makers. Indeed he argues that educational policy in the UK tends to be crude inasmuch as it is 'formulated at the expense of much thought' (Stenhouse, 1985, pp. 263–264) on the assumption that it applies to all cases. An exclusive reliance on the findings of psycho-statistical research is unlikely to challenge this assumption since such findings will tend to be used to justify pre-formulated policies. Stenhouse argues that in case study research, as opposed to sample studies, the relationship between the case, or a collection of cases, and any population to which similar meanings may apply is a matter of discernment and judgement. Such general insights are therefore the product of reflective thought. Stenhouse is careful to distinguish the 'insights' that emerge from the comparative study of cases from the general law-like principles derived from the study of samples. The latter may appear attractive to policy-maker's as a basis for confidently predicting the outcomes of policy, but in the realm of human affairs they promise more than they can deliver (see Stenhouse, 1979c, pp. 5–6). Insight rather than law Stenhouse argues is a more appropriate basis for understanding. The policy-maker's grasp of actualities is not so much enhanced by the straightforward application of general principles as by judgements that are tutored by the comparative study of cases. We will return later to Stenhouse's account of the distorting effects of an over-reliance on the findings of sample studies on education policy and practice.

At the time when Stenhouse was writing about the problem of disciplining illuminative research in the field of education many who subscribed to this approach appealed to ethnographic methods developed by social anthropologists. These included participant observation, through which the researcher became familiar with the meanings that participants attributed to the social setting he or she sought to understand, and grounded theorising through which theory building proceeds interactively with field observations and the constant comparison of cases. Stenhouse expressed worries about the use of ethnographic methods in the context of educational research on a number of counts (Stenhouse, 1979a, pp. 6–7 and 1985, p. 266).

Firstly, ethnographic methods presuppose a particular standpoint on the part of the researcher: namely, that (s)he is unfamiliar with the kinds of situations (s)he sets out to study. Educational researchers, on the other hand, and their readers have a lot of first-hand experience of life in classrooms and schools as pupils. They have already absorbed many of the meanings that shape the transactions between teachers and their students in classroom and school settings. Illuminative educational research will throw new light on familiar educational situations as opposed to throwing light on the unfamiliar.

Secondly, the ethnographer will tend to employ second order theoretical constructs from her discipline—'ritual', 'rites of passage', etc.—to render the social experience of participants intelligible to her peers. Hence, Stenhouse tends to go along with the view that the ethnographic methods of the social anthropologist tend 'to increase the power of the community to which the ethnographer belongs without making a similar contribution to those who are studied'. In the context of education the outcomes of ethnographic research would tend to be inaccessible to practitioners. Stenhouse argues that illuminative research that supports practical judgment 'calls for parsimony of theory, and theory which is within the literacy of the actor.' In other words theoretical insights should be expressed in the vernacular non-technical language of participants if they are to inform judgment. They may build out and extend this language but in terms whose meanings are continuous with and fit into the network of meanings it consists of.

Thirdly, ethnographers tend not to make their field notes available, and for Stenhouse this constitutes a problem for verification. He suggests that verification can be tightened up in ethnographic research by preserving field-workers' records. However, such records present an issue. Many of them are analytic records containing data that has already been processed in the course of field research, and that do not separate data from analysis. Hence, it is not clear how exactly the inclusion of field notes tightens up the verifiability of ethnographies, since it would imply separating 'interpretation' and 'evidence'.

The verification problems of ethnography are, according to Stenhouse (1979a), compounded by the difficulties of replication. It is rarely possible for a study to be replicated by other ethnographers, so that one can compare the consistency of interpretation/analysis across studies of the same situation or setting. Situations change or die away over time. This is why he looks to historical methods as a source of standards for illuminative case study research. The verification of case studies that follow the historical tradition would rest on the meticulous keeping of records of evidence, that were relatively free of the researcher's own interpretations. In the interpretative case study the researcher would footnote references to the relevant sources of evidence (both primary and secondary) that are held to warrant a particular interpretation of a situation or event. These sources would then be systematically organised in the form of a *case record* for the purpose of enabling others to critique the case study and to judge the extent to which it could be verified as a reasonable interpretation of the available evidence. Stenhouse defined the case record as a selection from the totality of the sources gathered, the *case data,* for the purpose of enabling others to verify the study. Of course, the researcher would also list all the case data gathered to enable others to check the sample selected as the case record for bias.

Stenhouse claimed that an appeal to the kinds of verification procedures embedded in the historical tradition of inquiry helped to resolve the problem of utilising case study accounts beyond the boundaries of the case. They enabled generalisable insights across cases to be cumulatively constructed on the basis of verifiable case studies in a way he believed was problematic for ethnographic case studies, unless they incorporated elements from the historical tradition. The existence of records of evidence ensures that people can have confidence in a case study as a source of insight into present circumstances, in spite of the fact that the situation it depicts may have changed and sometimes changed beyond all recognition. There may still be lessons that can be learned from such a case study, but this will depend on the trustworthiness of the account. Hence the significance for Stenhouse of the *case record*.

Becker *et al.* provide a counterpoint with the claim that 'the analysis of participant observation data can, and usually does, proceed in a careful way to test hypotheses in ways that can be communicated and replicated' and that case study often provides 'evidence for conclusions in field research [that] is usually better than critics think' (Becker *et al.*, 1977 [1961], p. 30). This does not necessarily invalidate the concerns of Stenhouse and others but, if correct, it should put them in a proper perspective.

One advantage for Stenhouse in conducting educational case studies in the historical as opposed to the ethnographic tradition is that they will present education 'in a language comprehensible to the educator'

(Stenhouse, 1979a, p. 7). This is because the researcher gathers documents or creates them through interviews with 'a parsimony of interpretation in the field' (p. 8). This enables the educational researcher to engage in a reflective interpretation 'of a second record' (ibid.) that can be shared with his audience, which Stenhouse believed should largely consist of educators and not merely academic educationalists.

CASES VERSUS SAMPLES

Stenhouse regarded case study research as complementary rather than an alternative and oppositional paradigm to the study of samples (see Stenhouse, 1979b, p. 3 [1980]). There was room in educational research for both the study of samples and the study of cases, and he wanted the proponents of each to talk to each other. For him the discourse of educational research should be woven in terms of this distinction. He regarded it as of greater significance than distinctions between 'quantitative' and 'qualitative', 'psycho-statistical' and 'ethnographic', 'positivism' and 'humanism'. He was particularly concerned to leave space for quantification and numbers in his account of educational case study research.

Stenhouse spelled out very clearly what he regarded as the limitations of sample studies in educational research, and argued that they were not simply technical limitations that could be overcome. The problems went deeper than that. Hence,

> Statistically significant preferences for one treatment as opposed to another generally meant that in a substantial minority of cases—as many as 40% it could be—the treatment which showed better overall was in fact worse. What was sauce for the goose proved not to be source for the gander! (1979b, p. 5 [1980]).

Others concur. In fact, as Becker (1992) suggests, a complete symmetricity and generality (of 100%) in quantitative research is an indicator of an imperfection (either in measurement or the mathematical procedure applied). It has even been used to uncover scientific fraud (see Gould, 1996). Therefore, the psychometric approach to research is just as much compelled to defend its generality as the case study approach.

Stenhouse argued that sample studies in education based on probability statistics could provide guidance for decision-makers but that:

> To make refined judgments about what educational action to take in particular cases lodged in particular contexts, we need much more information than can at present be reduced to indices and we need to present our conclusions in a way that feeds the judgment of actors in the situation, a way that educates them rather than briefs them (Stenhouse, 1979b, p. 6).

The role of educational case study research was therefore to complement rather than supplant the study of samples. It was to contextualise the findings of sample studies in ways that educated the judgment of professional educators.

Stenhouse's view echoes that of Cronbach in his seminal article on 'Course Improvement through Evaluation'. Cronbach argues that the improvement of educational programmes depends on gathering kinds of information that depart 'from the familiar doctrines and rituals of the testing game' (Cronbach, 1963, p. 672). He claims (pp. 672–683) that many varieties of information are useful to decision-makers in effecting improvements to a programme, and that standardised achievement testing was of limited usefulness in this respect. Programmes have multiple effects which vary according to context and decision-makers need to know what these are and how they are produced. Information gathering requires the educational researcher to deploy a variety of different research measures and instruments to capture effects and processes. Cronbach, the measurement expert, critiqued a particular ideology governing the use of measurement in educational evaluation (see Nussbaum's (1990) account of the 'Science of Measurement' below) rather than the use of all measurement. The critique was very influential in paving the way for the development of Case Study research in the field of educational programme evaluation.

The implication of Stenhouse's view of the relationship between the study of samples and cases is that government has tended to place too much confidence in sample studies as a basis for predicting educational outcomes.[6] The tendency to use findings from such studies as a basis for prescribing educational action and marginalising professional judgment in the process cannot be warranted by any defensible theory of knowledge. Educational policy may profitably use the findings of sample studies to frame agendas for case study research that can yield cross-case comparisons capable of educating professional judgment. Such evidence-based frameworks for case study research may do more to improve educational practice than the current standards-driven reforms that exclusively rely on 'the science of measurement'.

Helen Simons has been somewhat critical of efforts to integrate case study into large-scale research designs using a sampling framework. For her such efforts go too far in accommodating policy-maker's views of their information requirements. Of case study research she writes that:

> . . . along with its acceptance and widespread use in a number of fields . . . has come a weakening of the very characteristics of case study which prompted its emergence in the first place . . . one of the reasons for this has been the ever-present worry over generalizations . . . and the pressure in current times from sponsors who do not value qualitative data, let alone that stemming from a single case (Simons, 1996, p. 225).

Simons sets out a rationale for the single case study as a form of research in its own right. As a research genre, she claims, the value of case study research does not solely depend on its use to complement large-scale sample studies. A single case study she claims can paradoxically generate both unique and universal understandings (p. 225), a distinction that has more recently been contested by Evers and Wu, who argue that:

> ... case study research is not different in kind in its use of the epistemic resources we regularly employ to successfully understand and navigate our way around in the world. (Evers and Wu, 2006, p. 524)

Simons on the other hand argues that the use of a single case study within her community of educational programme evaluators has been a means of establishing claims to knowledge that cannot be accommodated in traditional paradigms of evaluation. Such claims refer to universal understandings of human situations and events that can only be evidenced by *holistic portrayals* of the unique features of a case. Such portrayals, she argues, 'strive to know and represent complex educational situations' and thereby constitute a form of understanding that matches the decision-maker's 'vocabulary of action' (p. 226). Simons is articulating a tradition of case study research (Simons, 1980) that transcends the boundary between art and science. She claims that 'this form of knowing is not divorced from science nor is it to be seen as the antithesis of it' and cites MacDonald and Walker (1975):

> Case study is the way of the artist, who achieves greatness when, through the portrayal of an instant locked in time and circumstance, he communicates enduring truths about the human condition. For both the scientist and artist, content and intent emerge in form (1975, p. 3).

Simons points out that MacDonald and Walker are very aware of the implications of their definition of case study. The choice of the word 'instance' for them implies a goal of generalisation. Moreover, as Simons points out, the researcher who played a leading role in forging the portrayal tradition of case study, Robert Stake, has argued that such generalisations are 'naturalistic' rather than 'formalistic' (See Stake, 1978, reprinted in Simons, 1980 p. 64). It is not the researcher that does the generalising but the reader. The good portrayal provokes its readers into a new way of understanding their own practical situation. The claim that such situational understanding also embodies knowledge of universal truth is validated when readers of a case portrayal come to think differently about their own experience. It renders the familiar qualitative world they live in strange. This is why programme evaluations that relied heavily on thickly descriptive portrayals of cases became known as 'illuminative evaluation'.

We have already noted Stenhouse's reservations about the case study research that fell into what he and others called the 'illuminative' paradigm. It is this paradigm that chiefly emerged in the context of educational programme evaluations that Stenhouse regarded as insufficiently disciplined and rigorous to warrant confidence in their interpretations and findings. He was sceptical even about attempts to inject methodological rigour from qualitative social science methods like 'ethnography' into educational research methodology; hence, his search for rigour in historical method. Simons, however, has persisted in defending case study as a naturalistic form of educational inquiry that does not depend on methods derived from the academic disciplines as a guarantor of truth. Indeed she points out that portrayals of cases avoid that distancing from experience involved in the use of objectivist methods of data analysis.

The philosopher John Macmurray (1957) lends support to the portrayal tradition of case study. Macmurray distinguishes between the *intellectual* and *emotional* modes of reflection (pp. 198–202). The former implies a certain 'analytic distancing' from direct experiences of situations and events, while the latter involves an attempt to understand what is being directly experienced. The emotional mode seeks to understand a practical situation as a 'system of new possibilities for action'. The greater the particularisation of the understanding of the situation the more the complexities of making wise judgments and decisions are taken into account and its practically relevant features discerned and discriminated. Macmurray echoes the psychologist Rollo May (1994), who is cited by Simons (1996) as providing an account of the kind of 'creative understanding' involved in case study portrayals. May, she points out, argued that '. . . reason works better when emotions are present; the person sees sharper and more accurately when his emotions are engaged' (p. 49). The philosopher Joseph Dunne also lends support to the portrayal tradition of case study research when he contends that the 'situational under-standing' that stems from direct experience—what Aristotle called *phronesis*—fuses a grasp of the particular with the discernment of universal truth, and he argues for 'richly descriptive studies' that possess 'epiphanic power' by 'illuminating other settings' as resources that support the development of understanding.

If holistic case study portrayals of the unique features of situations and events match the policy-maker's 'vocabulary of action' then how do we explain their rejection by the policy community? Simons (1996) argues that the reasons why educational programme evaluators utilised case studies in the 1970s are now being eroded in a contemporary policy context that is less concerned with understanding the complexities of effecting educational change in particular contexts of action, and more concerned with a search 'for generalisation, in the formal sense, for comparability, for certainty' (p. 227). This suggests that the level of confidence policy-makers do in practice place in case study findings and evidence may change considerably according to the prevailing policy culture.

MEASUREMENT VERSUS PRACTICAL PHILOSOPHY

The prevailing culture to-day is frequently depicted as a 'target culture' and is framed by a view of *practical reason* that Martha Nussbaum characterises as 'The Science of Measurement' She breaks down this 'scientific' conception of practical reason into four constitutive claims (Nussbaum, 1990, pp. 56–57). First, there is the claim of *Metricity*, that 'in a particular choice situation there is some one value, varying only in quantity that is common to all the alternatives'. The rational chooser is one who uses this single standard as a metric to weigh each alternative and thereby determine which will yield the greatest quantity of value. Secondly, there is the claim of *Singularity*, that one and the same metric or standard applies in all situations of choice. Thirdly, there is the claim of *Consequentialism*, that the chosen actions only have instrumental value as a means of producing good consequences. Fourthly, by combining each of these claims we have the principle of *Maximisation*, 'that there is some one value, that it is the point of rational choice, in every case, to maximize'.

Policy-making and research in the field of education has become increasingly shaped by this so-called 'scientific' picture of practical reasoning (see Schwandt, 2005, pp. 294–295; and Elliott and Doherty, 2001, pp. 209–221, in relation to the USA and UK respectively). Hence, the educational reforms initiated by many governments are viewed as devices for 'driving up standards' conceived in terms of *metricity* and *singularity*. Research increasingly takes the form of school and teacher effectiveness research aimed at determining how schools and teachers can 'add value' to student's learning. The *maximisation principle* is embedded in the idea of 'value added', which presumes that the practices of schools and teachers only have value if they produce good *consequences* that can be quantified in terms of a single metric that applies generally across the system. Hence the widespread use of standardised testing in school and teacher effectiveness research. The findings from such research are now widely regarded as furnishing the rational basis for modernising educational practice in schools and classrooms: hence the currently fashionable, widely circulating notion in many policy contexts of 'evidence-based practice' (see the chapter by Oancea and Pring in this volume for a full discussion).

Nussbaum claims that contemporary conceptions of practical rationality in 'almost every area of social life' are so dominated by the 'science of measurement' that we are in danger of losing sight of the Aristotelian conception of practical rationality as *phronesis* (Nussbaum, 1990, p. 55). We agree. The inroads that the evidence-based practice movement has made within the field of education in western countries, and even more globally, are testimony to this. However, this 'scientific' picture of rationality is also making it increasingly difficult to imagine any other relationship between science and practical reasoning. We will now argue that some policy contexts still leave space for a view of practical reasoning as *phronesis* and of the policy-maker as a 'man/woman of action' rather than a 'technocrat'. This implies a different relationship between science and practical reasoning. We will conclude that questions about the level of confidence or warrant that can be placed in different sorts of research evidence and findings cannot be answered independently of forming a view about the appropriateness of the policy culture that shapes political decision-making.

In some contexts findings based on comparisons between cases within a large-scale sample frame, and couched as formal generalisations, may command a certain level of confidence. Stenhouse's concern with issues of verification and utilisation appears to address such contexts. In other contexts a single case study may challenge existing policy frames, and open up for policy-makers new possibilities for action to effect change along lines suggested by Simons (1996, p. 231). In what kind of policy context might the policy-maker find single-case portrayals useful resources? We would suggest that it is a context that leaves cultural space for *phronesis* as a mode of practical reasoning. It is a case-focused rather than sample-focused mode of reasoning although it may eclectically draw on sample studies in the process. On the other hand we would suggest that Stenhouse's conception of case study fits a context in which space for *phronesis* cannot be presumed but needs to be opened up.

CASE STUDY AS GENRE AND AS A MODE OF REASONING

One of the problems with the assumptions around the generalisability of case study is that it suffers from a number of conceptual conflations both in the collective discourse and the individual practices in educational research. On the one hand, there is the case study as a research genre with its conventions and morphological properties that serve to identify it as such to participants in research discourse. In other words, in order for a case study to be (accepted) as a case study, it must 'look' like a case study. On the other hand, there is the notion of case study as a mode of reasoning (*case-focused reasoning*) that is seen as qualitatively different from the deductive reasoning assumed to be the exclusive domain of large-scale probabilistically controlled trials. Stake (1994) argues that the 'utility of case research to practitioners and policy makers is in its extension of experience' (p. 245) and claims that case studies provide both 'propositional and experiential knowledge':

> Certain descriptions and assertions are assimilated by readers into memory. When the researcher's narrative provides opportunity for vicarious experience, readers extend their memories of happenings. Naturalistic, ethnographic case materials, to some extent, parallel actual experience, feeding into the most fundamental processes of awareness and understanding[7] (Stake, 1994, p. 240).

Assumptions such as this make case study as a genre of research easily confused with case-focused reasoning and consequently it is easy to suggest that it offers superior results for situational judgment. While an argument can be made that situational judgment is in fact an example of case-focused reasoning, there is ample evidence that the mental and social construction of cases is not dependent on the format of a case study and can be (and frequently is) just as easily built on sample-based quantitative data. Indeed it can be argued that case-focused reasoning is central to intelligent judgment as typified by the political 'man of action'.

Let us step back from viewing case study as a research genre and instead view it as a form of deliberative reasoning (*phronesis*) about a situation in which there is a political imperative to act. Paradoxically case-focused reasoning is oriented towards both socially and politically committed action, or praxis, and the clarification of universal conceptions of the good. Such reasoning has been depicted as practical philosophy (see Carr, 2006, pp. 421–436; Elliott, 2007, pp. 99–112). Gramsci, the Italian political revolutionary and intellectual, depicted such a process as lying at the heart of all authentic political discourse (see 'The Modern Prince' in Hoare and Nowell Smith, 1971, pp. 313–441). The 'man of action' he argued is also a true philosopher: one who clarifies universal political ends—equality, justice, and freedom—by deliberating about what constitutes an appropriate expression of them in a particular concrete situation. John Lloyd has recently pointed out in *Prospect* (July, 2007, pp. 24–28), that Gramsci's political 'man of action', cast in the mould of the practical philosopher, is not the professional intellectual or specialist philosopher that one finds in universities. Nor is he or she a French-style polymath public intellectual, like Derrida or Foucault, or the kind of bookish and cultured politician that was typified in Margaret Thatcher's UK government by Sir Keith Joseph. Lloyd's article portrays the UK Prime Minister Gordon Brown as a practical philosopher in Gramscian terms (Brown being a youthful admirer of Gramsci). He cites Gramsci's portrait of the philosopher as 'man of action' in 'The Modern Prince' as someone who:

> ... can affect his own development and that of his surroundings only so far as he has a clear view of what the possibilities of action open to him are. To do this he has to understand the historical situation in which he finds himself and once he does this, then he can play an active part in modifying that situation. The man of action is the true philosopher: and the philosopher must of necessity be the man of action (Gramsci, quoted in Lloyd, 2007, p. 24).

From Gramsci's point of view case-focused reasoning or practical philosophy has a strong historical dimension. The discernment of concrete ways of expressing in action conceptions of the universal good (situational understanding) depends upon the political agent's grasp of the historical dimensions of his/her situation.

In the light of this we can see case-focused reasoning as a process that stems from the experience of the moral or political imperative to act in a social situation, and that unifies universal and situational understanding. And we can also see descriptive/holistic portrayals of cases—normally referred to as case studies—as artefacts that may provide resources for such reasoning inasmuch as they help the political 'man of action' to discern new possibilities of action that are open to him or her in his/her situation. This essential independence of case-focused reasoning from the case study was, we believe, well understood by Stenhouse (see Stenhouse, 1979b). Not only does he regard the case study, conceived as a specific format, as simply one complementary resource to support case-focused reasoning, he also points to 'an acute need for attention to be paid to quantitative aspects of case study' (p. 8). He cautions that 'descriptive case studies should not confine themselves to words'. Rather they should ask questions along the lines of 'What indices might best be gathered to describe a school and to locate it within the population of schools?' (ibid.). The same claim was made by ethnographers and sociologists, for instance recently by Pole and Morrison who maintain that their concept of 'inclusive ethnography' also 'permits the use of quantitative methods' (Pole and Morrison, 2003, p. 9).

Stenhouse attempted to represent case study as a serious methodological option for educational research as well as an object of reasoning. From the standpoint of members of the portrayal school, such as Stake, 'Case study is not a methodological choice, but a choice of object to be studied' (Stenhouse, 1994, p. 236). For this school the case study is not a research genre that complements other research genres. It serves a quite unique and distinctive, if paradoxical, purpose in relation to the object of reasoning, i.e. 'the case'.

All this leaves us with three distinct views of case-study research operating in the discourse of educational research: contemporary history, ethnography and grounded theory, and those holistic narratives of experience called 'portrayals'. Each shapes what a case study looks like rather differently, establishing a subgenre, and implies somewhat different notions of case-focused reasoning.

Research by Kennedy (1999; see below) suggests that practitioners place greater emphasis on the direct relevance of research results over the procedural parameters of a particular research subgenre. Such a finding matches Joseph Schwab's seminal work *The Practical: a Language for Curriculum*. He argued that practical reasoning was case-focused and eclectic in its orientation, utilising a range and variety of intellectual and cultural resources in its search for better understanding of the practical situation (Schwab, 1970, pp. 1–5). From this point of view different kinds of case studies and other kinds of research may all have a role as resources for the policy-maker who creates and finds space in the policy context to be a practical philosopher.

Furthermore, we argue that quantitative data provide intrinsically no better source of generalisation because case-study-like stories need to be constructed about how samples are conceived and how they apply to a given situation. In fact, the same genre-led confusion is present: because large-scale (usually based on randomised sampling) quantitative studies appear to bear on situations where particulars of individuals need to be abstracted and generalised, it is assumed that they are better suited to providing generalisations such as may be needed by policy-makers. However, upon closer investigation, large-scale quantitative research is inexorably interconnected with case-focused reasoning at a number of levels. The construction of scenarios and cases is essential in the design of quantitative experiments and research projects both in the form of discursive assumptions and actual case-based pilot studies. But it is no more absent in the policy implementation of the resulting data. Case-like stories have to be told before a policy based on quantitative 'evidence' can be translated into prescriptive documentation, but they are also essential in the political justification of a policy. Thus, when a policy advocate says that 'x in y children cannot read' she is not referring to the properties of a population as exemplified by a sampled cohort but rather enumerating the frequency of an occurrence of a particular schematised story.[8] However, this knowledge has higher social acceptability in the ethnic structures of the groups interacting at the intersection of policy and research. This is an argument similar to that made by Hammersley's (2001) discussion of Bassey's (1999) notion of 'fuzzy generalizations'. Generalisations in the 'hard' sciences, Hammersley claims, are only approximate in their applications to the real world. And therefore fuzzy generalisations (such as those Bassey suggests should be drawn from quantitative research) are 'not a distinct type of generalisation but a mode of formulation that ought to be employed in all predictions for practical use derived from scientific generalisations' (Hammersley, 2001, p. 219). Hammersley takes his case further in suggesting that 'survey research cannot produce strong evidence for probabilistic laws unless the population conforms to the terms and conditions of the theory' (p. 221).

CASE STUDY AS A COGNITIVE AND SOCIAL ACTIVITY

Research by Kennedy into the way teachers evaluate different kinds of research evidence appears to back up this distinction between case-focused reasoning and case study as a research genre. She found that research genre was not as significant as the extent to which teachers could interpret the research findings in ways that enabled them to make sense of the complexities of teaching and learning in their own classrooms. She claims that her study casts doubt 'on virtually every argument for the superiority of any particular research genre, whether the criterion is persuasiveness, relevance, or ability to influence practitioner's thinking' (Kennedy, 1999, p. 536). For example, when she asked teachers about what persuaded them about the utility of a particular piece of research, the reasons similar to 'descriptions of teaching or of student work were sufficiently detailed that I could envision them and see how this would be so' (p. 530) were given more often for an experimental study than for a case study. Both of these left narrative studies far behind. The teachers' judgments of relevance were their own and were made along the lines of their immediate need rather than simply following the cognitive rails supposedly laid out by the genre. Kennedy concludes that 'teachers forged analogies between the studies they read and their own situations or practices and that they were able to do that for the experiment as well as for other genres of research. That is they did not need ethnographic studies or narratives to make these connections themselves' (Kennedy, 1999, p. 537). Hence, we can argue that policy-makers like teachers may employ case-focused reasoning to interpret research findings regardless of the research genre. We need to know what they need to make sense of in their particular policy context. There is nothing about case study as a research genre that disqualifies it as a source of useful insights for policy-makers, just as there is nothing about experimental or random controlled trials as a genre that would disqualify them also.

Becker illustrates this by describing an imaginary look at some local census data as a basis for creating an image about the people behind the numbers, concluding that '[i]maginative, well-read social scientists can go a long way with a little fact':

> I can work up, in my mind, a complete if provisional, picture of the neighbourhood. [...] My picture is more than a compilation of statistics. It includes details that are not in the books and tables I consulted, details I have invented on the basis of what those books told me. I 'know', for instance, what kinds of houses these people live in—I can practically see the flamingos, the furniture 'suites' from the credit furniture store and whatever else my stereotype of the population produces (Becker, 1992, p. 211).

Abbott (1992) makes a similar case when he observes that quantitative social scientists tend to start referring to 'real people' when their numerical data fails to account for some aspect of what they are interested in. How this process of causal imagination plays itself out in the process of policy building is addressed in more detail in their theory of frame reflection. They suggest that all policy disputes can be understood in terms of frames: 'Frames are not free-floating but are grounded in the institutions that sponsor them, and policy controversies are disputes among institutional actors who sponsor conflicting frames' (Schön and Rein, 1994, p. 29). These frames contain both rich and schematic images (Lakoff, 1987, 1996) and scenarios that are more than remotely reminiscent of the sorts of images social scientists construct out of qualitative as well as quantitative data. The notion of frame has a long pedigree and has appeared as 'horizon' in Gadamer (1975), 'perspective' in Becker *et al.* (1977 [1961]) and finally introduced as 'frame' by Goffman (1975 [1974]). Fisher (1997) provides a detailed overview of the different ways the concept has found its place in the social sciences. Gamson's (1992) work is of particular interest in this context, showing how frame construction can become independent of 'the message' in social movements. Although we do not make use of the concept here, an instrumental epistemological account taking into consideration both cognition and socialisation may have to proceed in the direction of frame analysis (see Lukeš, 2007).

That is why when we ask whether case studies are generalisable, what we are really asking is whether we can tell a sufficiently socially acceptable story about case-study based research as a basis of policy-making. Because epistemologically there is no doubt about the generalisability of case study. Not only is it generalisable, it is in every instance the basis of generalisations. Of course, this requires a non-normative and non-instrumental view of generalisation. In refusing to doubt the generalisability of the case study we are not assuming that all or even most generalisations derived from case

study will be 'good' generalisations just as most generalisations derived from quantitative studies turn out to apply to a much narrower scope of 'reality' than their scientific patina seems to imply. This underscores the central point of our chapter that we introduced from its beginning, viz., that the epistemology of case study is not transcendent of the complexity of the situation in which the researcher, practitioner and policy-makers find themselves. Indeed, it is possible to construct a set of criteria that will lead us to conclude that a case study is not generalisable but such a set will perhaps serve the purposes of a Platonic world of ideals but not the complex world in which researchers, practitioners and policy-makers are located. However, as we were reminded was Stenhouse's position, that also does not mean that rigour and objectivity are absent from the case study and should not be sought. Kennedy attempted to outline how qualitative research can draw on principles of generalisation established in qualitative research to guide case study design citing medicine and law as examples of disciplines where such a combination is possible. Kennedy contrasts the situation in social sciences where 'researchers and evaluators are not accustomed to the notion of leaving generalisation up to the practitioner' (Kennedy, 1979, p. 672) with that in other fields. Judges and juries in the legal system and doctors in medicine commonly have to do just that as Kennedy observes: 'generalizations are frequently necessary from single cases, but it is also clear that these generalizations are done by the user of the case data rather than by the person who originated the case data' (p. 676). Robinson and Norris assume the cognitive inevitability of generalisation but they see the role of method only as part of the practice of research:

> The warrant we have for making judgements on the basis of research can take a number of forms: political, legal, moral, methodological. For researchers, the first concern is often the methodological reasons we have for the judgements we make. This should be the case since other justifications only become an issue when we are clear what can be said on the basis of the research although, of course, when we generalise we have particular purposes and utilities in mind and these cannot be separated from moral or political considerations (Robinson and Norris, 2001, p. 308).

Kemmis points out that methodological discussions are not sufficient to address questions of warrant and generality. We must look to the situation of the researcher:

> In general, there are two kinds of justification: those concerned with justification of the truth-status of findings, and those concerned with the accountability of researchers for the conduct of the research. In both cases, public access to the processes and products of research should provide the grounds for deciding whether a given research study is justified (Kemmis, 1980, p. 97).

This makes methods of case study not particularly distinctive due to the pragmatic need to respond to the nature of the case. The person of the

researcher is paramount: 'Since the methods employed in the study will depend upon the hypothesized nature of the case, a "methodological" definition will always seem inadequate to the experienced case study worker—it will not grasp the problem of case study as the case study worker experiences it' (Kemmis, 1980, p. 108).

It is particularly telling that when faced with accusations of 'positivism', proponents (e.g. Hargreaves, 1997) of the evidence-based policy paradigm (allowing for controlled quantitative evidence only) tend to fall back on the slogan of 'evidence-informed', thus substantially diluting their claims to have discovered general rules to govern practice. They implicitly afford case-focused reasoning a role in generating universal practical insights while in the same breath appearing to deny it such a role. This applies as much to the researched practitioner as well as the researcher practitioner as was apparent even in the early days of educational evaluation:

> Many of the quite legitimate questions that are put to evaluators, especially by teachers, cannot be answered by the experimental methods and numerical analyses that constitute the instrumental repertoire of conventional educational research (MacDonald and Walker, 1977, p. 189).

CASE STUDY AS METHOD

The initial question was: 'What kind of confidence can we have in the ethnographic study and construction of a single case (or cross site analysis of a limited number of cases) as a basis for policy and practice?' The answer seems to be that an ethnographic case study unreservedly can be, and frequently is, used as a basis for policy decisions. The more interesting question should be what are the sources of confidence we place in a particular piece of research, a researcher and a policy-maker. Here the picture becomes much murkier. Stenhouse speaks of a need 'to establish conventions for the conduct and reporting of fieldwork in case studies, which attempt to secure a basis for verification and for cumulation' (Stenhouse, 1979a, p. 9).

The key issue should not be whether and how a collection of case studies can be of use to the policy-maker but rather how a single case study can and does enter into the world of knowledge and policy. What is doubly important is that a case can be made for the claim that at the moment of policy/practice decision-making any research data is epistemologically a kind of a case study. The only difference between different sources of data is then their social acceptability for using it as a basis for its intended purpose, the social reference frame being a combination of the views of the society at large, codes of the particular discipline, and the codified practices of a specific policy-making outfit. Stake sees a rather limited role for case study:

> Case study is part of scientific method, but its purpose is not limited to the advance of science. Whereas single or a few cases are a poor

representation of a population of cases and poor grounds for advancing grand generalization, a single case as negative example can establish limits to grand generalization. For example, we lose confidence in the generalization that a child of separated parents is better off placed with the mother when we find a single instance of resultant injury. Case studies are of value in refining theory and suggesting complexities for further investigation, as well as helping to establish the limits of generalizability (Stake, 1994, p. 245).

Ethnographers, on the other hand, have rather more confidence. Lacey enlists the anthropologist Frankenberg to make the point that far from being complementary, the study of an individual case can be made to illuminate the general concerns of an entire population:

> Though I am presenting a case study of one school, its significance is not confined to the particularistic concerns of this one school. It extends to general problems in sociology and education. I agree with Frankenberg when he argues that an essential ingredient of the social sciences is '. . . a methodology in which the discussion of small segments of society in great detail is used to throw light on the general.' He continues, 'It is my firm view that only the particularistic can illuminate the universalistic' (Lacey, 1970, p. xi).[9]

The question, again, is not whether we can be confident in the case study as a genre of research, but rather what sources of confidence can we identify in all the individuals involved. This is where most of Stenhouse's interest in illuminative research has its roots.[10] The utility of case study research (be it ethnographic or historical or holistic portrayal) can be illustrated on the subject of the student experience of university life. While surveys and other census-like data abound and are frequently used in denouncing the quality of today's tertiary education, deeper understanding will remain elusive until we have a careful look at the four major ethnographic case studies (Becker *et al.*, 1977 [1961]; Moffatt, 1989; Holland and Eisenhart, 1990; Nathan, 2005) dealing with university life. Unlike many of the quantitative surveys, these case studies provide sufficient information to make better generalisations about the subject at hand, particularly when it comes to situated judgment and practitioner action. Both Moffatt and Nathan employ a wide range of approaches to gathering data including participant observation, guided interviews, collection of artefacts, self-administered surveys, diaries, etc. Their work shows the great potential of case study research and provides a cautionary tale to large-scale probabilistically sampled studies whose ultimate result is the telling of case-like stories that are substantiated by not much more than the researcher's imagination. In particular, Nathan's revelations about the relegation of knowledge acquisition in the social lives of students to a ritualistic incantation ('I have to study', 'This is a difficult course' versus 'I found out that. . .', 'That course discusses. . .') cannot be revealed by a survey and yet it demonstrates universal features of the student experience through its depth and thickness of description.

Research by Moffatt, Becker and others from previous decades can serve as replication and a basis for predictive generalisation that does not rely on statistical sampling. Interestingly, Nathan (2005) and Becker *et al.* (1977 [1961]) offer suggestions for policy decisions based on their research that are remarkably similar despite the gulf of nearly half a century. By coincidence, Nathan's work allows us to compare case study with journalistic accounts. In the same year another treatment of student culture on campus appeared entitled *Binge* (Seaman, 2005). It was the result of investigative reporting done across US campuses by a retired journalist and on the surface provided descriptions of student activities similar to Nathan's (albeit generally with an unfavourable tinge). It could even be argued that since Seaman covered multiple campuses where Nathan only focused on one, it would be his account that provides the most generality. However, a close reading of both works makes it clear that it was Nathan's painstaking observation that provides insight into the situational complexity of student life whereas Seaman's volume only serves to establish stereotypes. The question remains, of course, on what criteria we can base this conclusion. Should there not be an objective measure of which piece of research is insightful and which superficial? The answer is no. Conclusions such as this one can only be based on the practice of reading and the situated practice of inquiry. In other words, they need to be made by a particular practitioner in the context of his or her work. An epistemological feature analysis of both books would leave the difference obscured.

DEFENDING THE CASE STUDY

Despite all this, case-study based research has been on the defensive as a basis for a politically acceptable procedure for making policy decisions. Most recently this has taken on the guise of 'evidence-based practice' as the only acceptable source of knowledge for policy-makers. While there is little to be contested about the sentiment that policy-makers should base their decisions on the available evidence, the domain of medicine, upon which this implicit metaphor is based, often serves as an inadequate analogue to the problems faced by education and other social domains. This is further compounded by the fact that the realities of evidence-based practice in medicine are often poorly understood by the most vocal exponents of the 'evidence-based' mantras. This was illustrated by Lerner's (2006) description of the role 'celebrity illnesses' play in shaping how funding for research is allocated and how patients' knowledge of ailments of the famous interacts with the decisions made by medical practitioners. Škrabánek's and McCormick's (1989) *Follies and Fallacies in Medicine* can hardly inspire more confidence, demonstrating that much of what counts as evidence in medicine is transmitted through tradition rather than the disembodied scientific method of hypothesis falsification the field presents as its mainstay. The medical metaphor of research-based policy is also problematic because on closer inspection many of the assumed correspondences do not hold up when applied to the lived experiences of practitioners.

The idea that teachers and educational policy-makers can behave like physicians in basing their decisions on the knowledge of the latest available evidence is doomed to failure from the start. Apart from what we know about the differences in the stability and individual transmissibility of sociological versus medical knowledge, both these types of practitioners operate in markedly different contexts. Evidence-based reasoning in medicine is based partly on the fact that the very training of medical practitioners is from the very start focused on teaching future doctors how to use research results (knowing the transitory nature of much medical knowledge). Furthermore, physicians are expected to keep abreast of the latest developments in their field either through self-study, conference attendance, and, not insignificantly, advertising from the pharmaceutical industry. Not one of these elements is consistently present in the context of education.

The 'educational practitioner is medical practitioner' metaphor brings up other undesirable inferences. One of them is the idea of the researcher as a provider of information, to whom the practitioners relate as clients. However, given what we know about the kinds of reasoning really available to policy-makers, it is probably necessary to stop thinking of them as clients of the research profession but rather to start thinking about them as researchers themselves. This may not be possible without first unpicking the industrial production metaphor based on the image of individual lines supplying parts that are then completed into a product. In line with this metaphor, policy-making bodies tend to structure themselves as modular production units, appointing individuals or departments to be 'responsible for research'. But what this metaphor does not provide as readily is a mechanism for ensuring that each and every policy-maker is engaged with research on a level much deeper than the occasional enquiry as to the well-being of the 'research guy(s)'. To achieve this, it is necessary to convince policy-makers that they can be researchers in the same way that teachers or students can be researchers of their own practice. This may be problematic because of the imagery (frames) associated with the concept of research, many of which are built around the structural necessities of publication and prestige-building necessary for survival in the academic world.

However, teachers and policy-makers can be researchers without engaging in activities that appear research-shaped on the surface (reflective practitioners in the original sense; not as people who think about their practice but those who construct situational knowledge equivalent to academic knowledge). It can be said that the way they do research in fact constitutes practical philosophy (a disciplined inquiry into knowledge) that should, in fact, be the sole basis for assessing the reliability of any kind of research results about to be put into the service of justifying policy decisions.

POLICY-MAKING AS PRACTICE

One of the features that has characterised our joint inquiry is an essential commitment to the continual questioning of and challenge to what we refer to as instrumental rationality. Streamlined rational judgment is often, and almost always in the context of policy-making, a convenient fiction, a ritual of justification, that is trying to ignore, or worse, disguise the complexities involved in situational judgment. We now realise that the design of the project, the merits of which we perhaps insufficiently questioned at the outset but which in many respects we are still prepared to defend, tends to reinforce the idea of an independent rational agent, the philosopher, who can swoop in onto the policy-making process in some consultative role and point out the 'irrationalities' of this or that policy. It is not, however, the philosopher's role to function as a vizier to the policy-maker's sultan. If philosophy has any role in the process of policy-making, it is through setting an example of a disciplined inquiry—in which a policy-maker as researcher[11] can find direct relevance to their practice. It is important, we feel, to look at the process of policy-making in its own terms, doing justice to its complexities, rather than just assuming an impartial 'rational' robotic process. It appears that the following words are as true today as they were a quarter of a century ago: 'Despite the considerable volume of work on the problematics of policy making and implementation, educational researchers are prone to underrate the constraints on policy makers which limit their ability to respond to research findings' (Nisbet and Broadfoot, 1980, p. 56). If Nisbet and Broadfoot are correct in assuming that '[t]here is as much of a gap between policy and practice as there is between research and policy or research and practice' (p. 57), we must focus our inquiry on policy-making as a practice in its own right that, as all practice does, generates its own knowledge and makes its own generalisations irrespective of the data research presents to it. And as such it can be subject to the same dynamic interrelation between action and reflection as any other professional activity. Nutley *et al.* (2007) offer an overview of research utilisation and reflections on the complexity of this relationship are also available in Pole and Morrison (2003) and Hammersley (2002). It is clear that policy-making needs to be treated as an area of practice with its own situated system of ethical action that is distinct from the practice of research and the practice of educators.

This is important given that each practice generates its own generalisations but only some of these provide us with universal insights such as those suggested above by Simons, Dunne, Lacey, and Nussbaum. This distinction is crucial whenever a practitioner asks the philosopher about the epistemological warrant of his or her generalisations. Generalisations are generated within a particular discipline (area of practice) and apply to data as construed by that discipline. Universal insights can be inferred from outside that particular discipline. However, they are always made by individuals situated in their own context of need, desire and requirement. Whereas the general can be subject to instrumental disciplinary rules, the universal is a human act for which no analogous normative ideal can be constructed. One way of viewing the interface between research and practice is, then, as a continuing conversation between the general and the universal.

SUMMARY AND CONCLUSIONS

Overall, we have informed our inquiry with three perspectives on case study. One is rooted in ethnography and built around the metaphor of the understanding of cultures the researcher is not familiar with (these are presented by the work of scholars like Becker, Willis (1977), Lacey, Wallace (1966), Ball (1981), and many others). Another strand revolves around the tradition of responsive and democratic evaluation and portrayal represented by the work of scholars such as MacDonald, Simons, Stake, Parlett, and others. This tradition (itself not presenting a unified front) aims to break down the barriers between the researcher, the researched and the audience. It recognises the situated nature of all actors in the process (cf. Kemmis, 1980) and is particularly relevant to the concerns of the policy-maker. Finally, we need to add Stenhouse's contemporary history approach into the mix. Stenhouse provides a perspective that allows the researcher to marry the responsibility to data with the responsibility to his or her environment in a way that escapes the stereotypes associated with the 'pure forms' of both quantitative and qualitative research. A comprehensive historian-like approach to data collection, retention and dissemination that allows multiple interpretations by multiple actors accounts both for the complexity of the data and the situation of which it is collected and interpreted.

However, we can ask ourselves whether a policy-maker faced with examples of one of these traditions could tell these perspectives apart. Should it not perhaps be the lessons from the investigation of case study that matter rather than an ability to straightforwardly classify it as an example of one or the other? In many ways, in the policy context, it is the act of choice, such as choosing on which case study a policy should be based, that is of real importance.

In that case, instead of transcendental arbitration we can provide an alternative test: does the case study change the prejudices of the reader? Does it provide a challenge? Perhaps our notion of comprehensiveness can include the question: is the case study opening the mind of the reader to factors that they would have otherwise ignored? This reminds us of Gadamer's 'fusion of horizons' ('Understanding ... is always the fusion of ... horizons [present and past] which we imagine to exist by themselves' (Gadamer, 1975, p. 273).

However, this could be seen as suggesting that case study automatically leads to a state of illumination. In fact, the interpretation of case study in this way requires a purposeful and active approach on the part of the reader. What, then, is the role of the philosopher? Should each researcher have a philosopher by his or her side? Or is it necessary, as John Elliott has long argued, to locate the philosopher in the practitioner? Should we expect teachers or policy-makers to go to the philosopher for advice or would a better solution be to strive for philosopher teachers and philosopher practitioners? Being a philosopher is of course determined not by speaking of Plato and Rousseau but by the constant challenge to personal and collective prejudices.

In that case, we can conclude that case study would have a great appeal to the politician and policy-maker as a practical philosopher but that it would be a mistake to elevate it above other ways of doing practical philosophy. In this, following Gadamer, we advocate an antimethodological approach. The idea of the policy-maker as philosopher and policy maker as researcher (i.e. underscoring the individual ethical agency of the policy-maker) should be the proper focus of discussion of reliability and generalisation. Since the policy-maker is the one making the judgement, the type of research and study is then not as important as a primary focus.

And, in a way, the truthfulness of the case arises out of the practitioners' use of the study. The judgment of warrant as well as the universalising and revelatory nature of a particular study should become apparent to anybody familiar with the complexities of the environment. An abstract standard of quality reminiscent of statistical methods (number of interviewees, questions asked, sampling) is ultimately not a workable basis for decision-making and action although that does not exclude the process of seeking a shared metaphorical perspective both on the process of data gathering and interpretation (cf. Kennedy, 1979; Fox, 1982). Gadamer's words seem particularly relevant in this context: '[t]he understanding and interpretation of texts is not merely a concern of science, but is obviously part of the total human experience of the world' (Gadamer, 1975, p. xi).

We cannot discount the situation of the researcher any more than we can discount the situation of the researched. One constitutive element of the situation is the academic tribe: '[w]e are pursuing a "scholarly" identity through our case studies rather than an intrinsic fascination with the phenomena under investigation' warns Fox (Fox, 1982, p. 32). To avoid any such accusations of impropriety social science cultivates a 'prejudice against prejudice', a distancing from experience and valuing in order to achieve objectivity whereas the condition of our understanding is that we have prejudices and any inquiry undertaken by 'us' needs to be approached in the spirit of a conversation with others; the conversation alerts participants to their prejudices. In a sense, the point of conversation is to reconstruct prejudices, which is an alternative view of understanding itself.

It should be stressed however, that this conversation does not automatically lead to a 'neater picture' of the situation nor does it necessarily produce a 'social good'. There is the danger of viewing 'disciplined conversation' as an elevated version on the folk theory on ideal policy: 'if only everyone talked to one another, the world would be a nicer place'. Academic conversation (just like any democratic dialectic process) is often contentious and not quite the genteel affair it tries to present itself as. Equally, any given method of inquiry, including and perhaps headed by case study, can be both constitutive and disruptive of our prejudices.

Currently the culture of politeness aimed at avoiding others' and one's own discomfort at any cost contributes to the problem. Can one structure research that enables people to the reflect about prejudices that they inevitably bring to the situation and reconstruct their biases to open up the possibility of action and not cause discomfort to themselves or others? We could say that concern with generalisation and method is a consequence of academic discourse and culture and one of the ways in which questions of personal responsibility are argued away. Abstraction, the business of academia, is seen as antithetical to the process of particularisation, the business of policy implementation. But given some of the questions raised in this chapter, we should perhaps be asking whether abstraction and particularisation are parallel processes to which we ascribe polar directionality only *ex post facto*. In this sense we can further Nussbaum's (1990) distinction between generalisation and universalisation by rephrasing the dichotomy in the following terms: generalisation is assumed to be internal to the data whereas universalisation is a situated human cognitive and affective act.

A universalisable case study is of such quality that the philosopher policy-maker can discern its relevance for the process of policy-making (similarly to Stake's naturalistic generalisation). This is a different way of saying the same thing as Kemmis: 'Case study cannot claim authority, it must demonstrate it' (Kemmis, 1980, p. 136). The power of case study in this context can be illustrated by anecdotes from the field where practitioners were convinced that a particular case study describes their situation and berated colleagues or staff for revealing intimate details of their situation, whereas the case study had been based on research of an entirely unrelated entity. In cases like these, the universal nature of the case study is revealed to the practitioner. Its public aspects often engender action where idle rumination and discontent would be otherwise prevalent. Even when this kind of research tells people what they already 'know', it can inject accountability by rendering previously private knowledge public. The notion of case study as method with transcendental epistemology therefore cannot be rescued even by attempts like Bassey's (1999) to offer 'fuzzy generalizations' since while cognition and categorisation is fuzzy, action involves a commitment to boundaries. This focus on situated judgement over transcendental rationality in no way denies the need for rigour and instrumentalism. We agree with Stenhouse that there needs to be a space in which the quality of a particular case study can be assessed. But such judgments will be different when made by case study practitioners and when made by policy-makers or teachers. The epistemological philosopher will apply yet another set of criteria. All these agents would do well to familiarise themselves with the criteria applied by the others but they would be unwise to assume that they can ever fully transcend the situated parameters of their community of practice and make all boundaries (such as those described by Kushner, 1993) disappear.

Philosophy often likes to position itself in the role of an independent arbiter but it must not forget that it too is an embedded practice with its own community rules. That does not mean there is no space for it in this debate. If nothing else, it can provide a space (not unlike the liminal space of Turner's rituals) in which the normal assumptions are suspended and transformation of prejudice can occur. In this context, we should perhaps investigate the notion of therapeutic reading of philosophy put forth by the 'New Wittgensteinians' (see Crary and Read, 2000).

This makes the questions of ethics alluded to earlier even more prominent. We propose that given their situated nature, questions of generalisation are questions of ethics rather than inquiries into some disembodied transcendent rationality. Participants in the complex interaction between practitioners of education, educational researchers and educational policy-makers are constantly faced with ethical decisions asking themselves: how do I act in ways that are consonant with my values and goals? Questions of warrant are internal to them and their situation rather than being easily resolvable by external expert arbitration. This does not exclude instrumental expertise in research design and evaluation of results but the role of such expertise is limited to the particular. MacDonald and Walker (1977) point out the importance of apprenticeship in the training of case study practitioners and we should bear in mind that this experience cannot be distilled into general rules for research training as we find them laid out in a statistics textbook.

Herein can lie the contribution of philosophy: an inquiry into the warrant and generalisation of case study should be an inquiry into the ethics surrounding the creation and use of research, not an attempt to provide an epistemologically transcendent account of the representativeness of sampled data.

Correspondence: John Elliott, School of Education and Lifelong Learning, University of East Anglia, Norwich NR4 7TJ, UK.
E-mail: j.elliott@uea.ac.uk
Dominik Lukeš, School of Education and Lifelong Learning, University of East Anglia, Norwich NR4 7TJ, UK. E-mail: dominik@dominiklukes.net

NOTES

1. It should be noted that words like 'confidence' and 'warrant' have their instrumental counterparts in lexemes like 'scientific' and 'verification'. However, although they are intended to provide a hedge, the underlying assumption frequently is that 'things' will eventually be clarified in a properly instrumental manner.
2. It would appear that Stenhouse's vision of illuminative research has survived most prominently in the arena of programme evaluation.
3. Also, it is to a large extent an empirical question. How people acquire and retrieve knowledge, e.g. is a question that can be asked at a cognitive level. Unfortunately, at the moment the cognitive and neural sciences can only provide a very sketchy image of how knowledge (indeed questions as to the nature of knowledge itself abound) is represented. However, there are at least some indications that the human brain is not reminiscent of a database in which knowledge is stored and neither is the "retrieval" and application of knowledge in a given situation driven primarily and exclusively by algorithmic processes of feature matching underwritten by the formal laws of logic (see e.g. Lakoff, 1987).
4. Kuhn (1996 [1962]) reminds us that the forgetting of important knowledge is an important part of paradigm shifts. Scientific knowledge, far from being straightforwardly cumulative, is embedded in its present situation of theory, method and social structure. This is equally true of the social sciences and humanities.
5. See for example a proposal to the ESRC by Carmichael and Elliott (2007) entitled *Learning from and about Case study: Developing a Teaching Archive for Educational Research* to be based on an initial archive of case-study based evaluation studies developed as part of the ESRC QUADS

Initiative and entitled *Representing Context in a Research Archive of Educational Evaluation Studies*, Re-346-25-3003.

6. There is a further disturbing element here. Not only do sample-based studies fail to account for much of the particular knowledge that could be used in practice, they often inform the policy-maker of properties that can be ascribed to populations alone (i.e. as specific configurational features of a given cohort) but that may not be 'true' in any meaningful sense of any individual in a single situation. This will diminish their utility for policy-making even further.

7. Note that Stake is making an essentially empirical claim about the nature of memory and the kinds of 'narrative' experiences that can trigger memories and connect them to other structures of knowledge, e.g. 'awareness and understanding'. However, not only does Stake not provide evidence that that is the case, he leaves it up to his readers' 'imaginations' to conclude that non-case study research is not as good at providing opportunities for 'vicarious experience'.

8. This is intensified by an English discursive convention to translate statistical data into the 'x in y' formula rather than reporting percentages as is more common for instance in Czech.

9. R. J. Frankenberg quoted from 1963 paper presented to the British Association titled 'Taking the Blame or Passing the Buck'. Reference to published work provided in Lacey, 1970.

10. Stenhouse's attempt at analogy of case study with history as opposed to ethnography has its justification but a careful study of historiography shows that just as often as not the historical record itself needs to be reexamined and/or deconstructed. On the other hand, the lack of detailed notes did not prevent Mead's or Whorf's hypotheses about other cultures being questioned.

11. Similarly to the notion of 'teacher as researcher'.

REFERENCES

Abbott, A. (1992) From Causes to Events: Notes in Narrative Positivism, *Sociological Methods and Research*, 20, pp. 428–55.

Adelman, C. (ed.) (1984) *The Politics and Ethics of Evaluation* (London, Croom Helm).

Adelman, C., Jenkins, D. and Kemmis, S. (1976) Rethinking Case Study: Notes From The Second Cambridge Conference, *Cambridge Journal of Education*, 6.3, Reprinted in Simons (1980) pp. 47–61.

Ball, S. J. (1981) *Beachside Comprehensive: A Case Study of Secondary Schooling* (Cambridge and New York, Cambridge University Press).

Bassey, M. (1999) *Case Study Research in Educational Settings* (Buckingham UK, Philadelphia Open University Press).

Becker, H. S. (1992) Cases, Causes, Conjunctures, Stories and Imagery, in: C. C. Ragin and H. S. Becker (eds) *What is a Case? Exploring the Foundations of Social Inquiry* (Cambridge and New York, Cambridge University Press), pp. 205–227.

Becker, H. S., Geer, B., Hughes, E. C. and Strauss, A. L. (1977) [1961] *Boys in White: Student Culture in Medical School* (New Brunswick, NJ, Transaction Books).

Carr, W. (2006) Philosophy, Methodology and Action Research, *Journal of Philosophy of Education*, 40.4, pp. 421–435.

Crary, A. M. and Read, R. J. (eds) (2000) *The New Wittgenstein* (New York, Routledge).

Cronbach, L. (1963) Course Improvement Through Evaluation, *Teachers College Record*, 64, pp. 672–683.

Elliott, J. (1984) Methodology and Ethics, in: C. Adelman (ed.) *The Politics and Ethics of Evaluation* (Beckenham, Croom Helm).

Elliott, J. (1990) Validating Case Studies, *Westminster Studies in Education*, 13, pp. 46–60.

Elliott, J. (2007) Educational Theory, Practical Philosophy and Action Research, in: *Reflecting Where the Action Is: The Selected Works of John Elliott* (Oxford and New York, Routledge, Chapter 6).

Elliott, J., Bridges, D., Ebbutt, D., Gibson, R. and Nias, J. (1981) Case Studies in School Accountability, Vols. 1–3 (Cambridge, Cambridge Institute of Education) (some are now accessible through a Digital Archive of Contextualised Case Studies, http://www.caret.cam.ac.uk/tel).

Elliott, J. and Doherty, P. (2001) Restructuring Educational Research for the 'Third Way', in: M. Fielding (ed.) *Taking Education Really Seriously, Four Years' Hard Labour* (London and New York, RoutledgeFalmer), pp. 209–222.

Elliott, J. and Kushner, S. (2007) The Need for a Manifesto for Educational Evaluation, *Cambridge Journal of Education*, 37.3, pp. 321–336.

Evers, C. W. and Wu, E. H. (2006) On Generalising from Single Case Studies: Epistemological Reflections, *Journal of Philosophy of Education*, 40.4, pp. 511–526.

Fisher, K. (1997) Locating Frames in the Discursive Universe, *Sociological Research Online*, available at: http://www.socresonline.org.uk/2/3/4.html

Fox, T. G. (1982) Applying Mathematics to the Study of Educational Cases, Mimeo (Madison, WI, University of Wisconsin).

Gadamer, H-G. (1975) *Truth and Method* (London, Sheed and Ward).

Gamson, W. A. (1992) *Talking Politics* (Cambridge and New York, Cambridge University Press).

Goffman, E. (1975) [1974] *Frame Analysis: An Essay on the Organization of Experience* (Harmondsworth, Penguin).

Gould, S. J. (1981/1996) *The Mismeasure of Man* (New York, W. W. Norton).

Hamilton, D., Jenkins, D., King, C., MacDonald, B. and Parlett, M. (eds.) (1977) *Beyond the Numbers Game* (Basingstoke and London, Macmillan Education).

Hammersley, M. (2001) On Michael Bassey's Concept of the Fuzzy Generalisation, *Oxford Review of Education*, 27.2, pp. 219–225.

Hammersley, M. (2002) *Educational Research, Policymaking and Practice* (London, Paul Chapman).

Hargreaves, D. (1997) In Defence of Research for Evidence-Based Teaching: A Rejoinder to Martyn Hammersley, *British Educational Research Journal*, 23, pp. 405–419.

Hoare, Q. and Nowell Smith, G. (eds and trans.) (1971) The Modern Prince, *Selections from the Prison Notebooks of Antonio Gramsci* (London, Lawrence and Wishart).

Holland, D. C. and Eisenhart, M. A. (1990) *Educated In Romance: Women, Achievement, and College Culture* (Chicago, University of Chicago Press).

Kemmis, S. (1980) The Imagination of the Case and the Invention of the Study, in: H. Simons (ed.) *Towards a Science of the Singular: Essays about Case Study in Educational Research and Evaluation* (Norwich, Centre for Applied Research in Education, University of East Anglia), pp. 96–142.

Kennedy, M. M. (1979) Generalizing from Single Case Studies, *Evaluation Review*, 3.4, pp. 661–678.

Kennedy, M. M. (1999) A Test of Some Common Contentions about Educational Research, *American Educational Research Journal*, 36.3, pp. 511–541.

Kuhn, T. S. (1996) [1962] *The Structure of Scientific Revolutions*, 3rd edn. (Chicago and London, University of Chicago Press).

Kushner, S. (1993) Naturalistic Evaluation: Practical Knowledge for Policy Development, *Research Evaluation*, 3.2, pp. 83–94.

Lacey, C. (1970) *Hightown Grammar: The School as a Social System* (Manchester, Manchester University Press).

Lakoff, G. (1987) *Women, Fire, and Dangerous Things: What Categories Reveal about the Mind* (Chicago, University of Chicago Press).

Lakoff, G. (1996) *Moral Politics: What Conservatives Know That Liberals Don't* (Chicago, University of Chicago Press).

Lerner, B. H. (2006) *When Illness Goes Public: Celebrity Patients and How We Look at Medicine* (Baltimore, MD, Johns Hopkins University Press).

Lloyd, J. (2007) An Intellectual in Power, *Prospect*, 2, pp. 24–28.

Lukeš, D. (2007) What Does it Mean When Texts 'Really' Mean Something? Types of Evidence for Conceptual Patterns in Discourse, in: C. Hart and D. Lukeš (eds) *Cognitive Linguistics in Critical Discourse Studies: Application and Theory* (Newcastle, Cambridge Scholars Publishing).

MacDonald, B. (1976) Evaluation and the Control of Education, in: D. Tawney (ed.) *Curriculum Evaluation Today: Trends and Implications* (London, Schools Council Research Studies, Macmillan Educational).

MacDonald, B. and Parlett, M. (1973) Rethinking Evaluation: Notes from the Cambridge Conference, *Cambridge Journal of Education*, 2, pp. 74–81.

MacDonald, B. and Walker, R. (1975) Case-Study and the Social Philosophy of Educational Research, *Cambridge Journal of Education*, 5, pp. 2–11; Reprinted in Hamilton *et al.* (1977), pp. 181–189.

Macmurray, J. (1957) *The Self as Agent* (London, Faber & Faber).

May, R. (1994) *The Courage to Create* (New York, W.W. Norton and Co).

Moffatt, M. (1989) *Coming of Age in New Jersey: College and American Culture* (New Brunswick, NJ, Rutgers University Press).

Nathan, R. (2005) *My Freshman Year: What a Professor Learned by Becoming a Student* (Ithaca, NY, Cornell University Press).

Nisbet, J. D. and Broadfoot, P. (1980) *The Impact of Research on Policy and Practice in Education* (Aberdeen, Aberdeen University Press).

Nussbaum, M. C. (1990) *Love's Knowledge: Essays on Philosophy and Literature* (Oxford, Oxford University Press).

Nutley, S. M., Walter, I. and Davies, H. T. O. (2007) *Using Evidence: How Research Can Inform Public Services* (Bristol, The Policy Press).

Parlett, M. and Hamilton, D. (1972) Evaluation as Illumination: A New Approach to the Study of Innovatory Programmes, Occasional Paper 9, Centre for Research in the Educational Sciences, University of Edinburgh, reprinted in Hamilton *et al.* (1977), pp. 6–22.

Parlett, M. and Dearden, G. (eds.) (1977) *Introduction to Illuminative Evaluation: Studies in Higher Education* (Cardiff-by-the-Sea, CA, Pacific Soundings Press).

Pole, C. and Morrison, M. (2003) *Ethnography for Education* (Buckingham, Open University Press).

Robinson, J. E. and Norris, N. F. (2001) Generalisation: The Linchpin of Evidence-Based Practice?, *Educational Action Research*, 9.2, pp. 303–310.

Schön, D. A. and Rein, M. (1994) *Frame Reflection: Toward the Resolution of Intractable Policy Controversies* (New York, Basic Books).

Schwab, J. J. (1970) *The Practical: A Language for Curriculum* (Washington, DC., National Educational Association, Centre for the Study of Instruction).

Schwandt, T. A. (2005) A Diagnostic Reading of Scientifically Based Research for Education, *Educational Theory*, 55.3, pp. 285–305.

Seaman, B. (2005) *Binge: What Your College Student Won't Tell You: Campus Life in an Age of Disconnection and Excess* (Hoboken, NJ, John Wiley and Sons).

Simons, H. (1971) Innovation and the Case Study of Schools, *Cambridge Journal of Education*, 3, pp. 118–124.

Simons, H. (ed.) (1980) *Toward a Science of the Singular: Essays about Case Study in Educational Research and Evaluation* (CARE Occasional Publications No.10), (Norwich, CARE/University of East Anglia).

Simons, H. (1987) *Getting to Know Schools in a Democracy: The Politics and Process of Evaluation* (London and New York, The Falmer Press, Chapter 3).

Simons, H. (1996) The Paradox of Case Study, *Cambridge Journal of Education*, 26.2, pp. 225–240.

Stake, R. E. (1978) The Case Study Method in Social Inquiry, *Educational Researcher*, 7, pp. 5–8. Reprinted in Simons (1980).

Stake, R. E. (1994) Case Studies, in: N. Denzin and Y. Lincoln (eds) *Handbook of Qualitative Research* (Newbury Park, CA, Publications).

Stake, R. E. (1995) *The Art of Case Study Research* (London and Thousand Oaks, CA, Sage Publications).

Stenhouse, L. (1978) Case Study and Case Records: Towards a Contemporary History of Education, *British Educational Research Journal*, 4.2, pp. 21–39.

Stenhouse, L. (1979a) The Problem of Standards in Illuminative Research. Lecture given to the Scottish Educational Research Association at its Annual General Meeting, Stenhouse Archive, Norwich: University of East Anglia, available at: http://research.edu.uea.ac.uk/stenhousearchive

Stenhouse, L. (1979b) The Study of Samples and the Study of Cases, Presidential Address to the British Educational Research Association, Stenhouse Archive, Norwich: University of East Anglia, available at: http://research.edu.uea.ac.uk/stenhousearchive. Published version (1980) in *British Educational Research Journal*, 6.1, pp. 1–6.

Stenhouse, L. (1979c) Case Study in Comparative Education: Particularity and Generalization, *Comparative Education*, 15.1, pp. 5–10.

Stenhouse, L. (1985) A Note on Case Study and Educational Practice, in: R. Burgess (ed.) *Field Methods in the Study of Education* (London and Philadelphia, The Falmer Press).

Škrabánek, P. and McCormick, J. (1989) *Follies and Fallacies in Medicine* (Glasgow, Taragon).

Willis, P. E. (1977) *Learning to Labour: How Working Class Kids Get Working Class Jobs* (Farnborough, Saxon House).

Wallace, W. L. (1966) *Student Culture: Social Structure and Continuity in a Liberal Arts College* (Chicago, Aldine Publishing Company).

6

Personal Narratives and Policy: Never the Twain?

MORWENNA GRIFFITHS AND GALE MACLEOD

In this chapter the extent to which stories and personal narratives can and should be used to inform education policy is examined. A range of studies describable as story or personal narrative is investigated. They include life-studies, life-writing, life history, narrative analysis, and the representation of lives. We use 'auto/biography' as a convenient way of grouping this range under one term. It points to the many and varied ways that accounts of self interrelate and intertwine with accounts of others. That is, auto/biography illuminates the social context of individual lives. At the same time it allows room for unique, personal stories to be told. We do not explicitly discuss all the different forms of auto/biography. Rather, we investigate the epistemology underlying the personal story in the context of social action. We discuss the circumstances in which a story may validly be used by educational policy-makers and give some examples of how they have done so in the past.

1 CONTEXT

In this section the range and variation of research that is included under the designation 'narrative research' is considered along with reasons for adopting the alternative title of 'auto/biography'.[1] The current enthusiasm for 'narrative research' more generally in education is outlined. Finally, and briefly, the purposes of educational research are examined along with implications for the usefulness of auto/biography arising from different views about what research is for.

Narrative research is generally contrasted with positivist accounts of research and seen as part of the move away from the search for a generalisable objectivity to a valuing of, and interest in, individual experience and personal stories (e.g. Casey, 1995/6; Fraser, 2004). As Kvernbekk (2003) notes, the concept of narrative is 'crucially vague'. If humans are conceptualised as 'storytelling organisms' who lead 'storied lives', any attempt to understand their experiences—as individuals or in social groups—may be seen as an enquiry into their stories (Connelly and Clandinin, 1990). As a consequence it would appear that, for some, almost any qualitative research could reasonably come under the heading of narrative. However others have sought to be more prescriptive in defining narrative: for Polkinghorne (1995) narrative is a storied text in which events are brought together into a unifying sequence in which there is a plot, and for most this notion of causal sequence is a necessary element of a narrative (Kvernbekk, 2003). For Polkinghorne a narrative analysis need not be based on data that take narrative form; rather the narratival element is to be found in the story that the researcher constructs or re-constructs to make sense of data in any form. Here the narrative is the product of the analysis and not the starting point. Smeyers and Verhesschen (2001) draw on the work of Polkinghorne (1995) and Bruner (1986) in distinguishing between the analysis of narrative, in which the narratives are the data and the aim is to identify *common* themes and their interrelation, and narrative analysis in which the aim is to understand the *particular* instance.

We have chosen to use the phrase 'auto/biography' to describe the approaches to research that we examine. This marks our focus, which is specifically on personal, individual stories, within the broad category of 'narrative research'. 'Auto/biography' may be used to cover life-stories and life history (e.g. Atkinson, 1998; McNulty, 2003; Chaitin, 2004; Thompson, 2004; Arad and Leichtentritt, 2005; Sanders and Munford, 2005; Stroobants, 2005) life-writing and personal histories (e.g. Bullough, 1998: Couser, 2002; Eick, 2002), narrative analysis (e.g. Reissman, 1993; Franzosi 1998) and the representation of lives (e.g. Richardson, 1992; Santoro, Kamler and Reid, 2001). In practice it would seem that some writers use these terms interchangeably, whereas for others a key aim of the project is to distinguish between terms (e.g. Jolly, 2001; Smith and Watson, 2001). Drawing such distinctions is not a purpose of this chapter. Rather, in using the term auto/biography, we distinguish our focus on personal and individual accounts from those accounts such as vignettes and fictionalised stories that are intended to present a generalised picture of qualitative data: these are forms of 'boiled down' qualitative data that no longer embody the particular (e.g. Clough, 1996, 2002).

The 'narrative turn' in the social sciences is usually fixed at around the early 1980s (Casey, 1995/6; Czarniawska, 2004), following a similar narrative turn in literary studies in the 1960s. The interest in narrative research has touched all of the social sciences—even in the apparently unlikely case of economics (McCloskey, 1990). It has particularly taken root in the areas of health (or, more accurately, illness) studies (Jordens and Little, 2004; Wetle *et al.*, 2005), social work (Fraser, 2004; Glasby and Lester, 2005), and education (Pollard, 2005; Lawson, Parker and Sikes, 2006). It can be argued that the fundamental tenet of good practice in these disciplines is an assumption that development (learning, healing, personal growth) can only take place in the context of a relationship between practitioner and client, and so these 'helping' services are often delivered in the context of a personal relationship. Hence biography is already an accepted and valued aspect of work in these fields (Froggett and Chamberlayne, 2004). An alternative explanation for the popularity of narrative approaches in these practitioner areas is that they are disciplines dominated by women both in practice and in research, and there are close links between feminist research (along with other movements for social change) and auto/biography (Stanley, 1993; Casey, 1995/6; Mauthner, 2000; Townsend and Weiner, forthcoming).

As Oancea and Pring (this volume) make clear, we are living in the 'what works?' age of educational research in which the constant search is for interventions whose effectiveness has been scientifically 'proven'. The rise in interest in narrative research has been described as a 'clear reaction' to this breakdown of teaching into 'discrete variables and indicators of effectiveness' (Doyle, 1997, p. 94). This focus on 'objective' research has fed a tendency to disregard the expertise of teachers in favour of the search for the elusive 'one size fits all' solution to effective teaching. An important element of auto/biography is that it focuses on the intersection between individual experience and the social context (Fischer-Rosenthal, 1995; Stroobants, 2005). As Fraser observes, what she calls 'narrative approaches' have '... the capacity to attend to context as well as idiosyncrasy ...' (2004, p. 181). Likewise, Frogget and Chamberlayne (2004, p. 62) argue that 'Biographical methods can help restore the relationship between policy and lived experience by moving between the micro- and macro- levels'. In a similar vein, Avramidis and Norwich (2002) call for more research using alternative methods such as narrative and autobiography. They argue that it is only through these methods that our understanding of the complexities of human behaviour in the social context can be developed.

The main question addressed in this chapter is whether auto/biography can and should inform policy. This raises the prior issue of the purpose of educational research and how this links to the purposes of policy-makers. As Ozga (2004) notes, policy-makers and researchers have different agendas, a point echoed by Hammersley (2002). These agendas may conveniently overlap at times in the pursuit of knowledge that has a practical use, but educational research is not limited to this purpose. Hammersley (2002) advocates a 'moderate enlightenment' view of educational research that seeks to provide understanding rather than solutions and that makes claims that are tentative. Similarly Munn (2005) distinguishes 'blue skies' research that produces knowledge that filters into the received wisdom and so indirectly influences policy, from 'applied research' that seeks to address the 'what works and why?' question. Further, Munn (2005) argues for the particular importance of the 'why' part of this question since it allows researchers to explore specific contexts and examine the complexities of policy implementation.

In Hammersley's view, what educational research can provide is limited; in particular, he notes the well-known difficulties in deriving 'ought' from 'is'. The is/ought or fact/value distinction was first raised as problematic by Hume and has been widely discussed since. Dennett (1995) disputes Hume's argument in general. Earlier, Searle (1964) had argued that the distinction disappears in the case of some social facts such as promises. It may be argued, similarly, that in any case where there is agreement on normative judgements an argument can be made for empirical research having a role in showing that 'in order for x to happen you ought to do y'. (Or in showing that 'y has no influence on x happening so you ought not to do it'.) As Biesta (2007) argues, the 'what works' tradition makes the mistake of assuming the move from 'is' to 'ought' because it ignores the importance of normative practitioner judgements— which are not necessarily in agreement with those of the researcher or the policy-maker. The role for the empirical researcher moves to: 'If you want x to happen, y is one strategy you should consider'. (Or '. . . y is a strategy that is not worth considering'.) Biesta advocates a wider role for educational research that he terms 'cultural' and that is concerned with making problems visible and seeing things differently, and that, he argues, is rightly concerned with questions of ends as well as means. Indeed some traditions of research would see challenging orthodoxies as a fundamental purpose—rather than research being the route to getting politics out, it is seen by some as the way to get politics in (Gitlin and Russell, 1994). In a similar vein Ozga and Jones (2006) suggest that in the context of global 'travelling policy' there is a need to take account of research that addresses the normative question of what new education systems ought to look like in different contexts, taking into account issues such as poverty, life changes, and access to opportunities. Hogan (2000) deplores the vacancy in educational policy-making that arises if it is not informed by a rich, qualitative understanding of education itself.

Research, then, can be seen as generating understanding that may influence policy indirectly. Alternatively it can be seen as exploring the potential of solutions to problems. Moreover, it can explore reasons for why those particular solutions work and in what contexts. It has a role to play in challenging taken-for-granted assumptions about education, and in addressing the question of the proper understanding of education itself. Auto/biography has a different contribution to make to each of these research goals, and each goal will articulate differently with policy at different levels and at the different stages of formation, implementation and evaluation.

2 QUESTIONS OF CONFIDENCE

Having outlined a contextual description covering the nature of auto/biography and educational research as understood in this chapter, we now move to more precise questions about the evidential weight that can be placed on particular auto/biographies and whether policy-makers can have confidence in them.

Personal stories are sometimes dismissed as anecdotal. They are also criticised for distorting the wider picture by overemphasising one, perhaps unrepresentative, case. Anecdotes are short biographical or autobiographical accounts of incidents, told because they are thought to be interesting or amusing or in order to make a debating point. They take the form of crafted stories, sometimes, like the urban myth, passed on orally, purporting to be from the life of 'a friend of a friend'. While anecdotal evidence counts for little in research terms, it is, nevertheless, powerful in rhetorical terms. Such stories are known to have the power to affect the audience. No doubt this is why anecdotes are used in political presentations, such as party political broadcasts or policy pamphlets. 'Human interest' is said to hook readers of newspapers into reading an article. Indeed, anecdotes can affect policy. Anecdotes told to powerful people may change their minds about issues, where other sources of information and argument have not. In research terms, an anecdote (as in 'anecdotal evidence') may also be a personal story told and heard without critical attention being paid to questions of context or reflexivity.

We argue that although anecdotal evidence *can* be influential in policy terms it *should* not be. It is especially important to be able to distinguish auto/biographical research from anecdote since one looks superficially like the other and both can be powerful, at least in individual cases. One concern of this chapter is to explain and justify the distinction. This kind of concern is not peculiar to auto/biographical research. Similarly, researchers need to be able to distinguish eye-witness accounts taken at face value from well-designed observational research evidence. Indeed this kind of distinction is not peculiar to qualitative research. Quantitative research, too, needs to guard against putting too much weight on salient instances, for instance by over-generalising from one school, one year or one intervention.

If, as we are suggesting, auto/biographical research is more than anecdote, then the issue that becomes fundamental concerns how sound it is. We have chosen to use the term 'sound' because in logic it distinguishes truth from validity: that is, validity is a property of a logical argument, while truth is the property of a premise. So the question we are addressing in this chapter becomes:

What are the characteristics of sound auto/biographical research in relation to policy decisions?

Further, insofar as there are different kinds of auto/biographical research, they are likely to have a differential relevance to the various possibilities and stages of policy formation. So a supplementary question addressed in this chapter is:

What kinds of sound contribution can different forms of auto/biography make to what kinds and stages of policy decision?

These questions depend on assumptions about how soundness should be determined. And these assumptions are, in turn, dependent on epistemological positions. So we consider these first before returning to consider these two questions directly. We shall begin by looking at the epistemology of practical, human affairs. We then go on to look in more detail at epistemological issues underpinning auto/biographical research.

3 EPISTEMOLOGY OF THE POLITICAL AND PRACTICAL

In this section we argue as follows. (1) Human institutions are made up of a plurality of unique human beings. (2) Therefore policymakers need to use an epistemology of the unique and particular. (3) What is needed is the kind of practical knowledge we can call *praxis*. (4) This kind of practical knowledge is challenged by new perspectives that (5) will result in revisions. (6) Such new perspectives may be in the form of auto/biography. (7) The continuing process of revision means that *praxis* itself is historically specific.

This volume has as one of its broad purposes the identification of the kinds of knowledge policy-makers can properly use. It is, therefore, concerned with the political and practical, what Arendt calls 'the realm of human affairs' (1958, p. 13). That is, not only is it concerned with what ought to be done, and the place that knowledge has in determining that, but also it is concerned with the relationship that political decisions and actions have with knowledge. In Aristotelian terms, politics is concerned with practical wisdom rather than with contemplation of eternal truths or with expertise. Aristotle's useful distinctions are usually discussed using his original Greek terms because they have no simple translation in English (and were technical uses of common words even in ancient Greece). Aristotle distinguished the practical wisdom (*phronesis*) needed to work with practical knowledge (*praxis*) from the theoretical wisdom (*sophia*) and theoretical understanding (*episteme*) needed to carry out enquiry into timeless truths (*theoria*). *Praxis* is the kind of practical knowledge needed for the social and moral judgements made by the *phronimos* (the possessor of *phronesis*). Aristotle also distinguished practical wisdom (*phronesis*) from the expertise (*techne*) needed to apply technical knowledge (*poiesis*) when making things. We first discuss *praxis* in relation to *theoria* and then go on to discuss it in relation to *poiesis*.

Epistemology of the Unique and Particular: Action and Theory

Adriana Cavarero argues that the tradition of philosophy in which the unique and particular are subsumed in the universal is, at best, partial. In her (2002) article, 'Politicizing Theory', she argues that 'political theory' is an oxymoron. She draws on Arendt to point out that the kind of universalising theory that contemplates abstract and universal objects is opposed to politics. In Aristotelian terms, *theoria* results in *episteme* rather than in *praxis*.

Theory, Arendt points out, pertains to the *bios theoretikos*, that is explicitly distinguished from the *bios politicos* (Arendt, 1958, pp. 13-14). The former is concerned with the contemplation of eternal truths. The latter is a life of (public) action concerned with the 'shared and relational space generated by the words and deeds of a plurality of human beings' (Cavarero, 2002, p. 506). This plurality is to be sharply distinguished from any concept of the many that does not acknowledge individual differences. As Arendt writes, 'Plurality is the condition of human action because we are all the same, that is, human, in such a way that nobody is ever the same as anyone else who ever lived, lives, or will live' (Arendt, 1958, p. 8). Equally it is distinguished from a concept of the many that is simply an agglomeration of individuals who do not relate to each other (like, for instance, a cinema audience). The *bios politicos* is found in the web of relationships (ibid., p. 181) formed as a number of unique human beings come together to take collective action. As Iris Marion Young explains:

> For Arendt the public is not a comfortable place of conversation among those who share language assumptions, and ways of looking at issues ... The public consists of multiple histories and perspectives relatively unfamiliar to one another, connected yet distant and irreducible to one another. A conception of publicity that requires its members to put aside their differences in order to uncover their common good destroys the very meaning of publicity because it aims to turn the many into one (Young, 2000, p. 111).

Individuals do not bring about actions in the public sphere by themselves. As decision makers they are always part of a web of social relationships. Any action in the public sphere involves initiating change as part of that web of social relationships, and it is there that decision makers have an influence as unique individuals. Decision makers act in concert but it is a concert that is made up of distinct, different members. Their actions have an influence in the realm of human affairs, which is itself made up of webs of social relationship. These webs, too, are created by distinct and different human beings. This is the *bios politicos*, and it is where education policy-makers find themselves.

Cavarero expands on Arendt's argument, pointing out that to try to use *theoria* to generate *phronesis* is to have confused the object of knowledge for the two forms of life, *bios theoretikos* and *bios politicos*. *Theoria*, the pursuit of enquiry in the *bios theoretikos*, will not result in the *praxis* needed for the *bios politicos*. She writes:

> Politics asks to be studied according to its own principles insofar as politics is a field of plural interaction and hence of contingency. These principles, exemplarily illustrated by Hannah Arendt, have to do with the plurality of human beings insofar as they are unique beings rather than fictitious entities like the individual of modern political doctrine, and they have most of all to do with the relational dimension of reciprocal dependency (Cavarero, 2002, p. 512).

Cavarero goes on to consider how a unique human being may speak to decision makers. Using the metaphor of voice, she explores the power of a unique voice to provoke a human response in the listener. That is, the listener becomes fully aware of the humanity of the speaker: a speaker who is always unique but who is also always already in relation to other human beings.[2]

Cavarero contrasts the account of the openness of the realm of human affairs with the lasting philosophical inheritance of Plato's desire to control the uncontrollable world of action by taking refuge in the reassuring world of theory. This is, she argues, the meaning of the myth of the cave. Plato 'designs the just city taking as his model the idea of justice he contemplated in his mind (500e-501c)' (p. 507). She goes on to point out how influential the impetus towards control has been, as evidenced by the continued ascribed primacy of theory over practice. For instance, she writes: '[Hobbes and Locke] confirm that political theory recognises its specific object in an order—governable and predictable, convenient and reassuring, just and legitimate—that neutralises the potentially conflictive disorder inscribed on the natural or pre-political condition of human beings' (p. 511). This is a view in which theory means applying reason to find a system (or order) that can then be put into practice.

Cavarero has pointed to a reason for the failure of 'political theory' to produce control. The impossibility of the task is not merely a contingent fact of history. It is logically impossible: a search for a mirage—or a snark (Carroll, 1974). Human beings continually elude systems. If rational persons did agree they would assent to the same rational systems. However, they do not. Consider the Enlightenment in which both currents of political theorising can be found. On the one hand is the tradition of seeking control and order, grounded in theory. On the other there is a tradition of critique (Foucault, 1984) grounded in theorising. Bernard Williams points out that:

> A familiar theme of contemporary criticism of the Enlightenment ... [is] that it has generated unprecedented systems of oppression, because of its belief in an externalised, objective, truth about individuals and society. This represents the Enlightenment in terms of the tyranny of theory, where theory is in turn identified with an external 'panoptical' view of everything, including ourselves (Williams, 2002, p. 4).

He contrasts this with another current in the Enlightenment, critique, which he argues has been a main expression of the spirit of political and social truthfulness. This spirit need not lead to anarchy. Rather, the kind of openness required by the *bios politicos* makes room for individuals to instigate change in a process of co-construction with others. In her 1963 book, *On Revolution*, Arendt commends episodes in history that were marked by change and revolution as examples of true politics but she is far from advocating perpetual revolution.

Epistemology of the Unique and Particular: Action and Technique

We have drawn attention to the way theory (*theoria*) consumes the particular in the universal. Another way in which the particular can be consumed in the universal is through conflating the practical knowledge needed for dealing with human beings with the practical knowledge needed for dealing with things or with law-governed behaviour (for instance, building bridges or predicting solar eclipses). This distinction is particularly significant in exploring the limitations of research into 'what works'. Aristotle distinguishes *praxis* not only from *episteme* but also from *poiesis*. Both *poiesis* and *praxis* exercise practical knowledge but they have very different relations to policy. The first, *poiesis*, is productive and has to do with making. The second, *praxis*, has to do with how one lives as a citizen and human being and has no outcome separable from its practice. *Poiesis* requires the technical knowledge possessed by an expert. Aristotle calls this kind of knowledge *techne*. Dunne succinctly characterises this: '*Techne* then is the kind of knowledge possessed by an expert maker: it gives him a clear conception of the why and wherefore, the how and with-what of the making process and enables him, through the capacity to offer a rational account of it, to preside over his activity with secure mastery' (Dunne, 1993, p. 9). Just as *theoria* appears to offer the prospect of order and control so does *techne*. However *poiesis* and *praxis* are different. *Praxis* requires personal wisdom and understanding, not expertise. To quote Dunne again:

> [*Praxis*] is conduct in a public space with others in which a person, without ulterior purpose and with a view to no object detachable from himself, acts in such a way as to realise excellences that he has come to appreciate in his community as constitutive of a worthwhile way of life. ... *praxis* required for its regulation a kind of knowledge that was more personal and experiential, more supple and less formulable, than the knowledge conferred by *techne* (p. 10).

As the word 'excellences' indicates, to act with practical wisdom is necessarily also to act ethically. As Dunne writes, '[Aristotle's] novel conception of *phronesis* ... provided a rich analysis of the kind of knowledge that guides, and is well fitted to, characteristically human—and therefore inescapably ethical—activity (*praxis*)' (Dunne and Pendlebury, 2003, p. 200). To put this another way: as was remarked in the first section, 'Context', empirical research can only give information about what might work in certain circumstances, but the decision about what to do in any specific circumstance will always depend on normative judgements that have to be made by those who are there.

Provisional Knowledge and Little Stories

We have been arguing that the kind of knowledge needed by policy-makers is knowledge of particulars and specifics, rather than on the one hand, knowledge of universalisable theories and timeless truths, or on the other, knowledge of techniques and skills to turn out certain products. In Aristotelian terms, policy-makers need to rely on *praxis* rather than, on the one hand, *sophia* and *episteme*, or on the other, *techne*. In more Arendtian terms, it is an epistemology underlying a life of (public) action rather than of labour or of contemplation.

We now go on to remark that *praxis* is open to new perspectives and understandings. It is therefore open to revision, drawing on new perspectives offered by the singular and unique stories of individual human beings. Such revision means that any decision or policy is historically specific. So neither can ever be settled once and for all: both need to respond to changing circumstances and new ideas.

Practical knowledge is developed in the realm of human affairs. Arendt's concept of natality is relevant here (Arendt, 1958). Her concept of the realm of human affairs is one that is open to change, and indeed does change as new unique human beings are born, come into the world and use their voices to act in it in concert with others: 'The frailty of human institutions and laws and, generally, of all matters pertaining to men's living together, arises from the human condition of natality and is quite independent of the frailty of human nature' (p. 191). Natality means that each of us is unique at the same time as being born into specific social and political contexts. Therefore, it is not just that we have not yet worked out perfect systems and strategies for age-old problems, such as how best to educate young people. And it is not just human nature that gets in the way of getting it right. It is also that real newness enters the world because of natality. New institutions appear, whether as formal or informal social groupings. New ways of looking at things change our judgements and understandings about each other.

Natality means that practical knowledge is subject to revision as new perspectives are encountered: it is always revisable. New perspectives in themselves can change what we know and do as we make practical judgements and decisions—what we perceive, what we judge to be at issue, and what we take our role to be. As Smeyers and Verhesschen argue, educational problems arise in particular situations and contexts that are always subject to change, leading to new interpretations and new meanings. They give the example of the family: 'Wide coverage of cases of child abuse ... have perhaps inevitably cast the family in a different light ... The context of trust has been undermined ... In education we hear again the language of (children's) rights' (Smeyers and Verhesschen, 2001, p. 82). Decisions about what to do, at every level from teachers in the classroom to national policy, will change as a result of such changed perceptions and understandings.

Such changes in perceptions and understandings may be expressed in the auto/biographies of everyone involved. And their stories will capture something of the specificity and context of these changes. Cotton and Griffiths (2007) argue that auto/biographies can be told in such a way as to have the power to change the understandings of their listeners—and indeed those of the tellers—about educational policy and practice. Cotton and Griffiths draw on research that presented auto/biographies told by marginalised people in specific social, political and historical contexts. One of these was told by a young woman articulating her feelings about being in school. Another was told by teachers about a disabled boy in a dance class. Both auto/biographies were told in the context of a changing curriculum (in the areas of mathematics and creativity, respectively) and illuminate some of the implications for social justice in schooling.

The continuing process of revision means that practical knowledge (*praxis*) is historically specific. Research of all kinds helps educators keep up with changing circumstances and ideas. We have made this argument focusing on auto/biography but it is also true of other research methods.[3]

4 QUESTIONS OF TRUTH AND VALIDITY IN AUTO/BIOGRAPHY

If auto/biographies are a necessary part of an epistemology suitable for policy, then there must be ways of determining whether they can be trusted, whether they are sound. There are two ways in which such soundness may be challenged. First it may be challenged on the grounds of truth. Secondly its validity may be challenged. We take each in turn.

Truthfulness

The question about truth is complicated by the academic arguments that rage in social sciences and the humanities about the nature of truth. These arguments are many-sided and complex. There is no space here to do more than allude to them. Bridges' influential article (2005) summarises some mainstream philosophical discussions about different theories of truth (correspondence, coherence, pragmatic, etc) in relation to education. These theories are discussed further in Heikkenen *et al.*, 2000, 2001. Other discussions are influenced by postfoundational philosophies. Walker and Unterhalter (2004) discuss the significance of multiple perspectives, experiences and interpretations when judging how far to trust a story or set of stories. MacLure (2003) draws on Derrida and Foucault to argue that truths are always textual, discursive and suffused with power relations. Such truths cannot be straightforwardly reported, she argues.

Bernard Williams suggests a useful strategy for sidestepping some of the arguments about the nature of truth. He proposes that we focus less on truth and more on truthfulness. He points out that sceptics about truth within the humanities and social sciences nevertheless exhibit 'this demand for truthfulness or (to put it less positively) this reflex against deceptiveness' even though 'there is an equally pervasive suspicion about truth itself' (Williams, 2002, p. 1). He usefully distinguishes two basic virtues associated with truthfulness: accuracy and sincerity. He points out that 'each of the basic virtues of truth involves certain kinds of resistance to what moralists might call temptation—to fantasy and the wish' (p. 45). It is relatively simple to judge accuracy and sincerity in the case of reporting facts about 'middle-sized dry goods', to use J. L. Austin's phrase. Similarly, it is relatively simple when discussing shared contexts. Judging accuracy and sincerity in the case of auto/biography is trickier. However, it is a familiar trickiness. In ordinary life we listen to and tell auto/biographies all the time. We need to judge how far the stories we hear are accurate and told with sincerity. We know, and indeed expect, them to be partial, self-serving, entertaining, persuasive and to draw on imperfect memories. All this is an inevitable part of understanding the unique and particular, the singular, individual voice. And it is routinely understood, as individual voices are, with the aid of intelligence and wisdom drawn partly from personal experience and partly from knowledge gained from other sources.

First it is necessary to be clear what there is in an auto/biography to be accurate and sincere about. Most obviously there are facts about the memories being recounted: time, place, observable behaviour, etc. Secondly there are the feelings that accompany these memories. Feelings can be reported and they will also affect how the facts are reported. Facts and feelings are rarely reported (or even reportable) in neutral terms. As Walker and Unterhalter observe: 'Our stories do not speak for themselves, nor do they provide unmediated access to other times, places or cultures' (Walker and Unterhalter, 2004, pp. 285–6). Interpretation is unavoidable,[4] and the feelings of the participant will affect the interpretations made. Finally, even as the facts and feelings are reported, the way they are understood and reported is responsive to who the audience is. Stroobants gives an example. Reflecting on research interviews about the learning process, she remarks:

> It was not only me as a researcher who was trying to understand the stories in terms of learning. When telling their life story, the women were actively giving meaning to their life experiences ... During the interviews some of the women gained insight ... they could see some work experiences in a different light (Stroobants, 2005, p. 50).

Walker and Unterhalter (2004) provide another example of the effect of the audience. They argue that the lack of a feminist ethos in the audience for the South African Truth and Reconciliation Commission changed how women's stories of rape and sexual humiliation were told.

Judging accuracy and sincerity is, then, precisely a matter for judgement, for weighing evidence, rather than a matter of rules or protocols. Researchers need to make such judgements and also to give an indication of how they made them, using evidence of how the auto/biographical accounts were produced, with what intended audience, for what purpose, and setting the judgment within as full an understanding of the cultural, political and personal contexts as could be obtained. We give two contrasting instances of how this may be done.[5]

The introduction to the hugely influential book, *Tell Them from Me*, is exemplary. Gow and McPherson begin by explaining that:

> [These accounts] have been written by young people who left school in Scotland in the second half of the 1970s ... The book is about their experience, their opinions and feelings, about their grudges and gratitude. It is about the way education, work and employment seemed to young people (Gow and McPherson, 1980, p. 3).

The following subheadings then structure the discussion preceding the accounts: 'Whose writings are these and why did they write?'; 'Is the writing honest? For whom did leavers think they were writing?'; 'How was the selection of writings made?'; 'How can we achieve better understanding and better practice?'. The second of these subheadings is particularly interesting. The questions of audience and accuracy/sincerity are taken together. Reasons for believing the young people had no reason to 'play to' any group are given, as are reasons for both trusting—and mistrusting—written accounts. Finally, Gow and McPherson write:

> We cannot, either logically or empirically, exclude the possibility that, once they had decided to comment, some at least commented mainly on what they had experienced as negative aspects of their schooling. Whether such an orientation constitutes bias can, in part, be left to the reader to judge. The writings that follow may occasionally read as resentful, unperceptive, hostile or partial. But do we feel in reading them that they were offered dishonestly, maliciously or frivolously? Their transparency seems evident and their cumulative impact is convincing. For example the disturbingly similar stories told by leaver after leaver in the opening chapters on belting, truancy and the neglect of non-certificate classes in fact reflect pupils' experiences of more than 80 schools; the events were experienced, and the accounts were written, mainly in isolation one from another (p. 13).

Stroobants describes another way of approaching the task of explaining how the stories told to her may be judged by the reader as accurate and sincere:

> I write in detail about how my grounded interpretation developed and grew, trying to do justice to ... the stories ... and to my own interpretation by alternately telling the life story of one particular woman in the story of my interpretive analysis process. I also systematically describe and account for the methodological steps I took, elaborating my considerations and reflections ... in order for the reader to be able ... to judge the quality of the research report, the research results and the craftsmanship of the researcher. (Stroobants, 2005, p. 56)

Validity

Like the question of truth, the question about validity is complicated by academic arguments within the social sciences. So far, we have been tacitly assuming a meaning for 'validity' that is derived from formal logic. That is, validity refers to reasoning rather than to facts. However, the term, like 'truth', is subject to fierce debate within social science and the humanities. Much of this debate seems to be a response to the specialised use of the term in the natural sciences. The natural sciences have developed a specialised, technical vocabulary suitable for themselves. In this discourse, 'validity' determines whether the research truly measures that which it was intended to measure or how truthful the research results are. One response has been postmodern playfulness. Suggestions for alternative understandings of validity include 'rhyzomatic validity' or 'ironic validity', as suggested by Patti Lather (1994). Altheide and Johnson (1998) list 'successor validity', 'catalytic validity' and 'transgressive validity' among others. Another response has been to ditch the concept altogether as being bound up with the quest for certainty (Altheide and Johnson, 1998). In some discussions, 'validity' appears to have been equated with 'quality', as in the two linked articles by Heikkinen *et al.* (2007) and Feldman (2007).

But social science and the humanities need not, and should not, be so reactive to definitions in the natural sciences. Instead we begin the discussion about validity from a more ordinary understanding of the term (which does not require either measurement or certainty) and go on to refine this into a more specialised, technical meaning suitable for discussing auto/biography.

We start from the common understanding of validity to be found in a dictionary definition. In this we follow J. L. Austin's comment that distinctions 'in ordinary language work well for practical purposes' and this is 'no mean feat': 'ordinary language is *not* the last word ... but it *is* the *first* word' (Austin, 1979, p. 185.) This strategy has the advantage that it builds on what generations of human beings have needed to say when making judgements about the stories they are told. The strategy leaves us free not to start from measurement. 'Valid' was not originally a word especially associated with measurement. Rather it comes from the Latin *validus*, meaning 'strong'. The dictionary definition makes clear that there are various well-known ways in which this can be understood. Merriam-Webster (2006–7) provides the following four current definitions: (1) legal efficacy or force; (2) well grounded or justifiable: being at once relevant and meaningful; (3) having a conclusion correctly derived from premises; (4) appropriate to the end in view—effective (as in 'every craft has its valid method'). The first of these is evidently not relevant here. The second, third and fourth are applicable, however. We take each in turn, briefly describing the kinds of issue that need to be taken into account.

The second definition of validity draws attention to the way that a story might be truthful—both accurately and sincerely told—and yet not be germane to the matter in hand. For an auto/biography to be relevant and significant it needs to be shown to be so with regard to its representativeness and/or the possibility it provides of re-framing the understanding of what is at issue. Sometimes auto/biographies are significant precisely because they are ordinary. That is, they show something of the lived experience of ordinary life in all its complexity and everyday differences between contexts. For instance, the stories of the student and the teachers in Cotton and Griffiths' (2007) study are like this. They are unique, individual, personal—but they are not atypical. That is their significance. In contrast, auto/biographies may be significant precisely because they are *not* ordinary. The significance may arise because auto/biography is rarely heard from such an individual. Think, for instance, of very high and very low achievers in educational terms. And, again, some voices are much easier to hear than others, as feminist and Black scholarship has demonstrated over the last few decades. The auto/biographies of people marginalised for reasons of gender, race, disability and social class have much to offer to those decision makers striving for equality in education. Finally, an auto/biography may be relevant because of the way it helps its audience reframe an issue, by make the familiar strange, and giving a different perspective on what was previously taken for granted.[6]

The third definition of validity draws attention to the kinds of conclusion that would be drawn from a truthful narrative, even after issues of representativeness, bias and the possibilities of reframing have been considered. This is the area of criticality, and it points to a very large area in narrative studies, one that we can only allude to here. The key issues here are representation, genre and literary quality. Representation refers to the way that an auto/biography is presented not only by the teller but also by the researcher who is re-presenting it. All representation involves choices and judgements. The editing and framing of the story obviously require judgement. But so does the form in which it is told, what choices have been made about the medium in which is presented, and whether it is presented as finished and definite or as just one possible presentation among many. Closely related to representation are the issues of genre and literary quality. The first refers to the way that any story is influenced by the genres available to the teller—both those of the original teller and those of the researcher. These include the wish for an expected happy and tragic ending, indeed for an ending at all: in short, for the auto/biography to work *as* a story. Literary quality draws on genre, but, for some researchers, it can also be a wider concern than this. For instance, one of Renuka Vithal's four conditions for what she refers to as a 'crucial description' is 'transformacy': the potential for it to effect transformative change in the reader (Vithal, 2002). This must be, at least partly, a matter of literary quality. Controversially, literary quality may also be associated with the use of fiction in the presentation of auto/biography. Walker and Unterhalter (2004) discuss the account of the Truth and Reconciliation Commission's evidence by the South African Broadcasting Corporation journalist, Antjie Krog (1998). In her book drawn from her two years reporting the Commission, she uses fiction about herself in order to present the stories more truthfully. This relates to the fourth of the dictionary definitions above, too, since literary quality is part of the craft of story-telling.

The third definition not only draws attention to criticality but also to reflexivity. Conclusions are never drawn straightforwardly from stories. They are layered, and subject to a range of interpretations. They may be constructed and re-constructed according to the intentions and ideologies of the audience and the researcher. Gaps are noted. The teller's intentions are assessed. The relation between the teller, audience and researcher is brought into focus. The personal story of the researcher also becomes significant, as does the relation that is drawn between the story and other educational research and policies. Explicit reflexivity on the part of the researcher allows the reader to be reflexive too.

Truthful and Valid Auto/biography

We have argued that it is the responsibility of the researcher to present an auto/biography in such a way that judgements can be made about its truthfulness and validity. And it is also the responsibility of the researcher to present the auto/biography so that the audience for the research is in a position to be able to make these kinds of critical assessment too. This is the difference between auto/biographical research and other kinds of personal story (auto/biography in general, anecdote, parable, gossip, etc). We have argued that sound auto/biographical research needs to show that the researcher has taken account of the following:

(1) Truthfulness: accuracy and sincerity
(2) Representativeness
(3) Representation
(4) Re-framing of the matter at hand
(5) Genre
(6) Literary quality
(7) Reflexivity

Finally, and crucially, epistemologically sound auto/biographical research should be presented in such a way that readers can form their own assessment of its soundness. As in all research the story the researcher tells has itself to be shown to be trustworthy.

5 CAN AND SHOULD POLICY-MAKERS USE AUTO/BIOGRAPHICAL RESEARCH?

In this final section, the chapter draws together the discussion on policy with that on the epistemological issues. It is proposed that at some stages of the policy cycle auto/biography and life writing research can, and in some cases can and should, be taken account of. Similarly it is suggested that auto/biography and life writing research is more or less appropriate for different levels and subjects of policy. Some examples are noted along with observations of where the scope of auto/biographical research could be extended.

In order to say that auto/biographical research *can* influence policy one might want to find examples of instances in which it *has* influenced policy. However assessing the impact of research is notoriously difficult (Nutley, Walter and Davies, 2007). As noted above the policy-making process is neither simple nor linear, and it is not always clear who is involved; even if it were linear and even if we had reports of what did or did not exert influence, we would probably not hear the full story. However perhaps all that is needed to demonstrate the potential to influence is examples of situations in which auto/biography had such potential in the past, and examples of this kind are easier to find. The work of Gow and McPherson (1980) has already been noted: this research continues to be cited in government documents over 20 years later (Scottish Parliament, 2002). Indeed government education departments throughout the UK are not only receptive to but actively seek out research that focuses on the experiences of individuals, much of which is collected in the form of personal stories. Munn *et al.'s* (2005) work on the deployment of additional staff to support behaviour in schools focused not only on what worked but also on why and in what contexts, exploring as it did the individual circumstances of staff and young people (Munn, 2005). The Department for Education and Skills (now the Department for Children, Schools and Families) has recently commissioned research on the experiences of young people permanently excluded from special schools and Pupil Referral Units in England and Wales, in which hearing the stories of these young people is a key element (Pirrie and Macleod, 2007).

So, taking our weaker criterion—that auto/biography might have influenced policy—it is clear that this is easily met. The question then becomes *ought* auto/biography to influence policy, and, if so, which types/levels of policy and at what stage. We have outlined the ways in which soundness can be established. We have shown that it is the responsibility of the researcher to show how readers can judge whether this has been done. We now go on to explore the different kinds of ways in which auto/biographical research might influence policy.

There are some areas of study to which auto/biographical research can be seen as being particularly well suited. First, the experiences of people at the margins, such as those whose lives intersect more than one dimension of difference such as race, class, gender, disability, or sexuality. Narrative research has been presented as a method for giving a stage to the voices of people who traditionally have had not been heard (e.g. Casey, 1995/6). As Biesta (2007) has observed, one of the roles of 'cultural' educational research is to allow the 'known' to be re-examined from a new perspective, perhaps shedding light on established hierarchies and problematising the taken-for-granted. Auto/biography, with its focus on examining the life of the individual in context, seems particularly well suited for this purpose. Studies that address the experiences of people at the margins of our education system examine what it is like for those for whom the generalisations generated by other forms of research are unlikely to hold true. Their 'little stories' have the potential to refine the 'bigger picture' drawn by other studies. But should taking account of the personal be restricted to those at the margins? What of the personal experiences of those who do not find themselves on the edge? If the political is indeed personal then that holds for all, including those in the 'mainstream' and so a case can be made for saying that policy-makers *ought* to take account of auto/biographical research conducted with 'the generality' and not only the extremes.

Secondly, research into experiences that unfold over time can be examined through longitudinal studies as people are followed over a number of years. However a number of years are not always at the researchers' (not to mention policy-makers') disposal. In such circumstances researchers who are interested in transitions often utilise life-history approaches. Examples of work of this type includes that by Watts and Bridges (2004) on aspirations of 16–19-year-olds, McDowell's (2001) work with working-class young men, and Jones, O'Sullivan and Rouse (2004) examining school-to-work transitions. All of these studies have at heart the questions of what it feels like being in those situations over time and what meanings people make of these experiences, and these cannot be answered except through an auto/biographical approach. Similarly Brannen, Stratham, Mooney and Brockmann's work on care careers, following the lives of childcare workers, is being conducted with the express purpose of informing policy on recruitment into this area of employment (Brannen *et al.*, 2007). So longitudinal accounts of what it is like to live through or in a particular system utilise research that draws on the stories of individuals involved.

Finally, there may be areas of research in which large-scale quantitative studies, whilst being able to paint broad strokes, fail to capture the nuances of extremely complex situations. An example of this is studies into youth resilience, in particular Michael Ungar's international work on the cultural specificity of resilience and the particular insights that can be gained from adding a narrative dimension to a research design (Ungar, 2004, 2006).

There are also stages of the policy process to which auto/biographical studies are particular suited. Bridges and Watts (this volume) describe the complexities of the policy-making process: it is an iterative process that can start at the bottom, in the middle or at the top (Nutley *et al.*, 2007).[7] Auto/biographical research may identify a problem that policy may be required to address, viewing things from a different perspective and thus identifying previously hidden issues—that is, it can contribute to the setting of the policy agenda. Auto/biography has a contribution to make to the refinement of policy, its evaluation and 'fine tuning'. Finally, because of the ability of auto/biography to capture the individual experience in the wider social context, and to represent complex and nuanced situations, this approach has a contribution to make not simply to questions of 'what works?' but issues such as why, when and in what circumstances what works works, and why, when and where it does not.

Thus auto/biography has a contribution to make to particular areas of study and to some parts of the policy-making process especially, but at the same time the policy discourse assumes that it lacks credibility as a sound way of conducting research to inform policy. The 'what works' agenda has become a discourse defining 'the limits of acceptable speech' (Butler, 1990) about the types of research that are taken seriously by policy-makers. However, whilst it has not been easy to find *evidence* of examples of auto/biographical research informing policy it is clear that contrary to popular belief auto/biographical research is alive and well. So dominant is the notion that the only research that is being commissioned is in the 'what works' tradition that examples of government-sponsored research that are more auto/biographical in approach pass under the radar; we assume it is not happening because, of course, it couldn't be. However, scratch the surface and there it is. For instance, consider the following: Evans, Pinnock, Beirens and Edwards, 2006; Brannen *et al.*, 2007; Cameron, Bennert, Simon and Wigfall, 2007; Cunningham and Hargreaves, 2007. They are all research projects using at least an element of auto/biographical method and all published on the Department for Children, Schools and Families website.

In short, research continues to use auto/biographical approaches where these are the best way of addressing the issue or question to hand. However the power of the policy discourse is such that these approaches barely dare to speak their name, but rather hide under blanket terms such as 'qualitative' and 'case-study'. Ungar (2006) gives some interesting examples. He writes about strategies he has used to persuade funders to give money for qualitative research (including life history work)—including 'dressing up' to make it look like quantitative research and 'sleeping with the elephant'—tacking a qualitative aspect onto a larger quantitative study. In this chapter we have suggested criteria by which the soundness of auto/biographical research may be assessed. It is hoped that by so doing policy-makers may be able to have more confidence in taking account of research of this type, without comparing it against criteria designed for different approaches.

On the grand level of what education is for auto/biographical research can offer insights. Smeyers and Verhesschen write that 'Freeing us from the idea that education must have a fixed and unified meaning will change what we want to do in education' (Smeyers and Verhesschen, 2001, p. 80). They are talking about philosophy, but their argument also works for auto/biography, not surprisingly since the title of the article is 'Narrative Analysis as Philosophical Research'.

Auto/biographical research has properly been used by policy-makers and could be used more. It should continue to be a significant part of the evidence base for policy. Auto/biographical research is an essential contribution to the practical knowledge needed by policy-makers. We have shown that it has a sound epistemological basis, when it is presented critically and reflexively, and with attention paid to how far it is truthful and valid: accurate, sincere, representative.

Correspondence: Morwenna Griffiths, Department of Curriculum Research & Development, Moray House School of Education, University of Edinburgh, Thomson's Land, Holyrood Road, Edinburgh EH8 8AQ, UK.
E-mail: Morwenna.Griffiths@ed.ac.uk; Gale.Macleod@ed.ac.uk

NOTES

1. Of course, with space limited we omit much more than we include. The decisions about what to leave out should not in any way be taken as a judgement of their importance or potential contribution to the question at hand: it is simply that the issues that we do take up are those which we judge most germane to the focus of this chapter. For example it is not within the remit of this chapter to conduct a detailed examination of the defining features of narrative research, e.g. Ricoeur's work on the relationship between temporality and narrative; the notion of human life as 'storied'; the rhetorical power of narrative; conceptualisations of the 'self'; developmental aspects of narrative; the general philosophical discussion of epistemology and 'testimony'; psycho-social approaches to narrative and memory; etc.

2. There is much more that could be added here about the phenomenology of human presence. For instance, see Sartre's (1958, especially pp. 258–9) influential discussion of the Look and how it cuts through the attempt to make the Other into an object. Similarly Gaita (1998) discusses the sense of the preciousness of each human being which he distinguishes from concepts such as

inalienable human rights, or persons as ends in themselves. There is also something to be said about how we can lose that sense or have it brought into our attention. He quotes Weil: 'if you want to become invisible, there is no surer way than to become poor' (Gaita, 1998, p. 10).

3. In a number of publications Griffiths has argued for the view that reliable knowledge is always provisional and revisable (Griffiths 1995a, 1995b, 1998, 2003).
4. For more on facts and their interpretation, see Griffiths, 1998, Chapter 4.
5. We have not included a discussion of the truthfulness to be found in fiction. It is an interesting, relevant subject but we have not the space to examine it here.
6. See Smeyers' useful discussion of 'opening up the sphere of responsiveness', drawing on Wittgenstein and Cavell (Smeyers, 2007).
7. As Nutley, Walter and Davies (2007) clearly show, policy-making is not a simple linear process which always operates from the top down, rather it is a complex and interactive process between practitioners, organisations and policy settings. Educational policy can be characterised as varying across four key dimensions. First is the substantive area addressed, e.g. pupil assessment, teacher training, social justice. Second is the level at which the policy is to be applied, e.g. pupil, classroom, school, or authority. Third is the stage of the policy cycle: identification of the problem and agenda setting, analysis, creation, legislation and/or adoption, implementation, and evaluation. Fourth is the source of policy change (Doyle, 1997; Nutley, Walter and Davies 2007): research; locally accepted mythologies and symbols; models of change (e.g. a technical-rational 'prescribe and intervene' versus a 'diagnose and understand' approach); and personal experience. All of these are moderated by the influence of global trends and the extent to which travelling policy becomes colonised by local context and embedded policy (Ozga, 2006).

REFERENCES

Altheide, D. and Johnson, J. (1998) Criteria for Assessing Interpretive Validity in Qualitative Research, in: N. Denzin and Y. Lincoln (eds) *Collecting and Interpreting Qualitative Materials* (London, Sage).

Arad, B. D. and Leichtentritt, R. D. (2005) Young Male Street Workers: Life Histories and Current Experiences, *British Journal of Social Work*, 35.4, pp. 483–509.

Arendt, H. (1958) *The Human Condition* (London and Chicago, University of Chicago Press).

Arendt, H. (1963) *On Revolution* (London, Faber & Faber).

Atkinson, R. (1998) *The Life Story Interview* (Thousand Oaks, CA, Sage).

Austin, J. L. (1979) *Philosophical Papers*, 3rd edn. (Oxford, Oxford University Press).

Avramidis, E. and Norwich, B. (2002) Teachers' Attitudes Towards Integration/Inclusion: A Review of the Literature, *European Journal of Special Needs Education*, 17.2, pp. 129–47.

Biesta, G. (2007) Why 'What Works' Won't Work. Evidence-Based Practice and the Democratic Deficit Of Educational Research, *Educational Theory*, 57.1, pp. 1–22.

Brannen, J., Statham, J., Mooney, A. and Brockmann, M. (2007) Care Careers: The Work and Family Lives of Workers Caring for Vulnerable Children, Thomas Coram Research Institute *Research Brief* available online at http://www.dfes.gov.uk/research/data/uploadfiles/TCRU-02-07.pdf [accessed 25/7/7].

Bridges, D. (2003) *Fiction Written Under Oath?* (London, Kluwer Academic Publishers).

Bruner, J. (1986) *Actual Minds, Possible Worlds* (Cambridge, MA, Harvard University Press).

Bullough, R. V. (1998) Musings on Life Writing: Biography and Case Studies in Teacher Education, in: C. Kridel (ed.) *Writing Educational Biography: Explorations in Qualitative Research* (New York, Garland), pp. 19–32.

Butler, J. (1990) *Gender Trouble: Feminism and the Subversion of Identity* (New York, Routledge).

Cameron, C., Bennert, K., Simon, A. and Wigfall, V. (2007) Using Health, Education, Housing and Other Services: A Study of Care Leavers and Young People in Difficulty, *Research Brief* available online at http://www.dfes.gov.uk/research/data/uploadfiles/TCRU-01-07.pdf [accessed 25th July 2007].

Carroll, L. (1974) *The Annotated Snark* (ed. and intro. M. Gardner) (Harmondsworth, Penguin).

Casey, K. (1995/6) The New Narrative Research in Education, *Review of Research in Education*, 21, pp. 211–253.

Cavarero, A. (2002) Politicizing Theory, *Political Theory*, 30.4, pp. 506–532.

Chaitin, J. (2004) My Story, My Life, My Identity, *The International Journal of Qualitative Methods*, 3.4, pp. 1–17.

Clough, P. (1996) 'Again Fathers and Sons': The Mutual Construction of Self, Story and Special Educational Needs, *Disability & Society*, 11.1, pp. 71–81.

Clough, P. (2002) *Narratives and Fictions in Educational Research* (Buckingham, Open University Press).

Connelly, F. M. and Clandinin, D. J. (1990) Stories of Experience and Narrative Enquiry, *Educational Researcher*, 19.5, pp. 2–14.

Griffiths, M. and Cotton, T. (2007) Action Research, Stories and Practical Philosophy, *Educational Action Research*, 15.4, pp. 545–560.

Couser, G. T. (2002) Signifying Bodies: Life Writing and Disability Studies, in: S. L. Snyder, B. J. Brueggemann and R. Garland-Thomson (eds) *Disability Studies: Enabling the Humanities* (New York, Modern Language Association of America).

Cunningham, M. and Hargreaves, L. (2007) *Minority Ethnic Teachers' Professional Experiences: Evidence from the Teacher Status Project, Research Brief No. RB853* (London, Department for Education and Skills).

Curtis, K. (2002) Review Essay of Cavarero and Riley, *Political Theory*, 30.6, pp. 852–857.

Czarniawska, B. (2004) *Narratives in Social Science Research* (London, Sage).

Dennett, D. (1995) *Darwin's Dangerous Idea* (London, Allen Lane).

Doyle, W. (1997) Heard Any Really Good Stories Lately? A Critique of the Critics of Narrative in Educational Research, *Teaching and Teacher Education*, 13.1, pp. 93–99.

Dunne, J. (1993) *Back to the Rough Ground: Practical Judgement and the Lure of Technique* (South Bend, IN, University of Notre Dame Press).

Dunne, J. and Pendlebury, S. (2003) Practical Reason, in: N. Blake, P. Smeyers, R. Smith and P. Standish (eds) *The Blackwell Guide to the Philosophy of Education* (Oxford, Blackwell).

Eick, C. J. (2002) Studying Career Science Teachers' Personal Histories: A Methodology for Understanding Intrinsic Reasons for Career Choice and Retention, *Research in Science Education*, 32.3, pp. 353–72.

Evans, R., Pinnock, K., Beirens, H. and Edwards, A. (2006) Developing Preventative Practices: The Experiences of Children, Young People and their Families in the Children's Fund, *Research Brief RB735*; Department for Education and Skills.

Feldman, A. (2007) Validity and Quality in Action Research, *Educational Action Research*, 15.1, pp. 21–32.

Fischer-Rosenthal, W. (1995) The Problem with Identity: Biography as Solution to Some (Post)-Modernist Dilemmas, *Comenius*, 15.3, pp. 250–265.

Franzosi, R. (1998) Narrative Analysis—or Why (and How) Sociologists Should Be Interested in Narrative, *Annual Review of Sociology*, 24, pp. 517–554.

Fraser, H. (2004) Doing Narrative Research: Analysing Personal Stories Line by Line, *Qualitative Social Work*, 3.2, pp. 179–201.

Frogget, L. and Chamberlayne, P. (2004) Narratives of Social Enterprise: From Biography to Practice And Policy Critique, *Qualitative Social Work*, 3.1, pp. 61–77.

Foucault, M. (1984) What is Enlightenment?, in: P. Rabinow (ed.) *The Foucault Reader* (London, Penguin), pp. 32–50.

Gaita, R. (1998) *A Common Humanity* (London, Routledge).

Glasby, J. and Lester, H. (2005) On the Inside: A Narrative Review of Mental Health Inpatient Services, *British Journal of Social Work*, 35, pp. 863–879.

Gitlin, A. and Russell, R. (1994) Alternative Methodologies and the Research Context, in: A. Gitlin (ed) *Power and Method: Political Activism and Educational Research* (New York, Routledge).

Gow, L. and McPherson, A. (eds) (1980) *Tell Them From Me* (Aberdeen, Aberdeen University Press).

Griffiths, M. (1995a) *Feminisms and the Self: The Web of Identity* (London and New York, Routledge).

Griffiths, M. (1995b) Biography and Epistemology, *Educational Review*, 47.1, pp. 75–88.

Griffiths, M. (1998) *Educational Research for Social Justice: Getting off the Fence* (Buckingham, Open University Press).

Griffiths, M. (2003) *Action for Social Justice in Education: Fairly Different* (Maidenhead, Open University Press).

Hammersley, M. (2002) *Educational Research: Policymaking and Practice* (London, Paul Chapman).

Heikkinen, H. L. T., Huttunen, R. and Kakkori, L. (2000) 'And This Story is True': On the Problem of Narrative Truth. Paper presented to ECER, Edinburgh, September, www.leeds. ac.uk/educol/documents/00002351.htm (Accessed 28 February, 2007).

Heikkinen, H., Kakkori, L. and Huttunen, R. (2001) This is My Truth, Tell Me Yours: Some Aspects of Action Research Quality in the Light of Truth Theories, *Educational Action Research*, 9.1, pp. 9–24.

Heikkinen, H. L. T., Huttunen, R. and Syrjälä, L (2007) Action Research as Narrative: Five Principles for Validation, *Educational Action Research*, 15.1, pp. 5–19.

Hogan, P. (2000) Virtue, Vice and Vacancy in Educational Policy and Practice, *British Journal of Educational Studies*, 48.4, pp. 371–390.

Jolly, M. (ed.) (2001) *Encyclopedia of Life Writing: Autobiographical and Biographical Forms* (Chicago, Fitzroy Dearborn Publishers).

Jones, G., O'Sullivan, A. and Rouse, J. (2004) 'Because it's Worth It?': Education Beliefs Among Young People and their Parents in the United Kingdom, *Youth & Society*, 36.2, pp. 203–226.

Jordens, C. F. C. and Little, M. (2004) 'In this Scenario, I Do This, for These Reasons': Narrative, Genre and Ethical Reasoning in the Clinic, *Social Science & Medicine*, 58.9, pp. 1635–1645.

Krog, A. (1998) *Country of My Skull* (London, Cape).

Kvernbekk, T. (2003) On Identifying Narratives, *Studies in Philosophy and Education*, 22, pp. 267–279.

Lather, P. (1994) Fertile Obsession: Validity After Poststructuralism, in: A. Gitlin (ed) *Power and Method: Political Activism and Educational Research* (New York, Routledge).

Lawson, H., Parker, M. and Sikes, P. (2006) Seeking Stories: Reflections on a Narrative Approach to Researching Understanding of Inclusion, *European Journal of Special Needs Education*, 21.1, pp. 55–68.

MacLure, M. (2003) *Discourse in Educational and Social Research* (Buckingham, Open University Press).

Mauthner, M. (2000) Snippets and Silences: Ethics and Reflexivity in Narratives of Sistering, *International Journal of Social Research Methodology*, 3.4, pp. 287–306.

McCloskey, D. N. (1990) Storytelling in Economics, in: C. Nash (ed.) *Narrative in Culture: The Uses of Storytelling in the Sciences, Philosophy, and Literature* (London, Routledge), pp 5–22.

McDowell, L. (2001) 'It's That Linda Again': Ethical, Practical and Political Issues Involved in Longitudinal Research with Young Men, *Ethics, Place and Environment*, 4.2, pp. 87–100.

McNulty, M. A. (2003) Dyslexia and the Life Course, *Journal of Learning Disabilities*, 36.4, pp. 363–81.

Merriam-Webster Online Dictionary (2006-7) 'valid', http://www.m-w.com/dictionary/valid [accessed 3 August, 2007].

Munn, P. (2005) Researching Policy and Policy Research, *Scottish Educational Review*, 37.1.

Munn, P., Riddell, S., Lloyd, G., Macleod, G., Stead, J., Kane, J. and Fairley, J. (2005) Evaluation of the Discipline Task Group Recommendations: The Deployment of Additional Staff to Promote Positive School Discipline. Research Report to the Scottish Executive Education Department. Available at www.scotland.gov.uk/Home

Nutley, S. M., Walter, I. and Davies, H. T. O. (2007) *Using Evidence: How Research Can Inform Public Services* (Bristol, Policy Press).

Ozga, J. (2004) From Research to Policy and Practice: Some Issues in Knowledge Transfer, *CES Briefing No.31*. Centre for Educational Sociology University of Edinburgh. Available online at www/ces.ed.ac.uk/PDF%20Files/Brief031.pdf [accessed 8th May 2007].

Ozga, J. and Jones, R. (2006) Travelling and Embedded Policy: The Case of Knowledge Transfer, *Journal of Education Policy*, 21.1, pp. 1–17.

Pirrie, A. and Macleod, G. (2007) Tracking Pupils Excluded From PRUs And Special Schools: Some Methodological Concerns. Paper presented at *Work With Young People Conference* Leicester 14th–15th June 2007.

Pollard, A. (2005) Explorations in Teaching and Learning: A Biographical Narrative and Some Enduring Issues, *International Studies in Sociology of Education*, 15.1, pp. 87–105.

Polkinghorne, D. E. (1995) Narrative Configuration in Qualitative Analysis, in: J. A. Hatch and R. Wisniewski (eds) *Life History and Narrative* (London, Falmer Press), pp 5–23.

Reissman, C. K. (1993) *Narrative Analysis* (Thousand Oaks, CA, Sage).

Richardson, L. (1992) The Poetic Representation of Lives: Writing a Postmodern Sociology, *Studies in Symbolic Interaction*, 13, pp. 19–29.

Sanders, J. and Munford, R. (2005) Activity and Reflection: Research and Change with Diverse Groups of Young People, *Qualitative Social Work*, 4.2, pp. 197–209.

Santoro, N., Kamler, B. and Reid, J. (2001) Teachers Talking Difference: Teacher Education and the Poetics of Anti-Racism, *Teaching Education*, 12.2, pp. 191–212.

Sartre, J-P. (1958) *Being and Nothingness*, H. Barnes, trans. (London, Methuen).

Saunders, L. (2003) On Flying, Writing Poetry and Doing Educational Research, *British Educational Research Journal*, 29,2, pp, 175–187.

Scottish Parliament (2002) http://www.scottish.parliament.uk/business/committees/historic/education/or-02/ed02-1902.htm [accessed 2nd May 2007].

Searle, J. R. (1964) How to Derive an 'Ought' from an 'Is', *The Philosophical Review*, 73.1, pp. 43–58.

Smeyers, P. (2007) The Hidden Homogenisation of Educational Research: On Opening Up the Sphere of Educational Responsiveness, in: P. Smeyers and M. Depaepe (eds.) *Educational Research: Networks and Technologies* (Dordrecht, Springer).

Smeyers, P. and Verhesschen, P. (2001) Narrative Analysis as Philosophical Research: Bridging the Gap Between the Empirical and the Conceptual, *International Journal of Qualitative Studies in Education*, 14.1, pp. 71–84.

Smith, S. and Watson, J. (2001) *Reading Autobiography: A Guide for Interpreting Life Narratives* (Minnesota, University of Minnesota Press).

Stanley, L. (1993) On Auto/biography in Sociology, *Sociology*, 27.1, pp. 41–52.

Stroobants, V. (2005) Stories about Learning in Narrative Biographical Research, *International Journal of Qualitative Studies in Education*, 18.1, pp. 47–61.

Thompson, P. (2004) Pioneering the Life-story Method, *International Journal of Social Research Methodology*, 7.1, pp. 81–84.

Townsend, L. and Weiner, G. (forthcoming) *Deconstructing and Reconstructing Lives: Using Autobiography in Educational Settings* (London, ON, Althouse Press).

Ungar, M. (2004) *Nurturing Hidden Resilience in Troubled Youth* (Toronto, University of Toronto Press).

Ungar, M. (2006) 'Too Ambitious': What Happens When Funders Misunderstand the Strengths of Qualitative Research Design, *Qualitative Social Work*, 5.2, pp. 261–277.

Vithal, R. (2002) Crucial Descriptions: Talking Back to Theory and Practice in Mathematics Education Through Research, *Proceedings of the Third International Mathematics Education and Society Conference*, pp. 501–511. Helsingor, Denmark. Available at http://www.mes3.learning.aau.dk/Papers/Vithal.pdf [accessed January, 2008].

Walker, M. and Unterhalter, E. (2004) Knowledge, Narrative and National Reconciliation: Storied Reflections on the South African Truth and Reconciliation Commission, *Discourse: Studies in the Cultural Politics of Education*, 25.2, pp. 279–297.

Watts, M. and Bridges, D. (2004) *Whose Aspirations? What Achievement?: An Investigation of the Life and Lifestyle Aspirations of 16–19 Year Olds Outside the Formal Educational System* (Cambridge, East of England Development Agency).

Wetle, T., Shield, R., Teno, J., Miller, S. C. and Welch, L. (2005) Family Perspectives on End-of-Life Care Experiences in Nursing Homes, *Gerontologist*, 45.5, pp. 642–650.

Williams, B. (2002) *Truth and Truthfulness: An Essay in Genealogy* (Princeton, NJ, Princeton University Press).

7

Action Research and Policy

LORRAINE FOREMAN-PECK AND JANE MURRAY

This chapter examines the relationship between action research and policy and the kind of confidence teachers, policy-makers and other potential users may have in such research. Many published teacher action research accounts are criticised on the grounds that they do not fully meet the conventional standards for reporting social scientific research, and by implication are held to be less trustworthy. Action research is nevertheless often seen by some academics and policy-makers as a potential method for developing theory, disseminating good practice, or raising standards. Through a discussion of three major approaches to action research—seen variously as professional learning, practical philosophy and critical social science—it is argued that judgements about confidence depend upon understanding the various kinds of knowledge claim that can be made by action researchers, and appropriate judgements concerning the strength of evidence or reasons.

INTRODUCTION

The move to make teaching an evidence-based profession has led to a proliferation of government sponsored research initiatives, encouraging teachers to engage with the research findings of others, including teachers' own research, and to undertake research themselves.[1] Teachers have often responded positively to such a refocusing of attention, but they do not always see the usefulness or relevance of educational research findings to their own situations. Indeed it has been argued that generalisations derived from much educational research based on large samples may be positively misleading, since findings derived from large-scale studies are not necessarily reflected in the much smaller numbers that teachers are concerned with (Bassey, 1995 but see also Smeyers in this volume). To generate one's own findings, or to read the research findings of other teachers in similar situations, may seem a much better option, in terms of relevance and usefulness. But are teachers who are attracted to researching their own practice right to be confident in their findings? Are their fellow professionals right to be confident in the findings of their colleagues?

Generally speaking, the confidence we place in any knowledge claim based on research findings is rooted in an evaluation of the reasons, evidence and argument that support the claim. The concern of this chapter is to examine the kind of claims that action researchers may make, and hence what considerations teachers and others would need to take into account in judging their adequacy.

ACTION RESEARCH

In the most general terms, 'action research' names a form of practitioner research that is carried out by professionals into a practice problem that they themselves are in some way responsible for. Unlike other forms of practitioner research, which involve studying a situation in retrospect, action research involves a process part of which is carried out simultaneously with taking action with the intention of improving a situation. For example, to confine ourselves to classroom-based action research, a teacher investigating an aspect of assessment may introduce an innovative method of assessment and use recorded class discussions, work produced, student diaries, and so on, not only as part of the process of teaching but also as research evidence. This forms the evidential basis for making a knowledge claim. Findings may be discussed with colleagues or students who may themselves be actively engaged in the research. Some action research involves a partnership with an 'outsider' researcher. Starting points for such inquiries may be a perceived problem with current practice, or simply a desire to find a more solid basis for making decisions.

First, however, we should emphasise that action research does not pick out a particular set of research methods or have a common methodology (Noffke, 1997, p. 308); a wide range of data collection methods may be employed, including classroom observation, questionnaires, research logs, and interviews of various kinds. Action researchers employ cameras, sound or video recorders, field notes, score sheets. They may employ qualitative or quantitative analysis. Like any other researchers they may do any of this more or less thoroughly, systematically or rigorously. It is therefore not easy to generalise about the soundness or otherwise of the findings of action research. We would expect the way in which action research reports invite acceptance of their findings to exhibit differences in research methods and purposes and differences in the care and thoroughness with which it has been carried out.

However, most action researchers would acknowledge that the research is framed by a cycle of steps typically described as including problem definition; planning an intervention; implementing and evaluating the outcome (in some sense of those terms); and (in the full cyclical model) a reformulation of the problem to be researched further.[2] In addition it is a form of research that involves others, usually one's students or colleagues, who have a stake in the solution, unlike conventional research in which the researcher is most likely to be unknown to participants in the research and uninvolved, as a worker, in the site of the research (Cochran-Smith and Lytle, 1993).

Within this broad framework action research theorists draw on different intellectual and research traditions developing distinctive approaches.[3] Noffke likens action research to a 'large family' in which 'beliefs and relationships vary greatly' (1997, p. 306). Moreover theorising about action research is continuously evolving as new perspectives are suggested (see e.g. Edwards, 2000; Coulter, 2002; Phelps and Hase, 2002; Walker, 2005; Radford, 2007).

In the following we shall distinguish three different conceptions of action research and discuss the kind of knowledge characteristic of each.

ACTION RESEARCH AS PROFESSIONAL LEARNING

Teachers do not always see themselves as contributing, first and foremost, to a shared body of public knowledge, in a conventional sense. Their written studies are often (but not always) limited to accounts of professional experiential learning, rather than the production of fully substantiated research reports.

The conceptualisation of action research as professional learning is clear in one UK Government sponsored initiative, at least. In the case of the DfES-sponsored Best Practice Research Scholarship programme the reporting framework for 'teacher-scholars' suggests that they report what they did, what they learnt and the evidence they had for their learning. They were not asked to provide a literature discussion or to identify where there were gaps in current knowledge. Neither accounts of methodology nor the analysis of data were required (Costello, 2003).[4] Thus in their evaluation of the BPRS, Furlong *et al.* commented that of the 100 teacher reports they examined, the majority did not 'resemble research products' (Furlong *et al.*, 2003). Furlong *et al.* argued that the majority had produced what is sometimes referred to as Mode 2 knowledge, i.e. knowledge that is problem based and contextualised to a specific location and time, as opposed to Mode 1 knowledge that is academic, researcher rather than practitioner led, and discipline based (Gibbons *et al.*, 1994).

As a result, as Noffke observes, some forms of action research, where the emphasis is on highly localised social change, will not be visible through official sources such as academic publications (Noffke, 1997, p. 309). Much action research occurs 'outside of the usual circles of academic publication and indexing' (Noffke, 1997, p. 333). Action research is often only recorded in the 'memories of those who participated' (Bassey, 1999, p. 41). Clearly many teachers' reports are accounts of their professional learning that are not intended to meet conventional standards of empirical research reporting such as those provided by the American Educational Research Association (AERA, 2006).

Critics of such accounts see them as deficient research (Foster, 1999; Roulston *et al.*, 2005; Bartlett and Burton, 2006). However, some action research reports published in refereed journals by academics exhibit the same lack of conformity to traditional conventions (e.g. Fielding, 2001). Some writers argue that conventional 'academic' ways of judging knowledge claims are inappropriate (Temperley and Horne, 2003); some that new criteria are needed (Heikkinen, Huttunen and Syrjala, 2005).

Nor are such teacher action research reports properly understood as 'professional' papers intended for a professional audience. The British Educational Research Association's guidance points out that a policy or professional audience will want confidence that the research is not 'flawed', and so 'a reference to the refereed academic paper is appropriate' (BERA, 2000, p. 7). A professional paper is a condensed account drawing on fully substantiated research published elsewhere.[5] This is not, on the whole, what action research reports set out to provide.

However, many teachers' research accounts, whether intended or not by their authors to be a contribution to a publicly shared body of knowledge, *are* published or otherwise disseminated. Sometimes this is because they provide an example of good professional learning or development, so that what is offered to a wider professional or policy community is an example, a story perhaps, which illustrates what is regarded as a useful approach to professional development. In other words, it is not so much the 'research findings' that are significant but rather the action research approach to professional development itself. Sometimes they are thought to offer for consideration what other teachers have learnt or found 'to work', perhaps because they offer an especially well-grounded illustration of a problem that other teachers will recognise and of an approach to it that they might try. In this last instance they will then raise some of the issues about learning from the single case discussed in the chapter by Elliott and Lukeš in this volume—and this brings us closer to a second conception of action research.

ACTION RESEARCH AS A FORM OF PRACTICAL PHILOSOPHY

The idea of action research as a form of practical philosophy directed to the realisation of educational values is most closely associated with Elliott (Elliott, 1982, 2005, 2006, p. 169, 2007). Here the aim is for the teacher to research her own practice, usually in collaboration with others, and to align it more satisfactorily with her own educational values and theories. On this model empirical evidence about what is happening in a classroom is collected, analysed systematically and subjected to validity checks, such as triangulation.

Where there are discrepancies between a teacher's values and what is occurring, solutions are trialled, data collected, analysed and evaluated. Elliott's 1982 diagram of the action research process shows three cycles of reconnaissance, planning, implementation and monitoring of action (Elliott, 1982). The emphasis in Elliott's early writing is placed on individual teacher autonomy. The presumption is that the teacher is free to investigate areas of curriculum practice that interest her. Since the introduction of the National Curriculum, the aims of education are not less contested (Winch, 2002; Pring, 2005) or, at least, less open to debate, but teachers' research questions are more likely to have become tied to problems arising from implementing government initiatives, such as the introduction of teaching assistants or the National Literacy Strategy.[6] In a later work Elliott acknowledges the importance of democratic and systemic factors that impinge on teachers' classroom practice. He suggests that administrators, parents, employers and others with relevant roles should be involved in deliberation on data about classroom practices (Elliott, 1993).

Elliott's model is clearly directed at teachers' professional learning and in some cases the development of school policy about some aspect of currently problematic practice. The kind of knowledge aimed at is self-evaluative, derived from reflecting on evidence and educational aims, in the context of developing curriculum initiatives intended to improve practice, in particular by aligning it more closely with the educational values and principles that the teacher or school community is trying to realise. Thus deliberation on ends or the aims of education (what are the educational values and principles that they are trying to realise?) is essential, as well as empirical evidence about what is happening and whether any intervention has been successful.

An example of such an approach is provided by Brearley and Van-Es (2002). As members of the Manchester and Salford Schools Consortium, they set out to understand factors affecting the speaking and listening skills of children in groups. They wished to find strategies that would not only improve their own speaking and listening, but also encourage children to listen attentively and talk fluently and coherently. They wished to examine the idea that their students' poor performance in science was linked to poor listening and speaking skills. Their method was to collaborate with one another to evaluate their own use of language, the children's use of language and the quality of the interaction in small group discussions, through reflecting on and discussing video evidence. Evaluations were made using an analytical framework provided by a university mentor. This enabled a systematic approach to the evaluation of the data, and comparisons could be made between episodes over time. The videos were analysed independently by another teacher and the university mentor, providing triangulation in judgements. The written case study takes the reader through the cycles of thinking, planning and action, the questions they were concerned with at each stage, and ends with a list of actions that they argued would benefit the children 'so that they were more able to participate in group discussions' (Brearley and Van-Es, 2002, p. 81).

As is the case with many teacher action research reports, no explicit model of action research is acknowledged. Brearley and Van-Es's research seems however to fit Elliott's action research approach, as we understand it. There are however omissions. The authors do not present any discussion of their aims or educational values. Although the research is systematic, no example of evidence of the verbal interaction is presented. As a piece of 'academic' research we could say that it falls short of conventional standards because there is no link to a theoretical body of knowledge. However the research reveals that the teachers gained insight into their teaching. Admitted shortcomings, such as talking over children, not allowing pupil to pupil talk and allowing boys to talk more than girls, were noted.

This study is a good example of action research being used to inform the decision making of the teachers involved. Although it aims at participants' self-knowledge, it seems likely that other teachers facing similar sorts of demands with similar classes would find this an interesting stimulus to thinking about their own practice (but not a substitute for such thinking!). The authors provide sufficient contextual information for this to be a possibility. Although the authors do not present an explicit discussion of the normative issues surrounding means and ends, the values that they hold can be inferred. This is important in terms of the interest and use to other teachers. It seems unlikely that teachers or schools will find an action research report pertinent if the educational values it subscribes to are not shared.

Such considerations highlight the point that 'what works' in classroom practice is not only shaped by local context (which is one part of the rationale for locally focused research) but also by the educational values and principles that teachers and school communities are trying to realise. Elliott's approach emphasises the local and not just national deliberation around such values and their significance for directing local research aimed at their realisation. Reports of such activity may inform wider policy deliberation but are never a substitute for such deliberation—on values as well as on functionality.

ACTION RESEARCH AS A FORM OF CRITICAL SOCIAL SCIENCE

An alternative to action research as practical philosophy, is action research as a form of critical theorising with emancipatory intent (Carr and Kemmis, 1986; Carr, 2006; Kemmis, 2006). Carr and Kemmis (1986) produced an influential epistemological typology, which has framed the way in which action research is discussed. In arguing for a critical theory version of action research, they delineated and criticised a technicist version and argued that a practical or interpretive version was insufficient for the development of teachers' knowledge and action. Very briefly, *technical* action research has positivist epistemological assumptions and seeks causal explanations and predictive generalisations. *Interpretative* or practical action research is hermeneutic, aiming at uncovering actors' meanings and aims and a deeper understanding of situations from actors' various perspectives. *Critical* action research is directed towards an idea of emancipatory knowledge and involves uncovering false beliefs about practice. It is carried out through a process of dialectical reasoning rather than systematic empirical research and aims at the development of theorems, that is 'propositions about the character and conduct of social life' such as 'cooperative teaching can only develop under conditions of continuing negotiation of the content and classroom practices through which the curriculum is expressed' (Carr and Kemmis, 1986, p. 146).

It is this last version, deriving from critical social science, that the authors wish to recommend as providing the most appropriate theoretical rationale for the teacher as researcher movement (p. 1). The authors distinguish action research as critical social science from those critical theories that simply aim at transforming consciousness without necessarily changing practice. Drawing on Habermas, the authors recommend a form of collaborative research that combines critique with political determination to overcome contradictions in the 'rationality and justice of social action and social institutions' (p. 144). Critical theorems are examined for their analytical coherence and must be tested against evidence. Critical social science is conducted by the group acting and reflecting; it is a 'systematic learning process aimed at the development of knowledge about the practices being developed and the conditions under which they take place' (p. 146).

The criterion for the success of such action research is that the insights achieved are authentic for the individuals involved and mutually comprehensible. The participants must aim at understanding on their own behalf (without constraint or coercion) and allow all involved the opportunity to raise questions, affirm or deny validity claims, and 'test their own point of view in self reflective discussion' (ibid.). Actions may be evaluated in terms of, among other things, their prudence, that is to say that the decisions are such that those involved can carry them out without unnecessary risks. Common commitment to action requires prudence. Decisions must be taken democratically and those involved must be freely committed to them.

The authors describe the epistemology of critical social science action research as constructivist: knowledge develops by a process of active construction and reconstruction of theory and practice by those involved. Unlike the other two versions of action research, the practical or interpretative and the technical, all the participants are researchers and are co-inquirers.

The authors are critical of positivist notions of rationality, objectivity and truth. They see truth as historically and socially embedded, located in the concerns of individuals in social situations. The orientation is not towards problem-solving narrowly conceived, but towards emancipation from inadequate practices through reflection directed at distinguishing those ideas that are ideological or systematically distorted from those that are not. The method of critique is used to 'identify and expose' those factors that 'frustrate social change'. Both the critical theorems and the organisation of action are aimed at eliminating or overcoming constraints on rational change (ibid.).

It should be apparent that this model of action research will be critical of institutional or national policies that prevent the realisation and development of a group's 'critical theorems'. The work of Melrose and

Reid (2000) and Donald and Gosling (1995) illustrates the kind of knowledge sought using a critical action research approach.

Melrose and Reid (2000) set out to recommend a way of organising collaborative action research that can accommodate changes in individual commitment and 'patchy resources'. It was developed during several such projects, the last being in 1997 when it was used for the collaborative improvement of policies and procedures for the recognition of prior learning at two New Zealand polytechnics.

The policy driver was the Education Amendment Act 1990 that charged the New Zealand Qualifications Authority (NZQA) with creating an accessible and equitable qualifications framework. Auckland Institute of Technology (AIT) had already developed principles of good assessment of prior learning practice. The NZQA funded the research to spread good practice about APL.[7]

The research reported here involved staff responsible for APL at each institution, AIT and the Bay of Plenty Polytechnic (BOPP). The authors claim that the model evolved from the work of Kemmis and McTaggart (1988). This sets out a way in which practitioners can develop grounded theory about an area of common practice. The authors were influenced by phenomenology in their approach and they set out to be critical of the historical, political and organisational settings in which they worked. They explicitly wished to adopt the critical action research model advocated by Carr and Kemmis (1986). They also analysed and critiqued the systems and social construction of the organisations to which they belonged with a view to improvement. For the authors critical action research involved combining collaborative self-study of a practice and social analyses in the social science tradition to reveal disempowerment and injustice and to point to action for improvement. Their intention was to test some principles of good practice in the assessment of prior learning and to contribute to the development of policy and procedures related to the gaining of academic credit by experienced learners (Melrose and Reid, 2000, p. 156). Some examples of the outcomes of their deliberation are presented as critical reflections. For example: 'We need to establish how much information is needed by the applicant at each meeting— and who provides it', and 'facilitators must build a positive relationship with the programme teachers as well as the applicant' (p. 162). The report's emphasis was on describing a method of organising action research collaboration between institutions and therefore provides only an indication of the kind of critical and dialogic work involved. Clearly the kind of knowledge sought is in the form of practical, ethically sound principles that will inform their actions in this very complex area.

The second example is drawn from a article by Donald and Gosling (1995). They report on a one-year action research project into the prevalence and nature of racism in two primary schools and the implementation of multi-cultural and anti-racist guidelines in Scotland. They describe their work as socially critical. The research was carried out by three teachers and a small group of local authority workers and academics, largely in their own time since there was no national funding available. The researching group drew upon the Scottish national guidelines that stressed the need for schools to create 'awareness of bias and prejudice' (Donald and Gosling, 1995, p. 2). The Central Regional Council had produced multi-cultural and anti-racist guidelines, and had stressed the need for effective action.

The teacher researchers carried out three studies. The first was an institutional 'audit' of one primary school. Here it was found that although the curriculum showed evidence of multiculturalism being taken on board, adults were 'blind' to racial abuse being perpetrated in the playground as evidenced by the interviews with the children. The teacher researcher made a series of policy recommendations (e.g. assertiveness training should be available to those who are bullied or abused). Action was taken; policies were revised and awareness increased. The authors noted, however, that the school remained reluctant to adopt anti-racist approaches.

The second study, in another school, used ethnographic research methods (questionnaires, interviews) and a true but anonymised story of a racist incident involving an attack on an ethnic minority girl at a party. It came up with similar findings to the first study. Racist abuse was 'invisible' to the adults. The school accepted that staff development was needed.

In the third school the fictionalised story was used in discussion with 52 pupils. The majority of children thought the incident was 'unfair' and 'nasty', but a small group thought that it was natural, claiming that a lot of people do this. While the children were under the impression that the girl in the story was white they put the bullying incident down to jealousy of either her party-dress or her friendship with the party-giver. When they were shown a picture of a black girl, they changed their minds and attributed the bullying to her colour. The authors conclude their study with observations such as that the children were ill-equipped to support the bullied girl, and that children need to be educated to accept and value differences between people.

The authors comment that action research in the Scottish context is more a 'tactic of resistance than transformation, a way of giving voice to policy silences that exist at the national level, and perhaps amplifying the policy whispers at the local level' (Donald and Gosling, 1995, p. 9). The kind of knowledge aimed at here was insight into socially unjust practices and the way in which these are maintained. Its stance in relation to policy is one of critique, with, in the example provided, little expectation of immediate transformation. Action research in this mode clearly engages with policy and has the potential to inform it, but its relationship to policy is more adversarial than one of service.

It should be apparent from the examples discussed so far that the knowledge aimed at by action researchers can include knowledge of self (one's educational values, one's practice), knowledge of ethical principles for action in complex areas of decision making, and knowledge of unjust practices and the conditions that sustain them. The next section examines some attempts to use action research to generate other sorts of knowledge.

ACTION RESEARCH IN THE SERVICE OF POLICY IMPLEMENTATION

Because action research involves practitioners in 'owning' a problem, and can sit outside the constraints of academic award systems, it has been seen by some academics as a particularly dynamic way of transferring, developing and theorising about aspects of practice (see, for example, Koshy *et al.*, 2006) or curriculum at a local level (for e.g. Torrance and Pryor, 2001; Pascal and Bertram, 1997). Policy-makers have also investigated the possibility of teachers as researchers as a means of improving teaching and raising standards.

The Best Practice Research Scholarship initiative (2000–2003) has already been mentioned. This was preceded by a Research Consortia Initiative (TTA, 2003), which comprised four three-year partnerships between schools, LEAs and HEIs. The aim was to understand the benefits to be achieved by teachers' engagement in and with research, and to gain insight into the processes of teacher involvement in research activities. Teachers worked collaboratively in their schools, across schools in their area and across the four consortia. Methodological support was provided by university mentors. In most cases, common research foci that appealed to the teacher researchers in a particular consortium (such as 'critical thinking' and 'mental maths') were chosen in order to bring some thematic coherence (McNamara, 2002). According to a TTA report, summarising the findings from each of the consortia, the initiative helped teachers develop a sense of creativity about teaching and learning, increased their willingness to exercise professional judgement and increased their capacity for self-criticism and self-questioning. Participants developed a shared language for talking professionally about teaching and learning with their colleagues and further developed skills of observation and analysis of teaching. Students also benefited, demonstrating greater engagement, extended talk, and transfer of learning between lessons. There was also a concern by the funders to determine whether test results improved, that is, whether the research resulted in more effective practices. Evidence of this was inconclusive (TTA, 2003; Kushner *et al.*, 2001).

It is clear that the initiative was conceptualised as personal and professional development for teachers but also explored the possibilities of generating generalisable professional knowledge across particular localised contexts. University tutors supported and guided teachers in writing up reports, although it seems the tutors were often the principal authors (Stronach and McNamara, 2002).

What is apparent is that teachers were (after the first year of the first consortium) constrained in their choice of research foci. For example in the Norwich consortium the theme of disaffected students was adopted after discussion with Headteachers as being relevant and allowing enough scope for the participating teachers to design their own inquiries. The management structure of the initiative is somewhat vague, but it is clear that Teacher Training Agency (TTA) Link officers and the TTA Research Director played a substantial role in determining the direction and character of the initiative (Elliott, Zamorski and Shreeve, 2001; McNamara 2002), creating problems of ownership for consortium directors.

Critical action research theorists see these moves—the cooption of action research by central organs of state management of education—as a misappropriation of action research. Action research as a policy 'tool' rather than as a social change method is, on their view, a regrettable development and a misuse (Groundwater-Smith, 2005, p. 335) aiming at the wrong kind of knowledge. Kemmis, for example, argues that action research should tell 'unwelcome truths' about schooling rather than 'smooth' schooling (Kemmis, 2006, p. 469). Post-positivist writers see the point of action research as being transformative and emancipatory for individuals and disadvantaged or oppressed groups as contrasted with producing generalisable knowledge of effective practices.

Critical social science-inspired criticisms of technical action or interpretative research typically highlight the seemingly uncritical acceptance of the legitimacy of the political and historical frameworks within which such researchers are conducting research (e.g. Coulter, 2002; Kemmis, 2006). They argue that technical thinking, or means-ends rationality, typical of positivist approaches, has no part to play in teachers' professional knowledge (Biesta, 2007; Elliott, 2007, p. 2). On the contrary, professional knowledge is best described as *praxis* (wise action), and the form of reasoning that supports this form of action is *phronesis* (prudence) (Carr, 2006). On Carr's account for example, *phronesis* is inseparable from the concrete situations in which it is applied. This means that 'it can only be advanced by a form of "practical philosophy" that is exclusively concerned with sustaining and developing the kind of practical knowledge that guides *praxis*' (p. 427). For Carr, as for Elliott, action research is not part of social science and has no methods: it is a form of practical philosophy.

Clearly, such claims are claims about what forms action research *ought* to take and what sort of understanding it *ought* to contribute and not merely descriptive accounts about what forms it *does* take. Some action research theorists claim that there is no correct version of action research (Noffke, 1997; Phelps and Hase, 2002, p. 518) and thus no 'proper' form of knowledge. This at least invites consideration as to whether action research *can* afford a form of knowledge which is not focused on self-evaluation, unjust practices, or ethical principles, but which is about the effectiveness of practices, in terms of improved measurable outcomes and which may produce knowledge that is potentially generalisable across different contexts.

It is hard to see why some action research employing the methods of social science should not be informative, useful and 'empowering', both to those who conduct the studies and to others, provided that teachers and policy-makers take the findings of such research, as with other research, as hypotheses to be tested in practice. For example, Jennings (2002) researched the problem of the poor performance at reading of some of her 10-year-olds who have reading ages of 8 or 9. She was concerned that that they would not have the requisite level of skill to be able to cope with the secondary school curriculum. She asks what knowledge does a reader with a reading age of 9 years 6 months possess that a reader of 8 years and 6 months does not. Jennings surmises that poor readers, at the age of 10 years, do not seem to have internalised those phonic rules that have not been explicitly taught at KS1. She used the Salford Sentence reading test to confirm that they had an inability to read polysyllabic words. An analysis of available reading schemes led her to conclude that they would bring a child to a reading age of between 7 years, 6 months to 8 years, half way to 'becoming a competent adult reader' (Jennings, 2002, p. 63). Jennings relates this deficiency in the curriculum to the problems of deprivation in her area of Salford. The school has 65% on free school meals and approximately 45% on the special needs register. She hypothesised that these pupils needed to be taught advanced phonic rules. She employed a pre-test post-test design. Four tests were administered to form a baseline assessment. The phonic rules (p. 70) and the lessons taught are described in detail. Efforts were made to make the lessons enjoyable by using poetry. The lesson materials used are given in an Appendix. She discusses the validity and reliability of the post-test results with other members of staff. One test gave counter-intuitive results. There were some doubts about the way the test was administered. The pupils were interviewed by a researcher attached to the TTA-funded consortium and the claim that the children enjoyed the lessons was substantiated. The findings, which are published in tables, showed an improvement in most but not all cases. The intervention proved to be successful: 'both (research) groups had made the same average rate of gain of 4 months per month (range -3 to $+14$). This is four times the rate of the average child, a truly remarkable achievement for these children' (ibid., p. 73). The unsuccessful child's performance was explained in terms of severe home problems.

This is an example of a substantiated research report, in that the data on which conclusions are based and the methods used are given. Because the tests are standardised ones, the design is easily replicable. The findings imply a critique of the current curriculum. The warrant or justification for the knowledge claim, i.e. that teaching advanced phonic rules improves reading levels for most pupils deemed poor readers, lies in a correct inference from the data. Unlike the previous examples we have discussed, Jennings is an example of knowledge about pre-determined outcomes and is therefore an example of putting action research to the service of technical rationality.

Although teachers in the particular setting in which the action research was carried out may be justified in having a high degree of confidence in these findings, there is no claim that similar results are guaranteed in other settings. Although the problem was situated in Jennings' classroom, it is one that is experienced by other teachers in other similar classrooms. The findings are therefore generalisable in the sense that other teachers can probably understand the problem, understand the proffered solution, understand how and why it might have worked, see parallels, perhaps, with their own situation and be motivated to try the same approach for themselves to see if it 'works' in their particular contexts. This is a professionally significant sense of 'generalisability' even if it does not come with any epistemological guarantees that what worked in one situation would also work in another.

We can see from the discussion of examples that action research can and does inform the theoretical and policy deliberations of individual teachers, academics and institutions and has the potential to influence the thinking of other practitioners.

However, the interesting questions posed at the start of this chapter are: Are teachers attracted to researching their own practice right to be confident in their findings? Are their fellow professionals right to be confident in the findings of their colleagues?

If we unpack these questions a little further we can see that they encapsulate two related questions that we have been touching upon, and to which we now turn. Firstly there is a question about the rigour and trustworthiness of the research in the sense of being well designed, argued and warranted, and secondly there is the question of whether there is a form of knowledge that is more useful than other sorts. In the next section we discuss these questions.

WARRANTS AND KNOWLEDGE CLAIMS

If action research is concerned with the production of knowledge, that is knowledge of why a practice counts as an improvement, it is not enough, on traditional accounts of knowledge, simply to assert that there has been an improvement. Standards for conventional social science require that the evidence on which claims are made are transparently reported and accessible to public scrutiny and criticism. The strength of warrants is assessed on two factors: the quality of the evidence and the claims made on the basis of the evidence. Research can have relatively poor quality evidence and still make warranted claims if these are suitably hedged by an acknowledgement of the limitations of the evidence. Conversely research can have good quality evidence and make unwarranted claims. Poor research occurs when the researcher's claims go beyond what the evidence will bear.

Research can therefore make valid but weak claims to knowledge and fulfil a useful function for others, in suggesting possibilities for practice. Strong claims to knowledge involve, amongst other factors, good quality evidence, claims that can be supported by that evidence and a coherent argument that rules out alternative explanations (Gorard, 2002). Of course a strong claim to know based on good quality evidence *and* justified claims is perhaps more interesting to those engaged in policy formation than a weak claim.

However, in practice, we do not base our judgements about trustworthiness solely on the quality of evidence and the validity of the inferences made. Other factors come into play, such as whether (in the light of wider understanding and experience) the findings are credible, plausible, useful, have a sufficient degree of verisimilitude, and are morally acceptable.

From the point of view of thinking about warrants for non-social scientific research 'evidence' is replaced by 'reasons'. Critical theoretical versions of action research, invoke consensual views of truth reached through a process of dialogue. Carr for instance draws on the work of Gadamer, to suggest that participants who share a particular tradition of thinking can through dialogue 'rationally revise their understanding so as to transcend the limitations of what within this tradition, has hitherto been thought, said and done' (Carr, 2006, p. 429). A simple example given by Titchen may illustrate this. In a presentation given to MEd students at Westminster College Oxford, she related how she had inquired with a group of nurses as to why their work was such a 'slog' and why they were obliged to 'look busy' the whole time, to the detriment of their patients. They argued that this experience and expectation had its roots in the militaristic history of nursing. Such understanding is historical and takes the form of recognising prejudices (assumptions) that are false or no longer apply (see also Titchen, 1997). Action research on this version is a form of practical philosophy, carried out by communities of practitioners working in a tradition.

Advocates might say that a warrant for this form of inquiry would rely heavily on the conditions of dialectical discussion, on all voices, including the less powerful voices, being heard, for example, and the credibility of the interpretations and argument being put forward (Heikkinen, Kakkori and Huttenen, 2001) As in history, interpretations are substantiated by evidence and valid reasoning.

Thus empirical and non-empirical claims are warrantable and may be judged to be more or less weak or strong.

A practical consequence of this for reporting, however, is that evidence and/or the process of dialectical reasoning should be presented in a way that can be assessed by the reader, or in the case of digests, by research experts in the field. Where these conditions are not fulfilled we are not in a position to make informed judgements, but are forced to rely on the testimony of the researcher that 'it worked'.

We are now in a position to attempt an answer to the question of the kind of confidence we are entitled to have in teacher reports that are not fully substantiated. It goes like this: there are degrees of strength in knowledge claims and thus corresponding degrees of confidence that teachers and others can have. Personal learning accounts, in so far as they do not provide sufficient evidence or sufficient reasons to support the claim that an innovation is desirable, may provide weak claims to know that are nevertheless useful. They may provide ideas that can be used, tested or developed. If the claims do not 'threaten' us as teachers and if they seem easily incorporated into our practice then we are unlikely to wish for more evidence or reasoning over and above a teacher's testimony that a practice 'works' or is desirable. If, on the other hand, a teacher's learning account seems to challenge or negate something in our own practice, we are likely to demand more substantial evidence. Heikkinen, Huttunen and Syrjala (2005) make helpful suggestions for presenting action research in narrative form so that others may understand and learn. They suggest that there should be an acknowledgment of the past course of events that have shaped the present practice, a reflexive account and a dialectical way of elaborating the events. They also propose a criterion of 'evocativeness', which would (presumably) allow the reader to appreciate any similarities with her own situation.

National policy-makers will almost certainly require the strongest form of warranting available, although there is, as far as we have been able to determine, no evidence that national policy is informed by the findings or the deliberations of action researchers.

We now turn to the second question. It has been argued by some that technical action research, employing a means-end rationality, typical of positivist approaches, has no part to play in teachers' professional knowledge (Biesta, 2007). However we have seen that Jennings' (2002) study does have the potential to contribute to a body of theory about the teaching of reading, even if that was not within the scope of the original investigation. We have argued that there is a substantive claim about 'what works' that can be tested in the work of other teachers and researchers.

In Carr and Kemmis's terms (1986), 'technical action research', employing an instrumental approach, implies a mistaken view about the character of teacher knowledge. But their argument only has force if one accepts that a means-end form of rationality necessarily implies that the means are not related constitutively to the ends and that the 'means' are necessarily morally neutral, and if one holds a morally neutral idea of 'effectiveness'. This analysis of the means—end relationship however is not the only nor the most compelling one. Dewey (1922) for example, argued that ends are only fixed *at a moment in time*: in the flow of one's life they are not fixed at all. We do not simply evaluate the means in relation to the end but the end in relation to the means available. For example, the end may become less desirable if the cost of achieving it is too high. The end is not properly assessed until the means are evaluated. It is false to suppose that the value of a means lies solely in serving an end and has no value in itself (Mounce, 1997, p. 131; Price, 1967, p. 562). This is a more apposite analysis for teaching, since the means as well as the ends should be educationally defensible (Peters, 1966). In Jenning's study there was a constant monitoring of the effect teaching advanced phonic rules was having on the well-being of the students.

CONCLUSION

Action researchers address questions that are likely to be of interest to teachers and other education professionals, and the move towards an evidence-based profession requires that we know how to evaluate knowledge claims made by action researchers whose reports do not fully comply with conventional standards for reporting empirical research or standards governing philosophical theorising about practice. It has been argued that such reports are valuable, but make weaker claims to knowledge than fully substantiated reports. At a minimum, knowledge claims should be clearly identified, and the warrant for the claim should be made available so that the reader can make an informed judgement. Depending on our current state of knowledge, our contexts and purposes, weak claims to knowledge can be useful and valuable. However all research findings, even when strong, should be treated by teachers, as Stenhouse urged, as hypotheses to be tested in the particular and perhaps unique conditions of their own classrooms—a conclusion that is itself an invitation to continue the cycle of action research (Stenhouse, 1979; Fielding *et al.*, 2005).

Correspondence: Lorraine Foreman-Peck and Jane Murray, University of Northampton, School of Education, Northampton NN2 7AL, UK. E-mail: Lorraine.Foreman-Peck@northampton.ac.uk

NOTES

1. For example, The Schools Directorate Research News from the DfES aims to keep policy-makers, practitioners and other partners up to date with relevant findings from DfES sponsored research. The Evidence for Policy and Practice in Education Centre (EPPI) publishes reviews of research based on user's questions. Condensed research reports are published by the National Teacher Research Panel with advice about how such research can be utilised and suggest ways in which teachers and teaching assistants can carry out their own research. There are also a number of web sites, such as Topic on line supplied by the National Foundation of Educational Research, Research of the Month, supplied by the General Teaching Council. Learning Exchange Online is set up for Networked Learning communities to share information on research done by their schools and networks. The Research Informed Practice Site consists of digests of academic papers. They claim to cover 'hot topics'. Practitioner action research is a requirement for higher-level school staff (DfES, 2004; TDA, 2006).

2. A repetition of the cycle is desirable but not always possible in practice. Where it is possible Somekh acknowledges that it may be carried out with less intensity (Somekh, 2006).

3. Somekh lists eight principles as being definitive of her action research practice, including the principle that 'action research is conducted by a collaborative partnership of participants and researchers' (Somekh, 2006, p. 7).

4. The suggested reporting format for the BPRS was:
   What were my original aims?
   In what ways did I refine my aims?
   Research processes I found helpful
   Research processes my pupils found helpful
   The learning points I gained from undertaking the research and what evidence I had to monitor this
   Questions for my future practice
   Questions for my school
   Questions for further research
   How did you disseminate your findings? (Costello, 2003, Chapter 6).

5. According to the British Educational Research Association (BERA, 2004) a professional paper should indicate the professional issues being addressed, summarise the findings, and suggest the potential value of the findings.

6.   Neither critical action research, nor practical action research aimed at values realisation, have become most prominent, as evidenced by research into action research carried out by teachers as part of a higher education awards: most teacher researchers doing action research as part of an award adopt a practical instrumental version, adopting systematic empirical investigation methods and aim to recommend concrete strategies (Elliott *et al.*, 1996).

7.   Assessment of Prior Learning (APL) is a process whereby an individual seeks formal recognition for achievements of past learning and experience, whether as a result of formal education, on the job training, work or life experience.

REFERENCES

American Educational Research Association (AERA) (2006) Standards for Reporting on Empirical Social Science Research in AERA Publications. American Educational Research Association. http://www.aera.net/uploaded.Pdf [accessed 1.1.08].

Bartlett, S. and Burton, D. (2006) Practitioner Research or Descriptions of Classroom Practice? A Discussion of Teachers Investigating their Classrooms, *Educational Action Research*, 14.3, pp. 395–405.

Bassey, M. (1995) *Creating Education Through Research: A Global Perspective of Research for the 21st Century* (Newark, UK, Kirklington Moor Press).

Bassey, M. (1999) *Case Study Research in Educational Settings* (Buckingham, Open University Press).

Brearley, S. and Van-Es, C. (2002) One Mouth, Two Ears, in: O. McNamara (ed.) *Becoming an Evidence-Based Practitioner: A Framework for Teacher–Researchers* (London and New York, RoutledgeFalmer).

Biesta, G. (2007) Why 'What Works' Won't Work: Evidence-Based Practice and the Democratic Deficit in Educational Research, *Educational Theory*, 57.1, pp. 1–22.

British Educational Research Association (BERA) (2000) Good Practice in Educational Research Writing, available at: http://www.bera.ac.uk/publications/pdfs/GOODPR1.PDF

British Educational Research Association (BERA) (2004) Ethical Guidelines, available at: http://www.bera.ac.uk/publications/pdfs/ETHICA1.PDF

Carr, W. and Kemmis, S. (1986) *Becoming Critical: Education, Knowledge and Action Research* (London, Falmer).

Carr, W. (2006) Philosophy, Methodology and Action Research, *Journal of Philosophy of Education,* Special Issue: *Philosophy, Methodology and Educational Research Part 1*, 40.2, pp. 421–437.

Cochran-Smith, M. and Lytle, S. L. (1993) *Inside/Outside: Teacher Research and Knowledge* (New York, Teachers College Press, Columbia University).

Costello, P. J. M. (2003) *Action Research* (London, Continuum).

Coulter, D. (2002) What Counts as Action in Educational Action Research?, *Educational Action Research*, 10.2, pp. 189–206.

Department for Education and Skills (DfES) (2004) *National Standards for Headteachers* (London, Department for Education and Skills).

Dewey, J. (1922) Human Nature and Conduct, in: J. Boydston (ed.) *John Dewey: the Middle Works*, Volume 14 (Carbondale, IL, Southern Illinois University Press).

Donald, P. and Gosling, S. (1995) 'No Problem Here': Action Research Against Racism in a Mainly White Area, *British Educational Research Journal*, 21.3, pp. 263–276.

Edwards, A. (2000) Looking at Action Research Through the Lenses of Socio-cultural Psychology and Activity Theory, *Educational Action Research*, 8.1, pp. 195–204.

Elliott, J. (1982) Action-Research: A Framework for Self-Evaluation in Schools, Working Paper No. 1, in: R. Winter (ed.) *Learning from Experience: Principles and Practice in Action-Research* (London, Falmer Press).

Elliott, J. (1993) What Have We Learned from Action Research in School-Based Evaluation?, *Educational Action Research Journal*, 1.1, pp. 175–186.

Elliott, J. (2005) Becoming Critical: The Failure to Connect, *Educational Action Research*, 13.3, pp. 359–373.

Elliott, J. (2006) Educational Research as a Form of Democratic Rationality, *Journal of Philosophy of Education*, Special Issue: *Philosophy, Methodology and Educational Research Part 1*, 40.2, pp. 169–187.

Elliott, J. (2007) *Reflecting Where the Action Is* (London, Routledge).

Elliott, J., MacLure, M. and Sarland, C. (1996) Teachers as Researchers in the Context of Award Bearing Courses and Research Degrees, UK Economic and Social Science Research Council End of Award Report No R000235294 (University of East Anglia, Centre for Applied Research in Education).

Elliott, J., Zamorski, B. and Shreeve, A. (2001) (amended June 2002) Norwich Area Schools Consortium: Final Report to the TTA (University of East Anglia, Centre for Applied Research in Education).

Fielding, M. (2001) Students as Radical Agents of Change, *Journal of Educational Change*, 2, pp. 123–141.

Fielding, M., Bragg, S., Craig., J., Cunningham, I., Eraut, Gillinson, S. M., Horne, M., Robinson, C. and Thorp, J. (2005) Factors Influencing the Transfer of Good Practice. DfES Research Brief no: RB615, University of Sussex, available at: http://www.dfes.gov.uk/research/data/upload files/RR615.pdf

Foster, P. (1999) 'Never Mind the Quality, Feel the Impact': A Methodological Assessment of Teacher Research Sponsored by the Teacher Training Agency, *British Journal of Educational Studies*, 41.4, pp. 380–398.

Furlong, J., Salisbury, J. and Coombs, L. (2003) The Best Practice Research Scholarship Scheme: An Evaluation. Final Report to the DfES. (Cardiff, Cardiff University School of Social Sciences).

Gibbons, M., Limoges, C., Nowotny, H., Schawrtzman, S., Scott, P. and Trow, M. (1994) *The New Production of Knowledge* (London, Sage).

Gorard, S. (2002) Warranting Claims from Non-Experimental Evidence. Occasional Paper series 48, ESRC Teaching and Learning Research Programme (Cardiff, Cardiff University School of Social Sciences).

Groundwater-Smith, S. (2005) Painting the Educational Landscape with Tea: Re-reading *Becoming Critical*, *Educational Action Research*, 13.3, pp. 329–345.

Heikkinen, H. L. T., Kakkon, L. and Huttunen, R. (2001) This is My Truth, Tell me Yours: Some Aspects of Action Research Quality in the Light of Truth Theories, *Educational Action Research*, 9.1, pp. 9–24.

Heikkinen, H. L. T., Huttunen, R. and Syrjala, L. (2005) On the problem of Quality in Narratives of Action Research. Paper presented at the European Educational Research Association Annual Conference, 7th–10th September, University College Dublin.

Kemmis, S. (2006) Participatory Action Research and the Public Sphere, *Educational Action Research*, 14.4, pp. 459–476.

Kemmis, S. and McTaggart, R. (1988) *The Action Research Planner*, 3rd edn. (Geelong, Deakin University Press).

Koshy, V., Mitchell, C. and Williams, M. (2006) *Nurturing Gifted and Talented Children at Key Stage: A Report of Action Research Projects. DfES Research Report 741* (London, Department for Education and Skills).

Kushner, S., Simons, H., James, D., Jones, K. and Yee, W. C. (2001) The Evaluation of the TDA School-Based Research Consortia, available at: www.tda.gov.uk/upload/resources/pdf/c/con sortia99.pdf

Jennings, S. (2002) Helping Weak Readers Up the Reading Ladder, in: O. McNamara (ed.) *Becoming an Evidence-Based Practitioner: A Framework for Teacher–Researchers* (London and New York, Routledge, Falmer).

McNamara, O. (2002) *Becoming an Evidence-Based Practitioner: A Framework for Teacher–Researchers* (London, RoutlegeFalmer).

Melrose, M. and Reid, M. (2000) The Daisy Model for Collaborative Action Research: Application to Educational Practice, *Educational Action Research*, 8.1, pp. 151–165.

Mounce, H. O. (1997) *The Two Pragmatisms: From Peirce to Rorty* (London and New York, Routledge).

Noffke, S. E. (1997) Professional, Personal and Political Dimensions of Action Research, *Review of Research in Education*, 2, pp. 305–43.

Pascal, C. and Bertram, T. (1997) *Effective Early Learning: Case Studies in Improvement* (London, Paul Chapman).

Peters, R.S (1966) *Ethics and Education* (London, Allen and Unwin).

Phelps, R. and Hase, S. (2002) Complexity and Action Research: Exploring the Theoretical And Methodological Connections, *Educational Action Research*, 10.3, pp. 507–523.

Price, K. (1967) *Education and Philosophical Thought*, 2nd edn. (Boston, Allyn and Bacon).

Pring, R. (2005) The Nuffield Review of 14–19 Education and Training. Annual Report 2004–05, October, University of Oxford Department of Educational Studies, available at: http//www.nuffield14-19review.org.uk

Radford, M. (2007) Action Research and the Challenge of Complexity, *Cambridge Journal of Education*, 37.2, pp. 263–278.

Roulston, K., Legette, R., Deloach, M. and Buckhalter Pitman, C. (2005) What is 'Research' for Teacher-Researchers?, *Educational Action Research*, 13.2, pp. 169–188.

Somekh, B (2006) *Action Research: A Methodology for Change and Development* (Buckingham, Open University Press).

Stenhouse, L. (1979) Using Research Means Doing Research, in: H. Dahl, A. Lysne and P. Rand (eds) *Spotlight on Educational Problems* (Oslo, University of Oslo Press), pp. 71–82.

Stronach, I. and McNamara, O. (2002) Working Together: The Long Spoons and Short Straws of Collaboration, in: O. McNamara (ed.) *Becoming an Evidence-Based Practitioner: A Framework for Teacher–Researchers* (London, RoutledgeFalmer, Chapter 12).

Teacher Training Agency (TTA) (2003) Teachers and School-based research. The Reports of the TTA/CfBT funded school-based research consortia initiative 1997–2000, available at: www.gtce.org.uk/research/ttaresearchhome.asp [accessed 21.10.04].

Titchen, A. (1997) Creating a Learning Culture: A Story of Change in Hospital Nursing, in: S. Hollingsworth (ed.) *International Action Research: A Casebook for Educational Reform* (London, Falmer Press).

Training and Development Agency (TDA) (2006) [Online] The Revised Standards for the Recommendation for Qualified Teacher Status (QTS), available at: http://www.tda.gov.uk/upload/resources/doc/draft_qts_standards_17nov2006.doc [accessed: 17.4.07].

Temperley, J. and Horne, M. (2003) Networked Learning Communities: Multiple Models of Enquiry and Research. Conference paper at International Congress for School Effectiveness and Improvement, Sydney, 5–8th Jan.

Torrance, H. and Pryor, J. (2001) Developing Formative Assessments in the Classroom, *British Educational Research Journal*, 27.5, pp. 615–631.

Walker, M. (2005) Amartya Sen's Capability Approach and Education, *Educational Action Research*, 13.1, pp. 103–110.

Winch, C. (2002) The Economic Aims of Education, *Journal of Philosophy of Education*, 36.1, pp. 101–117.

8
Philosophy as a Basis for Policy and Practice: What Confidence Can We Have in Philosophical Analysis and Argument?

JAMES C. CONROY, ROBERT A. DAVIS AND
PENNY ENSLIN

The purpose of this chapter is to suggest how philosophy might play a key, if precisely delineated, role in the shaping of policy that leads educational development. The argument begins with a reflection on the nature of confidence in the relationship between philosophy and policy. We note the widespread resistance to abstract theorising in the policy community, disguising the enormous potential of a philosophical approach. Defending a philosophically equipped approach to policy, which is inevitably theoretically laden, we argue that philosophical investigation should be construed not as an initial step anterior to the task of research, but as a way of standing in relation to evidence and policy-making throughout the process of investigation and adjudication. To illustrate the distinctive contribution philosophy can make, we propose five interrelated stages where philosophical thinking plays a constitutive role in the full process of policy development, critique and instantiation.

INTRODUCTION

Michael Fielding and Terry McLaughlin present two contrasting views of the relationship between philosophy and policy. For Fielding, 'without philosophy, education policy is more likely to be muddled and inconsistent, overly concerned with the tangential or trivial, and so tremendously busy with getting things done that the possibility of foolishness outweighs the likelihood of wisdom' (2000, p. 377). Fielding goes on to describe a range of reasons why philosophy is important in relation to both the production of policy and reflection on policy. McLaughlin took a more circumspect view, warning that the contribution philosophy can offer is modest and that we should not artificially bring philosophical considerations to bear on educational policy (McLaughlin, 2000, pp. 443–444). While we tend to favour Fielding's somewhat more expansive perspective, we nevertheless acknowledge that McLaughlin's approach is likely to be more productive given the hermeneutic of suspicion about philosophy in the policy community. (It is possible as we suggest below that this suspicion has been something of a self-inflicted wound.) In the best formulated and executed policy, philosophy can offer a vital if modest contribution to deliberation in the policy arena. In the most egregious examples of poor policy formation, we still encounter the deployment of abstract and conceptual thought, but in such instances it is too often inadequately formulated or open to inspection. The purpose of this chapter is to suggest how philosophy might play a key, if precisely delineated, role in the shaping of policy that leads educational development/innovation. The argument begins with a reflection on the nature of confidence in the relationship between philosophy and policy. We note the widespread resistance to abstract theorising in the policy community, disguising the considerable potential of a philosophical approach. We defend a philosophically equipped approach to policy, which is inevitably theoretically laden.

ON THE NATURE OF CONFIDENCE

The disagreement between McLaughlin and Fielding masks a rather deeper question than whether we are to be modest or immodest in our claims as to the relative importance of the contribution of philosophy to policy. That deeper question is—'can we have any confidence *at all* in philosophy as a basis for policy and practice?' Of course this appears on first look to be a question about the bona fides of philosophy as an enterprise, but, on closer examination, we can see that it may in fact be a question about the nature of confidence itself. Might it not be that, as faith in the processes, procedures and claims of an ever-widening range of public endeavours and institutions has diminished, the socio-psychology of confidence itself has suffered a loss of meaning? Arguably the widespread introduction of a substantial range of monitoring and surveillance measures in institutions from religion to politics, public transport to hospitals has undermined any common sense of what constitutes public confidence itself. Moreover, the re-shaping of what politicians and others are prepared to accept as evidence may well have a deleterious effect on an agreed or collective account of confidence. If we take David Bridges' point in the introduction that 'double blind' trials now appear to offer the only acceptable approach to social research in the United States, we are required to ask whether or not policy-makers and political operatives can have confidence in almost any kind of social research, much less the abstractions of philosophical enquiry. Why would one have faith in double blind trials but not in ethnography or anthropology or qualitative research in general? The answer must surely lie in a powerful attachment to a particular way of thinking about the world. That said, we might want to ask, 'why should one have confidence in one way of thinking about the world and not another?' To answer this we might want to reflect on some different senses in which we are inclined to use the term confidence. We may have, for instance,

> Confidence in winning the lottery;
> Confidence in the future;
> Confidence in the eschatological or other religious claims of a community;
> Confidence in some metaphysical claim such as the existence of God;
> Confidence in another person;
> Confidence in the evidence of my senses;
> Confidence in the reported evidence of another's senses;
> Confidence in my judgment;
> Confidence in the judgments of others;
> Confidence in a political or social system.

Is there any similarity between these examples given that the contexts in which confidence is experienced are so different? Some expressions of confidence—say in winning the lottery—may be seen as a synonym for 'I believe that I am going to win . . .' or 'I have faith that I am going to win'. In either case, confidence amounts to little more than a pious (or possibly impious) hope with little or no justification for the holding of it. Confidence in the future would seem superficially similar in that it too appears to be based on little more than pious hope. Here however, there are important differences to be highlighted since such a claim could be taken as describing a disposition towards the world: a way of standing in it. More prosaically, we might suggest that the well-qualified student may have justifiable confidence in her future based on her qualifications, experience and success to date. In this sense confidence offers a more substantive account of the person as person and how she relates to the world. In other words, unlike winning the lottery that is inherently irrational given the odds, hope in the future may represent something like a rational calculation with respect to anticipated outcomes. Here confidence might be seen as a synonym for justifiable optimism. Confidence in metaphysical claims is different yet again, combining as it does elements of the first two, their relative weight depending on a range of other critical factors, not least who makes the judgment. On the one hand, the sceptic looking at such confidence may want to say that the person who has it is yet more delusional than the one who is confident that they will win the lottery. On the other, a judge who is better disposed to such metaphysical claims may see such confidence as indeed a legitimate way of standing in the world. Here confidence is in some respects a synonym for a claim to value. Confidence in the evidence of the senses is also of a different kind, being more concerned with empiricist claims to know certain things about the world either by direct sensory apprehension or as reliably mediated by third parties. In this context, confidence becomes synonymous with a certain but very limited definition of knowledge. It is, however, rare for human beings in their interchanges to wish to so severely delimit knowledge. This is most manifest in collective enterprises such as education where societies invest confidence in a range of accounts of what would constitute the flourishing of students; accounts that are rooted in a range of philosophical and cultural antecedents that would leave us hard pressed to unearth any connection to empiricism. In the last three instances, indeed, confidence can be seen to be concerned with notions of trust.

This reflection on the nature of confidence is not as arcane as might be imagined. The timbre and imperatives of both this chapter and the TLRP project of which it is a part are concerned directly and indirectly with the twin set of relations embodied in the constructions of confidence and trust. The variety of senses of confidence identified here play different and often complementary roles in the shaping of policy. For example, it is not uncommon that a particular educational policy has been shaped on an indeterminate hope that certain aspirations can be realised if only we hold onto the aspiration itself. A range of reports and the educational policies they were designed to shape and energise have not infrequently been shaped in recent decades by a combination of confidence in the future and our capacities to realise certain kinds of goods. The 1944 Harvard Report (Harvard Committee, 1945), the 1949 Scottish Report on Secondary Education and the, highly influential, Plowden Report (Department of Education and Science, 1967) (all of which had a substantial impact on subsequent policy formation) are important examples of initiatives shaped by confidence in the future as the expression of a particular disposition. Here it is worthy of note that all three of these reports illustrate a robust interplay between the philosophical and normative on the one hand and the empirical on the other. Evidence-based policy formation was clearly to be grounded in stipulative accounts of how we might conduct our affairs as much as on claims about how the world appears. There was rather more confidence in the philosophical in the period covered by these reports than might be seen to be the case in the early 21st century. Despite the emergence of much scepticism about the efficacy of policy formulation grounded in such confidence (as is to be found in these reports) in the future and its displacement by putative 'evidence-led' policies confidence remains central to the relationship between philosophers of education and colleagues working in other areas of educational scholarship. The value or usefulness of philosophers of education to the enterprise of educational improvement and development has to be, in some important respects, dependent on a relationship of confidence in both the judgments and capacities of others.

Let us explore this a little further. In the effective cultivation of any kind of meaningful relationship mutual confidence is critical; most especially the one who seeks to offer advice or support must enjoy the confidence of the recipient. After all, were we to ask a patient if they had confidence in their general practitioner they might well answer that it depends on a number of conditions being fulfilled. Do I have evidence that his diagnoses are generally accurate? Can he refer me to another more expert physician when he feels that his expertise has been exhausted? Indeed, does he recognise when his expertise has been so exhausted? Does she

care? Important though all these questions are, the last is the most salient
for educationalists. After all, might one not be a little reluctant to place
one's confidence in a practitioner whose engagements were conditioned
by an obvious disdain for both the ailment and the description of the
ailment? It is precisely this problem to which Denis Phillips (2005) directs
our attention in his essay on why philosophy of education offers so little
help to empirical educational research. He observes that for too long
philosophers of education (of whom he lists quite a number) have chosen
to ignore the issues raised in the empirical domain. It is too often easy for
philosophers to focus their energies on some of the most egregious
examples of poor empirical research and extrapolate from these a sense
that all such research is so fatally flawed as to be useless. But this is hardly
the most propitious starting point. As Phillips observes, 'it certainly takes
a great deal of hubris to suggest that the work of thousands of our
colleagues is pointless but some philosophers of education rise to this
daunting challenge!' (ibid., p. 587). Indeed, it might be suggested that if
philosophers of education wish to secure the confidence of other scholars
working in the field then they should be prepared to subject their own
normative claims to some scrutiny. This is a *sine qua non* of establishing a
working relationship between philosophy of education and the rest of the
educational research and policy community: philosophers are, after all not
immune from error in their deliberations. It is a mistake to assume that the
contribution of philosophers of education is to validate or otherwise the
contribution of others—after all, it is not as if philosophers' own
hermeneutical and normative claims are not subject to disagreement. More
than this, when philosophers of education stipulate something like 'human
flourishing' are not others entitled to ask, 'What would this look like?' or
'How might we best secure such flourishing?' and so on.

 In the light of these observations, the first part of the question to which
this essay addresses itself might be re-phrased as 'Are the deliberations of
philosophers the kind of thing in which politicians can put their trust?'.
The answer might be a rather brief, 'no!'. We can then ask whether or not
they should do so. Again, the answer might be the same. As we have
already indicated, however, this might be a little too hasty. Smeyers,
Smith and Standish (2007) offer a useful insight here when they argue that
much empirical research may be reduced to the status of laying claim to
the blindingly obvious. In their discussion of the example of an
ethnographic study of beginning teachers, the list of a range of conclusions
offered by the research included the finding that beginning teachers feel—
well—that they are beginning! Do we really need to invest in research that
is likely to tell us little more than that which we already know? That most
people who are inexperienced feel their inexperience? But here the really
interesting question is, 'Why would the policy-makers or the Research
Council that funded the project require this kind of ethnography to verify
what professionals have known from generation to generation?' While
empirical research can offer counterintuitive insights, serendipity not
withstanding, this may only hold in those cases where both the issue and
the methods of investigation and determination are sufficiently nuanced as

to unearth the nature of that being investigated. Arguably, this is true of any piece of research, but here we see an interesting example of how the conclusions were already contained within the premises. With a little more consideration of the premises surely we could have seen that such an effort might not be entirely necessary. Might not the masked issue here be that policy-makers have no confidence in our everyday commonsense claims about life? May it not also be the case that affirmation of pre-existing judgments and claims has displaced confirmation as a dominant purpose of research sponsored by the policy community? Stories abound in the research community of commissioned research where publication has been delayed, findings re-written or pressure placed on the researchers to modify their findings because they fail to affirm the policy or policy direction desired by those commissioning the research.

Let us, however, attribute to the vast majority of those in the 'policy community'—a somewhat disparate and diffuse body (if body at all)—benign intentions, and a general desire to do good things and improve the lives of those in the wider polity whom they serve. Such people are rarely Mephistophelian characters but people who may be genuinely uncertain as to what version of the good society they are intended to realise on behalf of this wider polity. Moreover, even where they have some clear understanding of the 'good society' they may not be at all clear on how to realise it. However, this does not prevent them from focusing on a series of local or intermediary steps that may be constitutive of that wider vision. On that basis, they turn to research. There, to compound their lack of certainty about what it is that we are trying collectively to secure, they find that much of the research is limited and partial. As people brought up, however, in an age of number they invest some faith in the numbers. Cornelius Castoriadis (1997) suggests that number has assumed an ontologically originary significance for moderns. By this he means that 'the arithmetic', at least since Descartes, has been endowed with a certain transcendence and consequently assumes the status of an article of faith. Hence we are encouraged to think that the arithmetic holds the key to unlocking certain solutions to socio-educational problems and challenges. Confidence then becomes confidence that the arithmetic uncovers the real world, overcoming the poverty of our subjective judgments.

Why might we need such an atelic attachment? Might it be because we are unsure of the normative judgments by which we have chosen to live our public lives? Numbers seem so solid; valuing integrity appears so nebulous when laid alongside it. We have an anxiety about accepting that our own normative claims have any intrinsically enduring qualities and fret that they are much too prey to scepticism about value. The arithmetic appears to offer some buffer against our own loss of confidence in our own beliefs. If I believe that we should live in X way or by Y value then this is too often construed as a private matter subject only to my own confir-mation and of no import or interest to others. This is of course a too often encountered fallacy in much post modern thought. When we place this apparent uncertainty alongside the 'fixed' appearance of number, number tends to be accorded a superior status. Most people have little difficulty in publicly agreeing that $2+2=4$ is publicly agreed once we all accept the numbering systems and base convention. We cannot have faith in the work of the philosopher precisely because she brings us up against the vulnerability of our own commitments. Moreover, she asks us to clarify these, to intimate what they might mean and so on. And yet, it is precisely these commitments that distinguish us as human. John Lukacs puts it thus:

> It is sufficient for us to recognise that understanding is of a higher order than accuracy. Measurement depends on numbers. Its aim is accuracy. But understanding, including imagination, is immune to measurement (and imagination may be immune even to neurological experimentation). Numbers are devoid of wisdom: to give them meaning, to reconcile them with life, we have to think about them and clothe them in words (Lukacs, 2002, p. 138).

Policy formation is, in some important respects, an act of the imagination—after all we imagine particular kinds of social goods (including economic) are going to conduce to particular states of well-being. And well-being can be no other than the product of the collective imagination. So, then, is the task of the philosopher to restore to the policy-maker a belief that those values to which she is attached implicitly, and/or declares publicly offer something like a ground for judgment about certain social and educational practices? In other words philosophy helps policy through assisting in the clothing of numbers. In this context confidence is to be seen as trust; trust in one's own instincts about the capacity to make normative judgments where the rules have, at best, been left a little ragged. This further entails the invocation of two fundamental philosophical principles: the demand for a richer sense of what constitutes 'evidence' and the introduction of the sceptical pause in the face of that evidence and the conclusions it may appear to prompt. Both large data sets and fine-grained ethnographies offer the policy-maker sources upon which to draw, but neither may readily substitute for thoughtful reflection and engagement where such thought is conducted not as a private exercise but as a form of a public deliberation. To perform this function, philosophical intervention needs to be construed not simply as an initial step anterior to the task of research, but as a way of standing in relation to the world of evidence and policy-making (taking these as conjoined if not singular) throughout the process of investigation and adjudication. Too often, policy-making is driven by exigency. Here we wish to suggest that such political exigencies as there are should be tempered by the sceptical pause of philosophical reflection.

THE CONSTRUCTIVE CONTRIBUTION OF PHILOSOPHY

In this part of the chapter we now turn to the particular contribution(s) that philosophy can make to policy deliberation. In a sense philosophy does this by exploring the spaces in-between the statistics. But what exactly constitutes this space? Evidence-informed policy has as its ground a concern with understanding human behaviour; that is, understanding how people react to particular stimuli, how they behave in particular contexts and so on. This ground is used to predict future behaviours. Policy is then adjusted, developed and shaped to deliver a context in which such behaviours may be realised. While a distinction is often made in these debates between quantitative and qualitative research, it is not clear that in this respect there is very much difference. Of course, quantitative data is directly related to predicting patterns and qualitative data, among other things, to unearthing the nature and quality of an experience. Yet information derived from qualitative research is still to be deployed to inform and predict (otherwise why inform at all?) and in this way is still concerned with number, albeit indirectly. Qualitative data used in this way is, like quantitative data, a part of a materialist view of the world that stands in need of modification by the original and more expansive conception of quality—quality viewed as an expression of the judgments made with respect to human being and action. Both kinds of research under consideration here are used to assist in understanding the numbers of people who perform in particular ways, who react to particular stimuli or changes in context. Yet quality understood in its fullest sense is concerned, as we have suggested, with something significantly different. A range of recently developed tools for interrogating qualitative data sets (such as NUDIST) are concerned with categorisation, classification, demarcation—that is, with activities that are an extension of the numeric or arithmetic. But 'classification necessitates categorization and leads to homogenisation, whereby qualities and even differences become dependent on their preconceived and programmed capacities' (Lukacs, 2002, p. 139). To argue that much qualitative research is deployed quantitatively is not a surreptitious attempt to reinstate the manifest superiority of the philosophical turn and consequently reinforce old divisions and enmities. And we recognise that, of course, qualitative researchers whose work focuses on the particulars of a situation prefer to speak about transferability rather than generalisability.

Philosophy is that activity of the mind that can assist with understanding the nature of judgments. There is no self-evidently valid practice; all practice needs to be subjected to ongoing scrutiny, even as it works itself out. Judgement is not something anterior to policy but is integral to the ongoing enterprise that is discovery, decision and instantiation. We wish to avoid suggesting that conceptualisation and clarification (the work of the philosopher) are followed, in a quasi-independent way by the implementation of structures, practices and so on (the work of policy-makers and practitioners) between philosophical research and policy. We wish to suggest that it is naïve to assume that first comes conceptualisation, then implementation. The current tendency to see the 'reflective practitioner' as someone for whom we create a set of practices that validate themselves by their sheer efficacy, but who does not need to be too reflective herself is, we believe, to be resisted. What appears to be common sense is rarely if ever so straightforward.

In the first instance, the decision about the desirability or undesirability of any phenomenon is often in the eye of the beholder and rests on a set of normative assumptions about how things 'should be'. Geoff Whitty's (2003) work, *Making Sense of Education Policy*, offers an interesting example of the issue here. He plots the turn away from the neo-liberal economic and social policies and in the course of his discussion suggests that there had been increasing disquiet about the effects of such policies. This disquiet we are informed arose because there was concern among a number of people (Whitty included) 'about the damaging equity effects of the previous government's policies' (Whitty, 2003, p. 127). This concern is not actually amenable to any empirical scrutiny except in the sense that we might investigate how many, and the extent to which, people agree with Whitty's concern. Rather it is a claim—indeed a rather grand ethical claim—about how a polity should organise the distribution of resources and goods, including educational goods. Whitty had already established an *a priori* claim that 'equity' is itself a more important good than, say, 'free market choice'. Of course it can be argued that there are several means by which we may assess certain effects of particular socio-economic policies. But that is only to defer the question, 'why organise these resources in this way rather than in another?' Hence we may begin to see that in some important respects policy formation is prior to empirical research. The research itself does not necessarily give rise to the policy. Rather the policy emerges out of particular normative conceptions of the world in which we live and act. Consequently, if the research is to add anything to the process of policy formation it must continually weave back and forth between its own methods and the initiation of the quest to actualise a particular conception of how things 'ought to be'.

So then, given such complexities how are we to understand the role of philosophy as a practice in educational policy-making? In the next section we plot some tentative ways forward.

A SUGGESTED APPROACH

In this, the key section of our chapter, we take up some of the issues that are raised in both Fielding and McLaughlin's work. We take up McLaughlin's emphasis on the complexity of the relationship but also his reminder that philosophy can thus 'serve to illuminate complexities, sharpen dilemmas, undermine grounds for practical compromise and encourage further discussion and argument rather than decision' (McLaughlin, 2000, p. 451). We also apply Fielding's call for philosophy to provide its distinctive critical refection on the how, what and why of policy formation.

Our theme therefore prompts an inquiry: what kind of questions are we asked to ponder and what would count as answers to these questions? We will take it that we are responding not to educational questions that could be answered purely empirically. Indeed, we see the notion of 'inference' as manifestly problematic. One of the main targets in applying philosophical analysis to the work of educational policy-making may actually be underdeveloped or weak understandings of process concepts such as 'inference'. Inferential reasoning often performs an important, if inexplicit, function in the development of policy initiatives derived from the consideration of specific educational problems or from the interpretation of evidence—whether that evidence be formal research data or the commonplace observations of participants in any given educational experience. From the analysis of formal or informal data, inferences are commonly drawn as the basis for a particular policy intervention or perspective. If inference, broadly conceived, is the act of reaching a valid conclusion on the basis of what can be reliably known of any given problem or phenomenon, then one possible and primary task of philosophical analysis might be to question the steps by which any conclusion determinant of educational policy was reached and, more importantly, to require that the richest possible understanding of the known—with all its variables—has been assured in advance of any formulation of conclusions. A coherent understanding of the rules of inference—perfectly compatible with the prizing of commonsense insights and uncertainty margins—is likely to enhance the practice of inductive reasoning on which much policy formation rests. A philosophically aware position on inference will highlight for both researchers and the policy-makers whom they serve the importance of elements such a multiple observation tests (both confirmatory and disconfirmatory), multi-factoral observation, the complexity of causal relations, the presence of unacknowledged assumptions and the often counterintuitive nature of the explanatory frameworks emergent from educational research. On the basis of not only our understanding of the nature of quality and judgement (as discussed above) but also this 'thickened' understanding of inference, we have resisted a model of philosophy's relationship to policy that assumes that policy might develop its recommendations after some preliminary conceptual clarification, or statement of values, and nothing else. Just as inferential reasoning is operative throughout a research or policy-making process (whether admitted as such or not), so philosophical analysis more widely conceived ought to be in permanent ongoing dialogue with the policy-making enterprise.

Of the two dominant views of philosophy's contribution to activities such as policy-making, conceptual clarification as an application of philosophy has been exemplified in the well-known work of John Wilson (1963). Philosophy as conceptual analysis sets out to map areas of interest to education; most significantly in Wilson's case that of moral education. This involves the task of getting clear the meaning of concepts and their logical implications by probing what we normally mean when we use words—in particular, what counts as an instance of a particular concept (Wilson, 1963, pp. 4–5). These conceptual questions are distinguished from 'factual' ones as well as 'value' judgments and require an appreciation of the ways in which words serve human purposes (p. 6). As words may have more than one use, conceptual analysis pays attention to criteria that determine the ways in which we use them.

Wilson's view of philosophy as conceptual analysis has been criticised, e.g. by Bridges (2003), for its narrow focus on the definition and negotiation of terms. In its depiction of what philosophy can offer to educational research, it was both influential and useful in its heyday, encouraging debate, if not achieving consensus, about the meaning of key terms like 'teaching', 'indoctrination'—and 'education' itself. While the tools available for close attention to concepts and their meaning have widened since, sensitive attention to meaning has remained a practically useful dimension of philosophical research about education. Bridges mentions the example of developing criteria for the use of a concept like 'quality' as a case of such usefulness—as well as the importance of interrogating terms like 'democracy' and 'authority'. It is nonetheless now widely agreed among philosophers of education that philosophy's contribution is more expansive than Wilson insisted. Though related to philosophy as conceptual analysis, a further productive role lies in making distinctions that illuminate our understanding of issues of policy and practice. For example, Iris Marion Young's (2000) distinction between external and internal exclusion can be usefully employed in developing policies in education—distinguishing as it does between external exclusion as ways in which persons can be denied access (in Young's chosen example) to decision-making processes, and internal exclusion as exclusion of those who are allowed into discussions but unable to influence their outcomes. Drawing Young's distinction from political philosophy to philosophy of education, we may better understand the dimensions of exclusion in developing policies in, for example, inclusive education, recognising that even those physically brought into educational spaces may be as much excluded as they would if left outside.

Philosophers also contribute to the clarification, analysis and defence of values that do already, or in some cases ought to, underpin policy and practice. Although this task might seem like a more substantive contribution than those associated with the conceptual, it is also vulnerable to the perception that all such work is ultimately merely a preliminary to the 'real' research on which policy can be built. The vocabulary associated with this widespread view tends towards the foundationalism we have earlier eschewed, where the role of philosophy is strictly anterior to the tasks of research. The work of philosophy is deemed completed, according to this view, when the ground has been cleared and the concepts tidied up. Here, defining terms and resolving confusion is seen to be the primary task. While appearing to accord philosophical reason an important role in relation to policy and practice, such an approach tends to drive a wedge between this primary task and the ongoing deliberative process of policy-making. The seemingly high status role given to philosophical argument in this account in fact reproduces a division between the activity of the philosopher and the decisions of the policy community. In such circumstances philosophy fails to deliver on its potential to accompany the process of policy-making and confidence in its value is thereby diminished.

We can trace the origins of this disjunction back to a rupture between *archein* and *prattein*, (a rupture that, as Joseph Dunne suggests—following Hannah Arendt (1958)—goes back to Plato). '*Archein* [brings] out the element of beginning or opening up and prattein the element of carrying through or accomplishing that is, at the same time, an undergoing or bearing of the consequences that unfold from this beginning; both of these together had been intrinsic in the actions of everyone within the plurality of free agents' (Dunne, 1993, p. 94f). Plato begins the dissociation between the two, where the former (that is the initiation of a project) gets lodged in the notion of rule and hence in the ruler and prattein in that of the doer, the one who carries out the rule (Conroy, 2004, pp. 93 and 107). So it is that in educational research this disjunction gets played out in a series of moves that begins with a policy emerging from the particular normative claims of a policy-maker, with its corroboration and consequent instantiation being handed over to the professional policy-making community. This deprives the technician of the pre-platonic capacity to take responsibility for the ensuing policy implementation. Such dissociation serves neither the philosopher nor the policy-maker, making the parts less than their sum.

The philosophical method proposed here is not to be construed as a simple alternative to foundationalism, where the various stages of a policy project might invite philosophical scrutiny of, for example, the structural sequence of methodology, ethical implications and conclusions. There is no doubt that this can improve our confidence in the involvement of philosophy and offer a step beyond foundationalism, but it is not sufficient to sustain confidence in the efficacy of philosophy as a whole, which risks being reduced to an auditing role in the sequence, authenticating the credentials of the project to which it is allied. While we are content to accept the claim that such a function for philosophy might be a useful and necessary facet of policy development, if philosophical reasoning is to enjoy a substantial measure of confidence it must be seen to be an integral part of the total process of policy development, critique and instantiation. In this we see parallels between, on the one hand, the relationship of philosophy to policy and, on the other, the relationship of theory to practice. Philosophy is implicated in both.

Earlier we observed that the political endeavours in a liberal polity are, or attempt to be, constitutive in the search for human flourishing. More prosaically, this effort to realise such higher order goods often embodies the presumption that public policy initiatives are a response to particular cultural or political issues around perceived social or educational challenges. Hence the rise in the number of teenage pregnancies in Scotland has resulted in several government policy initiatives designed to reduce this trend because the phenomenon of increased numbers of teenage pregnancies is associated with a variety of social ills including poverty, reduced economic opportunity and future delinquency. On a foundationalist model, the likely contribution of philosophy to any policy response of this kind will be limited to some general normative claims as to what constitutes a good life, specifically for young people.

A number of examples of what might be termed popular educational policy initiatives of recent times serve to illustrate the focused contribution that philosophical analysis might have made to policy formation had the kind of extended dialogue we favour in this chapter been pursued from the outset. The work of Fay Smith, Frank Hardman and their colleagues on the assessment of the impact of Interactive White Boards (IWB) on whole class teaching addresses a major ICT innovation in UK schools. The initiative involved vast expenditure on an attractive high-tech teaching aid powerfully symbolic of the imagined consonance between progressive styles of pedagogy and leading-edge learning technologies. Yet Smith and Hardman's evaluation of the IWB programme highlights important gaps in the thinking applied to the policy when the appeal of these new instruments first impinged on education planners. Concluding from their research that 'such technology by itself will not bring about fundamental change in the traditional patterns of whole class teaching', Smith and Hardman suggest that policy-makers were 'seduced by the technology and assumed that IWBs will add motivation and change much of the ritualised teacher-pupil interaction that goes on in schools' (Smith, Hardman and Higgins, 2006, p. 455). They found instead that one of the paradoxical effects of IWBs was to reinforce 'traditional patterns of whole class teaching', actually leading to a reduction in group discussion among pupils. A philosophically literate reflection on the place of IWBs in classroom learning and teaching ought to have shifted attention away from the seductive multifuctionality of the IWBs themselves on to a deeper scrutiny of what Smith and Hardman call 'discourse moves' in the joint construction of classroom knowledge and participation. In furthering an enriched and variegated conception of teacher-pupil interaction, philosophical analysis would prioritise above the operational features of the IWBs themselves much deeper questions of meaning, value and the conditions of optimal learning. Why do we value interaction? What is the appropriate relationship of whole-class transmission modes to small peer-group discovery and experiment? What kind of learners do we wish to nurture in our classrooms and why? How should we understand and evaluate the relationship of human agents to the learning technologies at their disposal? By what criteria is the effectiveness of IWBs to be measured and to what extent are those criteria surreptitiously constituted by factors extrinsic to the processes of learning and teaching, such as the status of high-technology objects or the symbolic and material capital invested in them? Responding to these questions fosters a habit of intellectual enquiry within which philosophical analysis is seen not as an adjunct to policy development but as part of an integrated, critical appreciation of education and its broader purposes.

Another expression of this synthesis can be seen in scholarship that has emerged in the last few years to challenge a set of commonplace assumptions around notions of gender and racial identity in the practice of teaching. Once again, the broad policy themes operative in this area stem mostly from a set of popular perceptions of the role of the teacher in society and, particularly, the impact of the teacher on the lives and behaviours of pupils. A powerful folk wisdom has evolved, abetted by the UK mass media, which insists that the low educational attainment of certain sectors of the male pupil population in schools—and the social ills that appear frequently to accompany this failure—can be most effectively addressed by recruiting men into the teaching force to act as positive role models for disaffected boys. An analogous view is also commonly taken of the solution to under-achieving ethnic minorities in British schools. In both cases—and lent credibility by a cadre of concerned academics—expensive and elaborate policy measures have been taken deliberately to attract males and ethnic minority applicants to programmes of initial teacher education. A series of standard and seemingly self-evident principles accompany this strategy, in which heavily theory-laden yet supposedly commonsense observations about the dynamics of teacher-pupil relations prevail, to the effect that successful male classroom teachers will motivate boys just as successful ethnic minority teachers will similarly incentivise effort and achievement in ethnic minority pupils. This example is to be distinguished from the earlier example from Smeyers *et al.* (2007), where the conclusion was entailed in the premises. Here no such entailment exists and it is precisely this kind of distinction that it is the task of philosophical thought to draw.

In the face of this considerable accumulation of received opinion, the work of Carrington and Skelton has now shown that there is in fact no evidence that the predominantly white and female composition of the teaching force in England and Wales makes a significant difference to pupils' achievement. Counter-intuitively, they point to abundant yet scarcely acknowledged research evidence that the behaviour of male teachers can, indeed, subtly encourage forms of masculine behaviour that marginalise girls, some boys and women teachers:

> We have suggested that the term 'role model' is used uncritically and rarely, if ever, defined in official discourse. Yet, while there are funded strategies targeting men and ethnic minorities, there would not appear to be any clear explanatory framework underpinning them. Our own research suggests that, as a result of this woolly thinking, male and ethnic minority recruits to teaching may confront various dilemmas in schools. Indeed, such are these dilemmas that the focus on male and ethnic minorities as 'role models' might well act as a disincentive for entering the teaching profession (Carrington and Skelton, 2003, p. 258).

As their remarks imply, the whole 'role model' perception of the teacher, and the facile policy equations in which it has resulted, is for the most part barren of serious philosophical assessment. Large questions of imitation, resistance, patterns of influence, causal factors, suppressed variables, institutionalised authority, asymmetries of power, ratios of personal disposition to professional action, gender politics and the sheer irreducible complexity of interpersonal relationships in schools are all wildly neglected in this domain of policy. Basic philosophical analysis would surely induce the hermeneutical pause, opening out the possibility of both initial conceptual clarification at precisely the point where the issues are first described, whilst affording scope for ongoing alternative interpretations of the phenomenon and its underlying structures. The policy community's reflex recourse to easy solutions in seemingly obvious continuity with the problem under review can be tempered by this style of vigorous engagement with philosophical critique. Like the Smith and Hardman example, the repudiation of simplistic models of teacher-pupil interdependency presents philosophical analysis as a kind of hindcasting, exposing shortcomings in the definition of an educational issue of direct relevance to the policy community and debunking misguided efforts to address it. Nevertheless, both examples also contain within them the potential of a quite different and more positive synthesis of philosophical insight with policy development and it is upon this possibility that future research partnerships ought to be built.

THE PROCESS OF PHILOSOPHICAL ENGAGEMENT

In extreme forms, empirical research that is not conceptually informed reveals a lack of what might be termed 'curiosity'. A possible example of this can be seen in the emergence of citizenship as an influential concept in recent education policy. Britain, in common with other liberal democratic polities, has experienced what is popularly perceived to be a collapse of certain kinds of civic and democratic participation. This has induced a sense of social emergency out of which, and somewhat rapidly, a set of systemic and pedagogical prescriptions has emerged for swift implementation in schools. The leap from recognition to practice has seen an elision of the one into the other without a measured consideration as to what might count as citizenship in a mobile late industrial polity. It is here that philosophy may make a substantive contribution that is not reducible to the category of preliminary engagement but is rather a requirement that certain kinds of thinking accompany the processes of deliberation in move from identification of an issue to prescription for its solution. It is exactly this process that both Arendt and Dunne point us towards; it is a process by which the necessary engagement between policy formation and exploration into means and ends goes all the way down. As we have already suggested, too frequently the role ascribed to philosophy of education is that of a foundational task or tasks, or a somewhat clunky auditing device aimed at checking the coherence of the current and the next move at each stage of policy formation. Rather, we wish to suggest that philosophical thinking in educational policy formation may well begin with the task of exposition and clarification but should not remain there. Instead, philosophy may be seen to provide the bridge between initiation and completion precisely because it can recover and elucidate the connections through exploration, exposition, analysis and development. We can identify five interrelated stages where philosophical thinking plays a constitutive role in good policy formation and its concomitant practices. The typology suggested here should not be construed as a set of sequential auditing procedures but an intimation of the way in which we might stand in relation to thinking through the evolution of educational practices from the emergence of a question, through the formation of policy and development of strategies into social and pedagogical engagements.

Recognition—In the case of citizenship certain kinds of empirical data may suggest a decline or collapse in civic participation. It might be, and often has been, assumed that this heralds a dangerous loosening of attachments to the institutions of democratic society. At this stage and fairly immediately the philosopher might wish to ask, 'what is meant by participation?' She might also wish to surface what other factors might the concept of participation be related to that are not being illuminated. For example, 'what is the connection between attachment and participation?'. In its activity around questions of recognition, the philosophical method may be perceived once again as counterintuitive; indeed such counter-intuitions may themselves offer appropriate pause for thought. By this we mean to suggest that it is not uncommon that 'commonsense' notions of certain social phenomena may be felt to express particular causal relations that, under the kind of closer scrutiny encouraged by a philosophically informed appraisal, we might come understand as simplistic. In the Carrington and Skelton case might we not have begun by asking what kind of problem is being addressed; indeed, whether or not there is a problem here at all.

At this stage philosophy can assist, deploying the insights into a range of discursive practices to unearth other similar or overlapping patterns in the official discourses (e.g. between male students in general and particular groups or minorities such as the Afro-Caribbean community). Indeed Carrington and Skelton noted that the official discourse around gendered underperformance was at one with the rhetoric around Afro-Caribbean males.

Diagnosis—The present predilection in policy-making for eliding the distinction between apprehending the situation as it 'presents itself'[1] and an analysis of a causal track can occlude our capacity to speculate and offer alternative perspectives, and indeed alternative causal explanations. Too often this slippage results in a rush to judgement about the salient features of the social issue or educational problem under scrutiny. A failure to retain philosophical composure too often surrenders us to univocal explanatory frameworks. Again, in the Carrington and Skelton example the assumption made by the policy-makers/commissioners of the research was that there is a problem with academic male performance in schools. It was also noted that there are fewer men in teaching. Taken together these two features of contemporary schooling were seen to have a causal connection, the second in some way being responsible for the first. If we were to take more time in the diagnosis of the 'problem' might we not have avoided a rush to spend lots of taxpayers' money on attempts to recruit men into the teaching profession?

Prognosis—Once again, the temptation to offer peremptory prescriptions may leave us bereft of the capacity to project a range of possible outcomes that match the complexity of the social or educational question under consideration. Plato's Socratic dialogues offer a possible model for a style of philosophic prognosis. Socrates' interlocutors are held back from judgment by the careful consideration of a number of possible outcomes and by systematic interrogation of likely consequences. In the Smith and Hardman example we might want to suggest that the failure of IWBs to generate new pedagogical engagements requires us to offer a range of possible ways forward which are not necessarily reducible to a particular set or sets of practices but might require us to reach back and ask why we perceive particular practices to be both pragmatically and, we would suggest, morally superior to others.

Prescription—This is the stage where policies are formulated and where it might be assumed that the philosopher disengages from the process leaving the judgments to professionals. However, it is precisely here that a philosophical disposition may come into its own. This disposition presents itself in a number of complementary ways. First, it may appear in the form of an ethical engagement the effect of which is to subject intended prescriptions to an interrogation that receives its authority from an acquaintance with, and understanding of, a community's ethical traditions and its vision of a 'good society'. In liberal democratic polities more than one ethical ideal is likely to emerge in the course of our deliberations about proposed prescriptions. Such ideals may sometimes appear in tension one with the other. Here the philosophic attitude can critically reacquaint policy-makers with the resources of their own ethical tradition and in doing so enable them to test proposed prescriptions against those traditions. Secondly, the philosopher may assist in addressing some epistemological questions that emerge out of possible prescriptions. For example, the perception that contemporary education has failed in the context of a knowledge economy to deliver into the workplace young women and men who are fitted to the complex socio-engagements of a late industrial society. Here the deliberative engagements of philosophy may be helpful in disentangling some important epistemological questions. Primarily these may be concerned with the relationship between education as process leading to issues around the value and validity of metacognitive approaches as opposed to, for example, knowledge as cultural inheritance.

Social Practices—It is often assumed that when social practices (including pedagogical ones) are instigated they assume the status of theory-free action and that whatever claims the philosophic disposition might have had it is no longer relevant. Here, it is assumed, we are only concerned with 'what works'. However, social practices can themselves be recuperated into naturalised modes of behaviour that disguise their origins as culturally laden interventions. This blunts the edges and disguises the character of our more radical insights and engagements. Consequently, the social practices themselves are not an end or solution to a state of affairs recognised and diagnosed but a stage in an iterative process of ongoing re-cognition and insight.

Correspondence: James C. Conroy, Faculty of Education, University of Glasgow, 11 Eldon Street, Glasgow G6 3NH, UK.
E-mail: j.conroy@glasgow.ac.uk

NOTE

1. Of course we are conscious of the not inconsiderable hermeneutical difficulties attached to a claim that experience or the world presents itself in an unmediated form but would nevertheless for heuristic reasons wish to suggest that the distinction acts as a useful explanatory device.

REFERENCES

Arendt, H. (1958) *The Human Condition* (Chicago, University of Chicago Press).

Bridges, D. (2003) Six Stories in Search of a Character? 'The Philosopher' in an Educational Research Group, in: P Smeyers and M. Depaepe (eds) *Beyond Empiricism: On Criteria for Educational Research* (Leuven, Leuven University Press).

Carrington, B. and Skelton, C. (2003) Re-thinking 'Role Models': Equal Opportunities in Teacher Recruitment in England and Wales, *Journal of Educational Policy*, 18.3, pp. 253–265.

Castoriadis, C. (1997) *World in Fragments: Writings on Politics, Society, Psychoanalysis and the Imagination* (Stanford, CA, Stanford University Press).

Conroy, J. (2004) *Betwixt and Between: The Liminal Imagination, Education and Democracy* (New York, Peter Lang).

Department of Education and Science (1967) *Children and their Primary Schools: Plowden Report Vol. 1* (London, The Stationery Office).

Dunne, J. (1993) *Back to the Rough Ground: Practical Judgment and the Lure of Technique* (South Bend, IN, University of Notre Dame Press).

Fielding, M. (2000) Education Policy and the Challenge of Living Philosophy, *Journal of Education Policy*, 15.4, pp. 377–381.

Harvard Committee (1945) *General Education in a Free Society*, J. B. Conant, Introduction (Cambridge, MA, Harvard University Press).

Lukacs, J. (2002) *At the End of an Age* (New Haven and London, Yale University Press).

McLaughlin, T. (2000) Philosophy and Education Policy: Possibilities, Tensions and Tasks, *Journal of Education Policy*, 15.4, pp. 441–457.

Phillips, D. C. (2005) The Contested Nature of Educational Research and Why Philosophy of Education Offers Little Help, *Journal of Philosophy of Education*, 39.4, pp. 577–597.

Smith, F., Hardman, F. and Higgins, S. (2006) The Impact of Interactive Whiteboards on Teacher-Pupil Interaction in the National Literacy and Numeracy Strategies, *British Educational Research Journal*, 32.3, pp. 443–457.

Smeyers, P., Smith, R. and Standish, P. (2007) *The Therapy of Education* (Basingstoke, Palgrave).

Whitty, G. (2003) *Making Sense of Educational Policy* (London, Paul Chapman).

Wilson, J. (1963) *Thinking With Concepts* (Cambridge, Cambridge University Press).

Young, I. M. (2000) *Inclusion and Democracy* (Oxford, Oxford University Press).

9

Proteus Rising: Re-Imagining Educational Research

RICHARD SMITH

The idea that educational research should be 'scientific', and ideally based on randomised control trials, is in danger of becoming hegemonic. In the face of this it seems important to ask what other kinds of educational research can be respectable in their own different terms. We might also note that the demand for research to be 'scientific' is characteristically modernist, and thus arguably local and temporary. It is then tempting to consider what non-modernist approaches might look like. The purpose of this chapter is to sketch a case for one particular reaction against modernist thinking: romanticism. How might our understanding (apprehension, sense) of education be changed by readmitting the insights and perspectives of romanticism? And, crucially, what confidence could we have in educational research that was thus inspired and that took the 'romantic turn'?

1 EPISTEMOLOGY

In common with the other contributions to this volume, this chapter emerges from and develops work done for a seminar dedicated to investigating the 'Epistemological bases of educational research findings' under the auspices of the Teaching and Learning Research Programme (TLRP) of the ESRC (Economic and Social Research Council). According to the TLRP's website[1] the central questions that the seminar will address:

... are to do with the warrant or level of confidence which educational research (of different kinds) can provide for decisions about what should be done in terms of general educational policy across a whole system or practice at classroom level. It will therefore address specifically the claims made by the contemporary discourses of 'evidence-based practice' and 'what works', but it will locate these within a wider framework of literature which examines the relationship between research, policy and practice (including considerations to do with the derivation of practice from policy as well as policy and practice from research).

There are, it seems to me, three things to welcome here: the invitation to subject the scientific model ('evidence based practice' and 'what works') to critique, the location of discussion within a wider literature about research (in social science, broadly conceived, as I interpret it) and the emphasis on 'warrant or level of confidence'. This latter, I shall argue, opens a particularly helpful and revealing perspective on the question of just what shape or shapes educational research might take.

Nevertheless there is a series of reservations to be entertained about the title, 'The Epistemological Basis of Educational Research Findings', which, while excellent for its political purposes, is in other ways heavily loaded. 'Epistemological' directs us to the theory of knowledge, which in the analytical form that 'epistemology' strongly implies (though it need not) suggests a traditional examination in terms of, for instance, justified, true beliefs, or the distinction between knowing how and knowing that. As I shall note below, knowing, in these sorts of terms, is only one of many relevant ways of relating to the world and of imagining the connection between us and it.[2] The idea of research having an epistemological *basis* clearly implies that epistemology is to be foundational, in a sense that many philosophers now identify as a decisive wrong turn in the history of philosophical thought (e.g. Rorty, 1980; Kolakowski, 1972/1989). The phrase 'research findings' carries a strong implication of empiricism, as if research essentially discovers facts and correlations (it would be odd to present, for instance, an interpretive perspective, a philosophical analysis or a set of creative insights as any kind of *findings*). Every one of these assumptions or loadings—that the world is to be scientifically known by agents separate and distinct from it, that epistemology will supply the basis for sound knowledge, and the assumption of empiricism—are entirely characteristic of modernism. For Rorty, in fact, it is Descartes' identification of epistemology as by its very nature a foundationalist enterprise that inaugurates modernity and modern philosophy.

Equally characteristic of modernity is the ambition to discover a universal method for science and what we now call social science. This enterprise can be traced back to Francis Bacon and his *Novum Organum* of 1620 (*Organum* meaning, revealingly, something like our 'handbook' or 'manual') and tracked through Descartes' *Discourse*, whose full title (in English) is *Discourse on the Method of Rightly Conducting the Reason and Seeking for Truth in the Sciences* as well as his *Regulae* or *Rules for the Direction of the Mind* whose Rule 4 declares 'We need a method if we are to investigate the truth of things'. The track leads to David Hume's eight rules 'by which to judge of cause and effects' (*A Treatise of Human Nature,* Book I, part 3, section 15) and John Stuart Mill's four 'experimental methods' (*System of Logic,* Book 3, chapter 8). I have argued elsewhere (Smith, 2006b) that much educational research is driven by recognisable descendants of the Baconian search for *method* at all costs. It takes place within a framework in which the search for *findings* (results and outcomes: 'what works?') is treated as unproblematic. It is driven by the demand for accountability, which often seems to involve the fantasy that an exhaustive audit might be made of reality: that reality could be completely known. The modernist credentials of educational research, as it is generally conceived, are clear and, in their own terms, impressive.

Two interesting questions to ask now are just what would educational research look like that is not 'enacted in a set of nineteenth- or even seventeenth-century Euro-American blinkers' (Law, 2004, p. 143), and what kind of confidence could we have in it? Law's own approach to these questions emphasises two points, and I want to add a third. First, as indicated by the title and subtitle of his book, *After Method: Mess in Social Science Research*, science and social science traditionally deal with relatively stable realities. Law instances 'income distributions, global CO_2 emissions, the boundaries of nation states' (p. 2). Educational research supplies the quest for equivalent stable realities such as Supporting Group-work in Scottish Schools; Learning Scientific Concepts in Classroom Groups at Key Stage 1; Widening participation in higher education: a quantitative analysis (these are all examples of TLRP projects). Although the world is sometimes structured in these stable ways, Law writes, sometimes it is structured (or, in his word, 'textured') otherwise:

> ... things that slip and slide, or appear and disappear, change shape or don't have much form at all, unpredictabilities ... If much of the world is vague, diffuse or unspecific, slippery, emotional, ephemeral, elusive or indistinct, changes like a kaleidoscope, or doesn't really have much of a pattern at all, then where does this leave social science? How might we catch some of the realities we are currently missing? (Law, 2004, p. 2)

Law's second major emphasis is on the fact that the way we do social science research does not simply constitute a set of procedures for reflecting and conveying knowledge about reality. 'Rather it is performative. It helps to produce realities' (p. 143). There are 'realities' out there, but our research 're-works and re-bundles these and as it does so re-crafts realities and creates new versions of the world' (ibid.). It creates 'new resonances, new manifestations and new concealments' (ibid.). There are familiar examples from educational research: research on school effectiveness creates a version of the world in which wider questions of social injustice and exclusion tend to disappear from view. Research into ways of improving test and examination results increasingly brings into being a world where it is taken for granted that this is the main or even the sole point of education.

The third point that I want to emphasise takes us back to the idea of epistemology. Law follows his question (above) about how we might catch some of the realities we are currently missing by asking 'Can we know them [i.e. these realities] well? Should we know them? Is "knowing" the metaphor that we need? And if it isn't, then how might we relate to them?' (p. 2). In considering the alternatives to 'knowing', we might begin by noting that there is acknowledging as well as knowing: a difference often alluded to in the literature of psychoanalysis[3] and extensively discussed, in the context of scepticism, by Stanley Cavell

(1969), for whom acknowledgement is the articulating and what might be called the truly experiencing of what—others' pain, their very personhood, our own embodiedness and mortality—in our experience demands to be felt and expressed but what at the same time we may try to suppress. Even if we were to talk of 'understanding' rather than of knowing there would not be quite so much suggestion of representing what is out there (nor the same sense that in the end true, justified beliefs will be at stake). Instead of knowing the world we might be attuned to it, sensitive to it. We might *resonate* with it, share its rhythms—the way we might be at one with the natural world if we opened ourselves to it instead of analysing it, reducing it to its constituent elements, as a certain kind of scientist does. Our knowledge then would be like the knowledge the Brangwens had of their world (D. H. Lawrence, *The Rainbow*, chapter 1):

> [they] felt the rush of the sap in spring, they knew the wave which cannot halt, but every year throws forward the seed to begetting, and, falling back, leaves the young-born on the earth. They knew the intercourse between heaven and earth, sunshine drawn into the breast and bowels, the rain sucked up in the daytime, nakedness that comes under the wind in autumn . . .

Knowledge such as this would clearly be more than a technical business that the researcher deployed during office hours. It would be inseparable from the question of how to live a life. Or did we think that the way we lived held no implications for how we saw things, how we responded to them, and vice-versa? 'Method goes with work, and ways of working, and ways of being' (Law, 2004, p. 10).

The research sites where Law finds exemplified the 'messy', unstable realities that he investigates, where the idea of 'knowing' is problematical, include the work of endocrinologists at a scientific laboratory, an alcohol treatment centre, the Ladbroke Grove railway accident, Quaker worship and the development of the Zimbabwe bush pump. The question of just what we might think of as similarly 'messy' educational realities is touched on in Section 3 below.

2 ROMANTICISM

The visceral kind of knowledge enjoyed by Lawrence's Brangwens is Romantic, in one sense of that word, and the idea of our human apprehension creating reality (or producing it or, in Law's way of putting it, crafting it into existence) rather than simply reflecting or reproducing it is also characteristically Romantic. In the remainder of this chapter I take Romanticism seriously as a form of research, odd though this may sound to our scientifically-conditioned ears. To repeat my way of putting it earlier, I ask what (educational) research would look like if it was set in the Romantic framework or perspective, and what kind of confidence we could have in it.

This perhaps is the point at which a more conventional chapter would attempt to say something systematic about Romanticism and particularly about its relation to education, perhaps offering some version of a traditional literature review. One difficulty here is that there is very little literature on the connections between Romanticism and education. Halpin, for example, in an article entitled 'Why a Romantic Conception of Education Matters' (2006) notes only a handful of relevant texts. Another is that what literature there is tends to focus either on the influence of Romanticism on formal education or on views of the nature of the child. Willinsky (1990), for example, writes that his edited collection 'documents the Romantic roots of such educational projects as child-centred curriculum projects, expressive language programs, Montessori schools and the alternative school movement' (p. 2). There are however two more interesting difficulties, which seem to arise when Romanticism and the systematic are required to keep too close company.

First, it is well known that Romanticism is a fluid term that means different things to different people. The central features of Romanticism have been variously identified. Most accounts foreground the idea of the imagination as a faculty that creatively constitutes reality, either to be contrasted with reason or understood as distinctively and perhaps uniquely uniting reason with feeling. Nature is of course important both as a refuge from the excesses of a civilisation grown utilitarian and mechanistic, and as a way into enhanced self-consciousness for the poet or artist who finds an analogue for his or her feelings in landscape and weather. Closely connected here is the interest in the self, leading to the individualism that culminates in such works as Byron's *Childe Harold*, that is also generally held to be a typical emphasis of Romanticism. But this is to say nothing about love, about the connections of Romanticism with nationalism, the interest in the Gothic and the exotic, the cultivation of feeling (the 'sensibility' that Jane Austen contrasts neatly with 'sense') and a range of other ideas and terms. So many and so diverse are the interpretations of Romanticism that F. L. Lucas in *The Decline and Fall of the Romantic Ideal* (1948) famously counted 11,396 definitions of the term. Some writers have concluded that 'romanticism' has simply become too broad to be helpful: Lovejoy (1941) for example finding it 'useless as a verbal expression'. More recent writers prefer to think not in terms of Romanticism in the singular but of Romanticisms in the plural. To take just two examples, Clark and Goellnicht (1994, p. 3) use 'Romanticisms' to label a plurality of 'quite distinct thought-complexes'. Peer and Hoeveler (1998) believe that we can only understand Romanticism if we cultivate an awareness of the 'myriad Romanticisms'.

The fluidity and diversity of the term can be further seen in one of the few recent articles (Halpin, 2006) on Romanticism and education. Halpin's interpretation of Romanticism can be judged from the title of an Internet version of his article, 'Search for the Hero Inside Yourself: Why a *Romantic* Conception of Education Matters', and from some of the 'keywords' listed: utopia, romance, imagination, love, heroism, rebellion, criticism. Halpin connects Romanticism with hope and hopefulness, and regrets the way that the loss of Romantic ideas and ideals has helped to 'frustrate consideration of progressive ways of thinking about the practice of education' (Halpin, 2006, p. 326).

The second difficulty in connecting Romanticism with education, a difficulty that is both perhaps more intractable and more interesting, involves the paradox of attempting to write systematically about Romanticism, when that movement regularly problematises the systematic and the methodical.[4] Halpin himself quotes Aidan Day: 'Attempts to summarise Romanticism inevitably end up over-systematising and simplifying the phenomenon' (Day, 1996, p. 327), yet he is happy to write of Romanticism making 'better sense of what it means to be an effective teacher and a productive learner'— the language of productivity and effectiveness being of course the unmistakeable language of that most systematic of enterprises, the institutionalised practice of the 21st century Western school. The point here is not to convict Halpin of insensitivity or incongruity: the quotation comes from the article's Abstract, and the preparation of an Abstract is part of the technology of academic writing that has a way of imposing system even on those most aware of its drawbacks.

This point is symptomatic, and worth dwelling on. The Romanticism of the early 19th century was in large part a reaction against modernity, its intellectual expression in the Enlightenment and their impressive but ugly child, the industrial revolution. What some writers (see especially Kompridis, 2006) call *philosophical* Romanticism is the critical response to modernity, drawing on or echoing the legacy of 19th century Romanticism, that is being articulated in our own time. 'It is the tendency of the lifeforms of modernity', Kompridis writes (p. 4), to become not just what I have described above as systematic and methodical, but, in Kompridis's words, 'rigid and inflexible' (ibid.). The necessary task, then, is to challenge these sclerotic life forms, whether the challenge comes from (philosophical) Romanticism, from the postmodernism that offers a critique of our 'postmodern condition', or from whatever other resources can be found. In this sense, 'To "romanticise" the world is to make room for the new, to make room for new possibilities' (ibid.)—an essential and ineliminable task of the project of education.

Such critique, furthermore, must be sensitive to the way that it is itself an enterprise shaped by modernity and always in danger of collapsing back into modernity's tropes and assumptions. Its concerns therefore must include what Kompridis (ibid.) calls its own 'expressivity', the way in which it is written and spoken, and this brings it close to the concerns of literature, and of art generally, in our own time. We sense that there are things that demand to be said, but that cannot be said in the ways characteristic of, and confirmatory of, modernity: things that cannot be seen in the kind of light we have come to take for granted, and that call for a different kind of illumination.

3 SIGHT OF PROTEUS

These considerations explain, to some degree, my approach in what follows, where the elements of the Romantic view that I want to emphasise are the opposite of the systematic. They are the creativity that consists in bringing reality into being, rather than faithfully representing it; the capacity to work with the protean and unstable; and—another dimension of moving beyond representation—the truth and knowledge that transcend the explicit. They also explain, if any explanation is still necessary, why the 'expressivity' takes the form that it does. I proceed by way of a short examination or interpretation of a poem containing some characteristically Romantic themes. This will lead to a discussion of what constitutes a sound and confidence-inducing example of such an examination. (It should be noted that there is no claim here to produce a particularly authoritative interpretation of the poem: in fact, as will be clear later, the point I want to make about literary criticism as a mode of research is in a sense strengthened if my own examination is open to critical discussion. The point is in the form of the approach and not in its substance, but it is impossible to indicate the approach without giving example of the substance.) The poem is William Wordsworth's 'The World is Too Much With Us' (1807).

> The world is too much with us; late and soon,
> Getting and spending, we lay waste our powers;
> Little we see in Nature that is ours;
> We have given our hearts away, a sordid boon!
> This Sea that bares her bosom to the moon,
> The winds that will be howling at all hours,
> And are up-gathered now like sleeping flowers,
> For this, for everything, we are out of tune;
> It moves us not.—Great God! I'd rather be
> A Pagan suckled in a creed outworn;
> So might I, standing on this pleasant lea,
> Have glimpses that would make me less forlorn;
> Have sight of Proteus rising from the sea;
> Or hear old Triton blow his wreathed horn.

The writer complains that humankind is too involved with the material things of this world. We have lost our sense of connection with nature; we are no longer attuned to its sights ('This Sea'), its sounds (the howling winds) and by implication its smells (the 'sleeping flowers'). Sea and wind in particular seem emblematic of our inability to cope with the formlessness and instability of the natural world ('If much of the world is vague, diffuse or unspecific, slippery, emotional, ephemeral, elusive or indistinct ...', in Law's words, above): we prefer to live in the accountant's dream of ordered, balanced columns ('late and soon', 'Getting and spending'). The opening words of the poem can be read to suggest that the world in all its worldliness is proving more than we can cope with (as we might say, 'It's all just too much'), but the rhythm of the line and our growing attunement to what is being said here move us to place a fraction more emphasis on the small word 'with': then the sense is less that we are out of sympathy with the world and more that we find it only too comfortable a companion. In somewhat similar fashion the third line, 'Little we see in Nature that is ours' is at first suggestive of simple dislocation from the (Romantically conceived) realm of nature, but there is a more mordant sense that, looking up at Nature from our book-keeping and bean-counting, we see nothing that can be entered as possession or profit and in consequence dismiss it (as the telling phrases have it, we 'discount' it, 'write it off'). The writer contrasts this dismal picture of civilisation with the vividness and magic of pagan mythology. Even 'glimpses' of such a world, or sound without sight ('hear old Triton'), would lift his spirits. Proteus is an especially significant figure here: he is a sea-god who can alter his shape ('things that slip and slide, or appear and disappear, change shape or don't have much form at all': Law, again, above). He will tell the future to anyone (such as Menelaus, in Book IV of the *Odyssey*) who has the power to hold onto him through all his shifts and transformations. A person who values a sight—this is not a sustained spectacle—of Proteus rising from the sea is perhaps disposed not to be daunted by formlessness and instability.

The poem is a sonnet and, as is often the case with the sonnet form, there is a break between the first eight lines and the last six. Often the first section sets out a problem to which the second proposes a kind of solution. Here the break is all the more marked in that the rhyme-scheme changes; yet the break is at the same time blurred in that the sentence that makes up the second half of the first section runs on into the second section. The effect is perhaps to suggest that the problem sketched in the first section threatens to be overwhelming; and then the postponed expostulation that begins the second section ('Great God!') has a particularly exasperated quality. The rhyme-scheme is striking: the first section is ABBA, ABBA while the second section is CDCDCD. The 'D' endings of the second section hold an echo of the 'A' endings of the first (from 'soon', 'boon' etc to 'outworn', 'forlorn' and 'horn'). To my ear the rhymes of the first section have a slightly monotonous quality, appropriate to the jaded state of things the poet describes. The diction of the poem is generally simple but becomes noticeably more distinctive and vivid ('A Pagan suckled', the mythical figures of Proteus and Triton) in the last six lines. The final flourish of the 'wreathed horn', especially since the adjective must be pronounced as two syllables, confirms the 'glimpses that would make me less forlorn', the experience that would redeem the mundanity of the poet's world, as exotic.

Now let us think of this poem as a piece of research. William Wordsworth has investigated the human condition, and these are his findings. (If the educational implications here are not thought clear enough, we might say: there are grounds for wondering whether education at all levels has become overly instrumental and rational, and lost touch with the sources of enchantment: cp. Wordsworth, 1807; Egan, 1990.) What confidence can we have in this poem, this research, this text? Or, if this poem of Wordsworth's does not appeal to the reader, what confidence can we have in any particular imaginative text that appeals to our feelings, demands a response; where we want to say 'yes, this catches something important'? Where we are moved by a sense of its truthfulness to how things are, in a way that is not a matter of simply being intellectually moved, but moved by the truthfulness of what we read to our own experience?

The oddity of this question about confidence is that it appears to require the invocation of some set of over-arching criteria to guarantee the soundness of the research and thus to warrant the confidence. In the context of medical research and the kind of educational research that takes medical research as its model such warranties are supplied by randomised control trials, and by formal and statistical analysis where appropriate. This is what allows research of this kind to be certified as robust, reliable and replicable—the descriptors that are so to speak its distinctive kite-marks—and approved by the accountants of academe. But these are not the terms in which we would register our approval of an interpretation of Wordsworth's poem or, by extension, of what I am here calling 'Romantic research'. Here talk of reliability and replicability are out of place: as if a second reading of the poem by the same reader would (or should in principle) produce the same results, or as if any other reader would interpret the poem in the same way. The idea of a reading of a poem being 'robust' is mildly risible, revealing the adjective as little more than a term of rhetoric, here as elsewhere, intended to suggest down-to-earth, no-nonsense tough-mindedness.

The qualities of a good interpretation of a poem are very different. They include being sensitive, attuned, flexible. The reading of Wordsworth's poem that I offer above is a good reading only if I have been sensitive to, for instance, the rhythms in the opening clause and if I am attuned to the poem as a whole. A good critic is one who has the flexibility (and humility) continually to re-visit the artwork, not least in the light of her growing experience and knowledge of other artworks, and test her earlier understanding of it again and again. The flexibility of her response—even its *pro tempore* nature as 'only the best understanding I have achieved so far'—is at virtually the polar extreme from the legendary 'robustness' of the scientific approach. There is furthermore something at least implicitly dialogical about this kind of research. The literary critic F. R. Leavis used to maintain that 'all critical statements are of the form, "This is so, isn't it?" and presuppose a response, "Yes, but"' (Matthews, 2004, p. 60). Leavis (1961, quoted ibid., p. 55) wrote that 'It will always be necessary to insist ... that criticism is a collaborative and creative interplay. It creates a community and is inseparable from the process that creates and keeps alive a living culture'. As I have noted before, much turns on the intonation of that 'This is so, isn't it?' where 'the first "is" can be emphasised appropriately to the importance of what is at stake, while the voice must rise on the final "it" to reflect the idea that any literary judgement, like any moral one, can be re-visited and re-appraised' (Smith, 1997, p. 111). The researchers and critics of literature and of the arts in general are divided into many schools (Marxist, feminist, Reader Response theorists, post-structuralists, deconstructionists ...) and it is hardly possible to imagine that the purpose of research and criticism is to secure final agreement among them, after which discussion can come to an end.

Of course there are aspects of a reading that can be plain wrong, as when a word is construed in a sense that was not available to the writer or contemporary reader, or when the interpreter makes any other clearly erroneous claim (for instance if the rhyme-scheme of Wordsworth's poem was manifestly other than as I describe it above). But the central point remains, which is that the qualities of a good reading cannot be stipulated 'from the outside'. You only know if a reading has been sensitive, subtle, perceptive and so on if *you* are in turn sensitive (and so on) to *this* particular poem. There are no independently specifiable procedures or techniques that the critic or researcher must show she has followed or implemented, on pain of being dismissed as second-rate ('insufficiently robust', no doubt): apart, that is, from such banal points as that her response must be to the work of art rather than to some imagined version of it (and Harold Bloom's notion of 'strong misreading' renders even this uncertain: see Bloom, 1973). There is no room here for experts who can adjudicate on the merits of research method without themselves engaging in the very same research and participating in the dialogues among researchers. This is very different from the situation in educational research and social science research more widely, where it is of course common to find both general prescriptions of appropriate methodology and magisterial judgements on existing research.[5]

4 RESEARCH AND POLICY

What has I hope become clear is that when we ask what confidence we can place in educational research—and, in the context of this volume, what grounds we could have for the basing of policy on it—we are drawn to a different set of answers than if we ask what constitutes 'sound' or 'good quality' educational research. The latter question tends to draw us back into the modernist, scientistic—and systematic—way of thinking. The former question however tends to release us from the debilitating assumption that this is the single legitimate form of thinking, or indeed that there is just any one, hegemonic, kind of educational research. It permits us to see that we can have confidence in—and so contemplate building policy on—ways of thinking, interpreting and researching that are quite different from the (supposedly) scientific. It then enables us to explore what I have called Romantic thinking and research, a dimension of thought that enables us to take with full seriousness, and to explore, three possibilities that could prove liberating for thinking about education, for educational research. These are, to repeat from Section 2, the possibility of doing justice to the unstable or protean, of grasping that our research may create reality as much as report or represent it, and of moving away from thinking of our relationship to these realities only in terms of 'knowing' them.

It must be emphasised that it is these possibilities that are important rather than the 'Romanticism' that I have conveniently grouped them under. Other writers, such as Gadamer and Heidegger, have come to a similar stance towards such possibilities without categorising them in this way. Corradi Fiumara for instance writes from the perspective of one concerned to find alternatives to Western logocentrism, the dominance of discourse over the capacity to listen:

> There is a demand here for a relationship with thinking anchored to humility and faithfulness, an approach which is unheard-of in our current thinking, revolving around grasping, mastering, using ... [this] philosophical perspective is characterised by the requirement that we dwell with, abide by, whatever we try to know; that we aim at co-existence with, rather than knowledge-of (Corradi Fiumara, 1990, p. 15).

Keeping, however, with the label of 'Romanticism' for the sake of convenience (and of course its power to disturb the scientistic, Western mindset), what might 'Romantic' educational research look like? In giving some examples I am conscious that I may appear to recommend some kind of programme, or to propose a new methodology. Of course that is not my intention. I merely want to indicate that there is nothing wholly unfamiliar about this 'Romantic' approach and by rendering it more visible as a way of thinking about education to show it as a live alternative to method-based research as it is commonly understood. I group my examples under the three headings or possibilities above: research that accepts that it creates reality, that works with the unstable, and that problematises our 'knowing' reality. In fact matters are not so neat since most of the examples illustrate more than one possibility. Half of the examples are from my own work: so at least one writer will not complain of misrepresentation.

Consider, first, how certain ideals of education as something that has no end beyond education, the ideal of education 'for itself' (the notion of liberal education, or 'the educated man' [*sic*] or the cultured human being) have to be brought into being, made real (Law, 2004, writes of 'crafting-into-presence'), and done so again and again in terms that speak to different generations and kinds of people. How different this is from showing that education is good for something else ('graduates can look forward to increased life-time earnings of £187k as against non-graduates') which is indubitably real and against which it can be correlated. Here is Richard Hoggart crafting, or perhaps we might say conjuring, the ideal into presence:

> I remember once, when I was in the Upper Fifth, for some reason he marked or looked at a set of essays. I had written one on Hardy and had begun it, 'T.H. was a truly cultured man ...'. He stopped me a day or two later, swung against the door of his study, and said, 'What is a truly cultured man, Hoggart?' I was baffled. I thought he was playing me up, because if our headmaster didn't know what a truly cultured man was, if the phrase wasn't absolutely cast-iron, where were we? And he said, 'Am I one? I don't think so. I don't feel myself "truly cultured"'. This was my first sight of a mind speculating, of thought as something disinterested and free-playing, with yourself outside it. I usually thought of a master as

somebody who said, 'This is what the such-and-such verb is, or this is what happened in 1762, and you have to learn it' (Hoggart, 1970).

This is insightful (*this is so, isn't it?*), it may help the reader to see something she has not seen before. Yet there is no 'research finding' here. Poetry, novel, film (*Dead Poets' Society* perhaps) might do as well.

Or again: what the contemporary university can be, at its best, despite the increasing bureaucracy and auditing, the insistence on pre-formed aims and outcomes (and perhaps in quiet opposition to these things), the university as a place of open-ended and collegial enquiry—here is something as much to imagine as to discover, an occasion for writing that is semi-fictive, partly autobiographical, to some degree utopian. Conjure a seminar of good-humoured and properly disrespectful students, insightful into their subject and eager to apply those insights to their own lives (Smith, 2003). *This could be so, couldn't it?*

Second, the protean and unstable. It is remarkable how much educational research depicts schools as in principle relatively stable (or stabilisable) places, to be made still more effective, still more highly reliable organisations, as a result of further research, naturally. There is a world for which children are to be prepared, whether in terms of examination results, transferable skills or attitudes, the only significant question being just what preparation will be most efficacious. A different (and much rarer) literature suggests otherwise. Mackenzie (2002), for example, depicts a certain kind of school as one characterised by an 'adversarial curriculum' where pupils' education 'includes, among other things, learning to evade, trick, and make fools of the teachers' (p. 616), not without some complicity on the part of the better teachers; and Mackenzie's suggestion is that, not least because 'our world is not stable' (p. 613), such a school preserves subtle and important insights into the nature of education.

Or again: the therapeutic dimension of education can seem both progressive and disastrous at the same time, an apocalypse and yet a kindly one. The language of self-belief in particular (including such terms as 'self-esteem' and 'diffidence') is, I have argued, 'turbulent and disorderly' (Smith, 2006a). It will always defeat attempts at comprehensive systematisation. It does not present us with stable realities to chart and measure, perhaps not even by the conceptual mapping of the analytical philosopher.

Third: the teacher of small children deals with large issues that cannot be directly known. Death, jealousy, obsessions and nameless fears are best handled through fairy-story, myth and legend. Watch the children as they listen, utterly absorbed, to the story of the Snow Queen. How Kay and Gerda played together happily on their roof balcony. But there was an evil goblin who had a mirror and, when he saw things reflected in the mirror, even the loveliest things in the world seemed ugly and hateful to him. One particularly bad morning he caught sight of himself in the mirror, hideous and distorted, and he smashed the mirror in rage. And the fragments of the glass descended down to earth, where one of them lodged in Kay's eye.

Immediately he looked around at the roof-garden, and the window boxes, and the picture book that he and Gerda had been looking at together, and he shouted 'I hate all this' and kicked over the window-box of geraniums ... Shortly afterwards the Snow Queen came though town on her sleigh, pulled by black horses, whose hooves' sound was muffled by the packed snow on the streets. The Snow Queen was dressed in furs, she was austerely beautiful, and Kay wanted nothing more than to follow her and be her servant ... When they arrive at her palace in the far north, the Queen sets Kay a puzzle. He is to manipulate blocks of ice from the frozen lake, called the 'Mirror of Reason', so that they make the word 'eternity'. When he has done this, the Queen tells Kay, she will give him the whole world, and a pair of skates.

There is a kind of truth here, we may think (*this is so, isn't it?*). But the good teacher does not ask the children what the author of the story is trying to tell us. There is nothing here to know in that sense. The story must be fully listened to, savoured and absorbed.[6] The dimension of myth saves us from what Nietzsche called 'Socratism', 'the ruinous tendency to rationalise, to rely on reason too much and in contexts where reason should not be our only guide' (Smeyers *et al.*, 2006, p. 143). Ours is an over-knowing culture, against which another myth, that of Oedipus (ibid., pp. 144 ff), is the classic warning. Forms of therapy, particularly those influenced by psychoanalysis, also employ the mythic, partly as a way of resisting the kind of knowledge, and of knowingness, which short-circuits deeper learning and makes it harder to achieve.[7]

5 CONCLUDING GLIMPSES

The above constitutes no more than indications of a way, tramps' signs rather than firm directions. Corradi Fiumara writes that we need to develop the habit of 'paying heed to formerly unheard-of messages, voices, clues' (Corradi Fiumara, 1990, p. 47). Tramps' signs may be more useful to tramps than accurate maps. What follows too are glimpses only. Might what we think of as social science, and its research—and so educational research—be in some respects closer to the Arts in its approach than to the physical sciences? How might things look different if literary criticism, rather than physics, was our paradigm of knowledge? Or even if Darwin, rather than Newton, had been our image of the scientist?

If it is not a matter of knowing, grasping, we shall need new ways of being with, compre- , appre- hending. Dwelling with, abiding with, co-existing with (Corradi Fiumara, p. 9 above). Glimpsing (that would make us less forlorn ...). Detecting. Listening (as if we knew what that meant). Shutting off the racket of evidence, data, research findings: the obvious, the replicable and of course the eminently fundable. Slow, hesitant, uncertain. *Diffident*. Making space for the indefinite. The ability to create a kind of silence. 'It takes considerable methodological discipline—but also imagination—to reduce the dazzle of noise and make the kind of silence that will allow the faint signal of the neutrino, or of spiritual mystery, to be revealed, made audible, and amplified' (Law, 2004, p. 118). This will require a bodily attunement and not just a mental one.

This implies different ways of writing. If we are creating reality we had better be careful what language we use, if crafting it into being (ibid.) meticulous with our tools, if conjuring it into existence attentive to our spells. *Be careful what you wish for, lest it come true.* Poetry, which creates (*poiesis*) reality, rather than the research report that purports to reflect it. Nietzschean celebration and mockery. Anger and irony. Use of the first person. Autobiography and confession. The particular, rather than the academic and international generalisation. Unhygienic writing (Latour, 1993), full of impurities and rough contingent jumbled stuff. Metaphors for the unthinkable, ways of doing justice to the unpresentable and the unrepresentable. Dialogue.

And are the policy-makers supposed to listen to this? Laws have been changed before now by poets and novelists and their unsystematic writings (Charles Dickens, the workhouse and the Poor Law are obvious examples), and as other contributors to this volume make clear, policy-makers have their own imperatives in any case. Educational researchers seem to long to make everything rational, systematic and tidy—neat columns of getting and spending—in order to give the policy-makers what the researchers imagine they want; and then so much passes unnoticed and unremarked, and is betrayed. Another poem and a painting come to mind: the painting is Pieter Brueghel's *The Fall of Icarus* (reproduced on the cover of this book), where the shepherd stares inland from the coast and the ploughman focuses stolidly on the turf his ploughshare is turning. Meanwhile the child Icarus, so nearly successful in his first flight on the wings cunningly designed for him by Daedalus, his teacher and father, has crashed into the sea and is drowning. The poem is W. H. Auden's *Musée Des Beaux Arts:*

> ... the ploughman may
> Have heard the splash, the forsaken cry,
> But for him it was not an important failure; the sun shone
> As it had to on the white legs disappearing into the green
> Water; and the expensive delicate ship that must have seen
> Something amazing, a boy falling out of the sky,
> Had somewhere to get to and sailed calmly on.

***

This image is, perhaps, an appropriate one on which to conclude not just this chapter but also this volume as a whole. Our recurring theme has been a call to attend to forms of enquiry that are 'systematically' excluded from attention by the narrowly defined requirements of 'evidence-based practice' and the terms of reference of many 'systematic' reviews. These forms of enquiry are here represented by case study, personal narratives, action research, philosophy and, in this chapter, 'the romantic turn' as well as, more conventionally, large population studies, but educational research takes many other forms as well. If policy-makers and those who are informing them focus too narrowly, like the ploughman, on the job in hand or, like the ship, on the 'somewhere to get to' will they notice the fall, the splash or the forsaken cry? Will they ever enjoy the most splendid of sights, that of Proteus rising?

Correspondence: Richard Smith, School of Education, University of Durham, Leazes Road, Durham DH1 1TA, UK.
E-mail: r.d.smith@durham.ac.uk

NOTES

1. http://www.tlrp.org/themes/seminar/bridges.html
2. Gadamer's remark is, I take it, to the same effect: 'In its concern to understand the universe of understanding better than seems possible under the modern scientific notion of cognition, [a reflection on what truth is in the human sciences] has to try to establish a new relation to the concepts which it uses' (Gadamer, 1979, p. xiv).
3. For example, 'both Freud and Rosenzweig give us the means to think the difference between holding ourselves responsible for *knowing* other minds and accepting responsibility for *acknowledging* other minds in all their insistent and uncanny impenetrability' (Santner, 2001, p. 23).
4. Nietzsche's famous words are exemplary: 'I distrust all systematisers, and avoid them. The will to a system shows a lack of honesty' (Nietzsche, 2003). Whether Nietzsche can be counted as a Romantic, as heavily influenced by the Romantic Movement, or neither, is of course a matter of continuing debate. See for example Yelle (2000) and Picart (1997).
5. I have in mind in particular the 'What Works Clearinghouse' in the USA: see http://www.whatworks.ed.gov/. The situation in the physical sciences appears, interestingly, to be closer to that in the Arts with many theorists, such as Popper, prepared to deny that there is any such thing as a general scientific method. See for instance Rowbottom and Aiston, 2006, p. 137.
6. Corradi Fiumara writes: 'Listening draws upon those depths where "truth" does not lend itself to representation by means of institutionalised languages' (Corradi Fiumara, 1990, p. 51).
7. At the conference where I first presented this contribution one of the audience came up to me afterwards and told me I really ought to include a reference to the original author of the story of the Snow Queen, Hans Christian Andersen. The work was published as a part of *Nye Eventyr. Første Bind. Anden Samling* (1845), and the text in the original Danish version can be found at: http://www.adl.dk/adl_pub/vaerker/cv/e_vaerk/e_vaerk.xsql?ff_id=22&id=2479&hist=fmS&nnoc=adl_pub (accessed June 2, 2007). While Hans Christian Andersen deserves his due, it is an interesting question whether such references normalise the distinctive truth of the stories to which they refer and drain it of its force.

REFERENCES

Bloom, H. (1973) *The Anxiety of Influence: A Theory of Poetry* (New York, Oxford University Press).
Cavell, S. (1969) Knowing and Acknowledging, in: *Must We Mean What We Say?* (New York, Scribner).
Clark, D. L. and Goellnicht, D. C. (1994) (eds) *New Romanticisms: Theory and Critical Practice* (Toronto, University of Toronto Press).
Corradi Fiumara, G. (1990) *The Other Side of Language: A Philosophy of Listening* (London, Routledge).
Day, A. (1996) *Romanticism* (London, Routledge).
Egan, K. (1990) *Romantic Understanding* (London, Routledge).

Gadamer, H-G. (1979) *Truth and Method* (London, Sheed & Ward).

Halpin, D. (2006) Why a Romantic Conception of Education Matters, *Oxford Review of Education*, 32.3, pp. 325–345. Available at http://www.ioe.ac.uk/schools/cpa/DavidHalpin/ROMANTICISMARTICLE.pdf [accessed 2 June 2007].

Hoggart, R. (1970) Growing Up, in: *Speaking to Each Other*, vol. I (London, Chatto & Windus).

Kolakowski, L. (1972/1989) *The Presence of Myth* (Chicago, University of Chicago Press).

Kompridis, N. (ed.) (2006) *Philosophical Romanticism* (London, Routledge).

Latour, B. (1993) *We Have Never Been Modern* (London, Harvester Wheatsheaf).

Law, J. (2004) *After Method: Mess in Social Science Research* (London, Routledge).

Leavis, F. R. (1961) A Note on the Critical Function, *Literary Criterion*, 5.1, pp. 1–9.

Lovejoy, A. O. (1941) The Meaning of Romanticism for the Historian of Ideas, *Journal of the History of Ideas*, 2, pp. 251–278.

Lucas, F. L. (1948) *The Decline and Fall of the Romantic Ideal* (Cambridge, Cambridge University Press).

Mackenzie, J. (2002) Stalky & Co.: The Adversarial Curriculum, *Journal of Philosophy of Education*, 36.4, pp. 609–620.

Matthews, S. (2004) The Responsibilities of Dissent: F.R. Leavis after *Scrutiny*, *Literature and History*, 13.2, pp. 49–66.

Nietzsche, F. W. (2003) *The Twilight of the Idols*, R. J. Hollingdale, trans., 'Maxims and Missiles' no. 26 (Harmondsworth, Penguin).

Picart, C. (1997) Nietzsche as Masked Romantic, *The Journal of Aesthetics and Art Criticism*, 55.3, pp. 273–291.

Peer, L. H. and Hoeveler, D. L. (1998) *Comparative Romanticisms: Power, Gender, Subjectivity* (Columbia, Camden House).

Rorty, R. (1980) *Philosophy and the Mirror of Nature* (Princteon, NJ, Princeton University Press).

Rowbottom, D. and Aiston, S. (2006) The Myth of 'Scientific Method' in Contemporary Educational Research, *Journal of Philosophy of Education*, 40.2, pp. 137–156.

Santner, E. (2001) *On the Psychotheology of Everyday Life* (Chicago, University of Chicago Press).

Smeyers, P., Smith, R. and Standish, P. (2006) *The Therapy of Education* (London, Palgrave Macmillan).

Smith, R. (1997) Judgement day, in: R. Smith and P. Standish (eds) *Teaching Right and Wrong: Moral Education in the Balance* (Stoke-on-Trent, Trentham Books).

Smith, R. (2003) Unfinished Business: Education Without Necessity, *Teaching in Higher Education*, 8.4, pp. 477–491.

Smith, R. (2006a) On Diffidence: The Moral Psychology of Self-Belief, *Journal of Philosophy of Education*, 40.1, pp. 51–62.

Smith, R. (2006b) As if By Machinery: The Levelling of Educational Research, *Philosophy, Methodology and Educational Research*, Special Issue of *Journal of Philosophy of Education*, 40.2, pp. 157–168.

Willinsky, J. (1990) *The Educational Legacy of Romanticism* (Waterloo, Ontario, Wilfrid Laurier Press).

Yelle, R. A. (2000) The Rebirth of Myth? Nietzsche's Eternal Recurrence and its Romantic Antecedents, *Numen*, 47.2, pp. 175–202.

Index